DANGEROUS SUPPLEMENTS

Post-Contemporary Interventions
A series edited by Stanley Fish and Fredric Jameson

DANGEROUS SUPPLEMENTS

Resistance and Renewal in Jurisprudence

**Edited by
Peter Fitzpatrick**

**Duke University Press
Durham**

Published in the United States by Duke University Press

Published in the U.K. in 1991 by Pluto Press

Library of Congress Cataloging-in-Publication Data
Dangerous supplements: resistance and renewal in jurisprudence/
[edited by] Peter Fitzpatrick.
(Post-contemporary interventions)
Includes bibliographical references and index.
ISBN 0–8223–1140–2 (cloth). – ISBN 0–8223–1121–6 (paper)
1. Jurisprudence–Methodology. 2. Jurisprudence–Study and
teaching. 3. Law–Methodology. I. Fitzpatrick. Peter. 1941–
II. Series.
K212.D36 1991   90-28393
340'.1–dc20   CIP

Printed in Great Britain

Acknowledgements

'The art of living,' meditated Marcus Aurelius, 'is more like wrestling
than dancing.' Several people made living through this collection more
like dancing than wrestling. In producing the book, Anne Beech, Mari
Roberts and Roger van Zwanenberg generously combined imagination
and dedication. Stanley Fish has initiated many of the meanings the
work will have. The contributors were kind and understanding throughout. And Sally Sheldon's creative index adds immeasurably to our
efforts.

Peter Fitzpatrick
Canterbury, December 1990

Contents

Contributors

ANTHONY CARTY is a lecturer in the University of Glasgow. He is the author of *The Decay of International Law* (1986) and he has edited *Post-Modern Law* (1990). He has strong interests in continental European social theory and has published extensively on the theory and practice of law in the Third World.

PETER FITZPATRICK is a Solicitor and Professor of Law and Social Theory at the University of Kent. Much of his work has been on legal imperialism. He is currently writing on the mythology of modern law.

PETER GOODRICH has taught Jurisprudence and Common Law at the Universities of Edinburgh, Newcastle Upon Tyne and Liverpool. He is currently Senior Lecturer in Law at Lancaster University. His books include *Reading the Law* (1986) and *Languages of Law: From Logics of Memory to Nomadic Masks* (1990).

YIFAT HACHAMOVITCH is Professor of Philosophy at Colorado College, Colorado Springs. She is author of *Bound Objects* (1991). She has published articles on semiotics and Talmudic Law.

ALAN HUNT holds Professorships in the Department of Law and the Department of Sociology at Carleton University in Ottawa. Publications include *The Sociological Movement in Law* (1978), and he has edited, with Peter Fitzpatrick, *Critical Legal Studies* (1987).

CAROL SMART is Senior Lecturer in Sociology at the University of Warwick. She has contributed a number of books and articles to the area of feminism and law. The most recent include *Feminism and the Power of Law* and *The Ties That Bind*.

DAVID SUGARMAN is Professor and Head of the Law Department at Lancaster University. His principal publications include *Legality, Ideology and the State* (1983), and *Regulating Corporate Groups in Europe* (1990) with Gunther Teubner.

ALAN THOMSON is a Lecturer in Law at the University of Kent. His main interests are in Legal Education and Law and Social Theory. He is currently working on a book on Hayek.

The Abstracts and Brief Chronicles of the Time: Supplementing Jurisprudence

Peter Fitzpatrick

Introduction: Supplementing Jurisprudence

Jurisprudence is the theorised prejudice of lawyers. Its proponents strive to ensure the viability of law and to maintain law's authority. Courses on jurisprudence continually raise and revert to the old motivating question of 'the nature of law' (Barnett and Yach, 1985, pp.155, 169). Increasingly, these courses also explore the 'social, moral and political context' of law (ibid., p.169). In such explorations, however, the focus resolutely remains on a pre-existent law. The context is brought to it. These voyages are never undertaken without the intention of returning more securely to the point of departure. Challenges from the surrounding context are thus either rejected or adjusted and absorbed: 'the essential nature of the process is for someone to venture forth from the intellectual milieu of the law and to come back with spoils from elsewhere and to present them in assimilable form' (Twining, 1974, p.157). Understandably, then, jurisprudence exhibits an 'elasticity' and 'a capacity for self-renewal' while retaining '"a core of certainty" despite the wide variation in areas on the penumbra' (see Barnett and Yach, 1985, pp.151, 168).

The simple idea behind this book is that on these voyages of intellectual acquisition in jurisprudence too much has to be jettisoned on the return journey. To supplement jurisprudence could be just a matter of making sure that valuable things are kept on board. The supplement provides what is lacking. It serves to complement and to complete that which is supplemented. In this bland sense of the supplement, feminism for example may show us that current conceptions of law in jurisprudence are inadequate. We could explore feminism by seeking to incorporate within jurisprudence such aspects of it as would make good the deficiency. But, as Derrida has it, the supplement is also 'dangerous' (1976, pp.144–5). It is not fully assimilable. It remains outside, challenging the completeness and

1

the adequacy of that which is within. So, the chapter by Smart in this collection indicates that jurisprudence would have to undergo 'a radical transformation' if it were to accommodate feminism.

I will raise the stakes by invoking a mainstream idea already securely accommodated, so it seems, within jurisprudence. For N.E. Simmonds, in an important text on the subject, 'studying jurisprudence is a matter of reading books by such authors as Rawls, Nozick, Hart and Dworkin' (1986, p.v). This accurately reflects the predominant emphasis in the teaching of jurisprudence (Barnett and Yach, 1985, p. 165). Each of these four writers espouses and brings to jurisprudence a variant of strong liberalism. Offhand, it is difficult to see why Hayek should not be in this list of the select. He is probably the most influential proponent of strong liberalism. He has written extensively on law and jurisprudential questions. Yet Hayek figures marginally at most in jurisprudence. The reason why and the disruptive challenge which Hayek's thought poses to jurisprudence can be discerned later in Thomson's chapter.

I simply mention the instances of feminism and Hayek to indicate what the supplementary jurisprudence of this volume aims to do. Minimally, it would keep open the connections between 'law' and 'context' and avoid the protective and premature closure around law which jurisprudence continually seeks to effect. In doing this, however, supplementary jurisprudence would evoke those otherwise suppressed, disregarded or marginalised perspectives which the writers of this book are seeking to bring into full consideration, thereby challenging both jurisprudence and that law which it encases. I will return to that challenge and to the purposes of the collection in my conclusion to this chapter (p.27). For now, I pursue the aspirations of supplementary jurisprudence in the danger it throws up for the supreme text of jurisprudence, H.L.A. Hart's *The Concept of Law* (1961). First I shall indicate the significance of that target and then outline my general line of argument.

The Concept *and the Supplement*

'In the English-speaking world', *The Concept of Law* now provides 'the standard position' in jurisprudence (Leith, 1988, p.85). From within jurisprudence and from without, superlatives have been showered upon it (see Moles, 1987, p.5). *The Concept* underlies 'Hart's position of pre-eminence among British jurists of the twentieth century' and his position as 'the focal figure ... for English speaking jurists' (MacCormick, 1981, pp.12, 19). It 'remains the most significant post-war text in jurisprudence' (Lloyd and Freeman, 1985, p.403). It also 'remains a central focus of jurisprudence teaching in the U.K.' (Barnett and Yach, 1985, p.158). Surveys of jurisprudence teaching place it very much on the top of the list of works used (ibid., pp.159–61). It remains, as well, remarkably intact as a text despite, or perhaps because of, the hundreds of papers which would seek to revise or undermine it. Those writers sympathetic to it have tended not to engage, or not to engage fully, with destructive criticism. The effect of their own contributions is difficult to pin down because it is usually not clear whether these are revisions or exegesis (see Hart 1982, Chapter X; MacCormick, 1987, p.105). The upshot is that both detractors and supporters still address *The Concept of Law* with its key teachings largely unchanged since its publication in 1961 (for example, Hart, 1987; Moles 1987).

There is good reason for this continuity and for the high regard in which *The Concept of Law* is held. In this book Hart restored and set new sustaining terms for a positivist jurisprudence that appeared increasingly impoverished in the face of jurisprudential tendencies which it was unable either to challenge or to contain. To sustain positivist jurisprudence, to endow it with the ability to deal with these tendencies, Hart provided it with a new foundation derived from linguistic philosophy. The difficulty here is that linguistic philosophy is incompatible with positivist jurisprudence. Hart accommodates the difficulty by ignoring it. When providing intimations of a new approach and when dealing with the inadequacies of other theorists, Hart adopts linguistic philosophy without reserve. In this adoption, linguistic philosophy supplements positivist jurisprudence by making up for its inadequacies. Yet when unveiling his triumphal alternative, Hart resorts to the idiom of positivist jurisprudence. Then linguistic philosophy is silently pushed into the margins where it waits as a dangerous supplement. If we bring it in from the margins, if we restore it to the position of primacy that Hart initially accorded it, then *The Concept of Law* simply 'self-destructs'.

The meaning of *The Concept*
I will now provide a description and running criticism of the main lines of argument in *The Concept of Law*. I want to show at the outset that Hart's standpoint and his claim to transform jurisprudence is founded in linguistic philosophy and especially in Wittgenstein's *Philosophical Investigations* (1968). This may seem a distortion because Wittgenstein's explicit part in *The Concept* is confined to two footnotes (Hart, 1961, pp.234, 249). Hart later provided a more general acknowledgement (Hart, 1983, pp.2–3). He more prominently acknowledges the influence of the linguistic philosopher J.L. Austin (see also Hart, 1954a). This influence is broadly compatible with (if overshadowed by) that of Wittgenstein, who created the domain of linguistic philosophy. It is, however, Austin whom I will draw on now to illustrate a dimension of linguistic philosophy

that will be central to my analysis: its claim to break from previous philosophy and to reorient the whole philosophical project. Prior philosophies would only retain worth to the extent that their contents were recast by linguistic philosophy. For Austin, linguistic philosophy was 'a revolution in philosophy' and '[i]f anyone wishes to call it the greatest and most salutary in its history, this is not, if you come to think of it, a large claim' (see Leith, 1988, p.85). As we shall see, Hart makes only somewhat less outrageous claims in his rejection and reorienting of prior jurisprudence. Having done this he cannot revert to the old ways of jurisprudence, but revert he assuredly does. The resulting incoherence means that his positivist jurisprudence is dissolved.

The Concept of Law is usually seen as an exercise in linguistic philosophy, one which secured Hart's renown as a linguistic philosopher as well as a jurist (MacCormick, 1981, pp.12–19). The first four chapters of the book are largely in the idiom of linguistic philosophy and impelled by its characteristic concerns. In looking initially at Hart as linguistic philosopher, I will give references to Wittgenstein that parallel Hart's resort to that philosophy. Hart begins securely within the tradition by addressing the question of definition (see also Hart, 1954b). He confronts and disposes of the old question, 'what is law?'. This puzzle has resisted resolution because it is founded in linguistic confusion (Wittgenstein, 1968, paras. 109, 119, 123). The origin of error lies in the experience of meaning which the question evokes. That is, a word like 'law' must name something to which it corresponds (Wittgenstein, 1968, paras. 26–7). A word has essential or inherent meaning. One way of testing such meaning would be to match the word against some empirically observable reality. Linguistic philosophy was created in opposition to such a view of meaning and such a way of testing it. Whether words stand adequately for things was only one kind of question that could be asked about them. If we placed words in their ordinary context, if we looked at their characteristic use, we would see that they did much more than just stand for things (Wittgenstein, 1968, paras. 19, 23, 146–8). So, some legal realists may see law in terms of a prediction of what judges will do. But this view of law does not capture the ways in which a judge uses a legal rule 'as his *reason* and *justification* for punishing the offender' (Hart, 1961, p.10; original emphasis). The multiple and complex uses of 'law' cannot be reduced to a simple statement of factual correspondence – reduced, in this case, to what judges are seen to be doing. Such a statement would explain something, but far from all, of what is going on. This attempt to capture an essence of law which would be the same in all situations where the word 'law' was used has merely reduced varied and multiple uses to one possible use.

Hart (ibid., p.234) quotes Wittgenstein's instruction for considering various 'games' and the question of what is common to all of them:

> Don't say: 'There *must* be something common, or they would not be called "games"' – but *look and see* whether there is anything common to all. – For if you look at them you will not see something that is common to *all*, but similarities, relationships, and a whole series of them at that. (as in Wittgenstein, 1968, para. 66; original emphasis)

Linguistic philosophy effects its revolution by showing that perennial questions posed in philosophy disappear or can be radically recast in a more tractable form. In the same way Hart finds prior jurisprudence to be wrongly oriented. The result is a 'record of failure and there is plainly need for a fresh start', which he provides (Hart, 1961, p.78). The record of failure is revised, in terms of linguistic philosophy, by looking at characteristic contexts in which 'law' and significant legal usages appear and by considering the diversity of jobs which they do. The aspiration of linguistic philosophy which Hart does pursue is that which would see the words and the functions they perform in their particularity, describing them as they are and not reducing them in other terms (Wittgenstein, 1968, paras. 19, 23). For use and context linguistic philosophers look to language. In the observation and evaluation of linguistic use, however, they also look to non-linguistic presuppositions of that use. For a judge to use a legal rule as a rule presupposes, as we saw earlier, a certain commitment to that rule. But there are limits to what can be presupposed. For linguistic philosophy use is prime and presupposition has necessarily to be related or relatable to use.

Hart brings the force of linguistic philosophy most immediately to bear on the work of John Austin, the ancestor figure of English jurisprudence. In Hart's estimation, 'Austin's influence on the development in England of the subject has been greater than that of any other writer' (Hart, 1954a, p.xiv). Much of *The Concept* is taken up with setting Hart's own standpoint in a critique of Austin. Austin is Hart's proper obsession. His positivist jurisprudence dominated the subject for close to a century until its displacement by *The Concept* and it still retains a position of prominence close to Hart's in jurisprudence teaching in the UK (Barnett and Yach, 1985, p.159). Yet Hart's version of Austin is strangely truncated. Austin attempted, Hart says, 'to analyse the concept of law in terms of the apparently simple elements of commands and habits' (1961, p.18). And 'we shall state and criticize a position which is, in substance, the same as Austin's doctrine but probably diverges from it at certain points' (ibid.). It certainly does diverge, but that for Hart is of no significance since 'our principal concern is not with Austin but with the credentials of a certain type of theory which has perennial attractions whatever its defects may be' (ibid.). These attractions lie in the siren call for definition, for encapsulating what law is in some factual formula such as one involving 'the apparently simple elements of command and habits' which Austin supposedly uses. The problem is that the 'elements he uses do not include the notion of a *rule* or the rule dependent notion of what *ought* to be done' (Hart, 1954a, pp.xi-xii; original emphasis). When we see rules operating in legal contexts it becomes evident that they cannot be reduced to a correspondence with certain observable facts about commands and habits any more than they could be reduced, as we saw earlier, to a prediction of what judges will do. What these reductions capture, at most, is how the operation of a rule could appear to an external observer. They do not capture the internal perspective of the operation of rules, the perspective of those who use rules. And it is this which is distinctive of rules and of law. Such, very briefly, is the next stage of Hart's argument, which I will now amplify and analyse.

To respond to demands for definition of law in terms of factual correspondences fails to account for 'the idea of a rule, without which we cannot hope to elucidate even the most elementary forms of law' (Hart, 1961, p.78). And we cannot, says Hart, claim to make adequate statements about the existence of a rule in terms of habit. (Neither Austin nor any other thinker Hart takes to task does this, but we must let that pass.) The idea of a habit relates to observable uniformities of behaviour. Following a rule may to an outsider look like a habit. If a group has a rule requiring its members to meet in a bar every Saturday night, then such a gathering of its members could look like – and even take on elements of – a habit. Yet it would always remain more than that. A habit would not oblige people to come, nor would departing from the habit be a cause for criticism, much less a good reason for criticism. Further, a rule does not correspond to a command, to orders that are backed by threats. We do not describe an order given by a gunman in a hold-up in the same terms as we describe a legal rule. For a start, not all legal rules require people to do or not to do something on pain of some harm that could result from not complying. Some rules enable people to do things. They enable people to make wills, judges to judge, and so on. Even where the legal rule is a requirement backed by a sanction it cannot be seen as 'the gunman situation writ large' (ibid., p.7). The immediate and transitory nature of the gunman's order does not, for example, accommodate the continuity of legal rules or the sustained commitments people have to rules in terms of rights and obligations.

With Hart, a conception of law in such terms as habits and commands would be confined to the 'external aspect' provided by an outside observer:

> For such an observer, deviations by a member of the group from normal conduct will be a sign that hostile reaction is likely to follow, and nothing more. His view will be like the view of one who, having observed the working of a traffic signal in a busy street for some time, limits himself to saying that when the light turns red there is a high probability that the traffic will stop. He treats the light merely as a natural *sign that* people will behave in certain ways, as clouds are a *sign that* rain will come. In so doing he will miss out a whole dimension of the social life of those whom he is watching, since for them the red light is not merely a sign that others will stop: they look upon it as a *signal for* them to stop, and so a reason for stopping in conformity to rules which make stopping when the light is red a standard of behaviour and an obligation. To mention this is to bring into account the way in which the group regards its own behaviour. It is to refer to the internal aspect of rules seen from their internal point of view. (ibid., pp.87–8; original emphasis)

It is this internal aspect which best encapsulates Hart's criticisms of the external conceptions of law (ibid., p.88). This aspect, to borrow MacCormick's influential assessment, is 'the most distinctive and valuable element in Hart's work as a jurist' (1981, p.29) and it is the same internal aspect that undermines Hart's conceptions of law and legal system, as we shall see. I should now look at it in a little more detail.

Drawing on the idiom of linguistic philosophy, Hart locates the internal aspect of rule in contexts where rules operate and in the use people make of rules. Looking at such a use and such a context is a very different operation to the search for supposed correspondences to a rule that the external examiner is limited to. The external description of people's behaviour at traffic lights 'cannot be in terms of rules at all' (Hart, 1961, p.87). This is, admittedly, an 'extreme external point of view and does not give any account of the manner in which members of the group who accept the rules view their own regular behaviour' (ibid.). But even the non-extreme observer 'who records *ab extra* the fact that a social group accepts such rules but does not himself accept them' has an external point of view, one which contrasts with the 'attitude of shared acceptance of rules' (ibid., p.99):

> What the external point of view ... cannot reproduce is the way in which the rules function as rules in the lives of those who

normally are the majority of society. These are the officials, lawyers, or private persons who use them, in one situation after another, as guides to the conduct of social life, as the basis for claims, demands, admissions, criticism, or punishment, viz., in all the familiar transactions of life according to rules. (ibid., p.88)

Yet again in the idiom of linguistic philosophy, Hart often resorts to games in order to make his point, the indicative preferences being for chess and cricket:

Chess players do not merely have similar habits of moving the Queen in the same way which an external observer, who knew nothing about their attitude to the moves which they make, could record. In addition, they have a reflective critical attitude to this pattern of behaviour: they regard it as a standard for all who play the game. Each not only moves the Queen in a certain way himself but 'has views' about the propriety of all moving the Queen in that way. These views are manifested in the criticism of others and demands for conformity made upon others when deviation is actual or threatened, and in the acknowledgement of the legitimacy of such criticism and demands when received from others. (ibid., pp.55–6)

The external observer, or at least the extreme external observer, would not be able to 'distinguish, as compliance with an accepted rule, the adult chess-player's move from the action of the baby who merely pushed the piece into the right place' (ibid., p.137). The external observer does not act in relation to the rules 'as a member of the group which accepts and uses them as guides to conduct' (ibid., p.86). So, we find that those following rules as guides to conduct make statements in terms of someone being 'out' in a game of cricket, of what 'must', 'should' or 'ought' to be done, of 'having an obligation' and of some action being 'wrong' (ibid., pp.9, 56, 84). Such participants adopt 'a critical reflective attitude to certain patterns of behaviour as a common standard', 'as a general standard to be followed by the group as a whole' or 'as standards for the appraisal of their own and others' behaviour' (ibid., pp.55–6, 96). Deviation from the standard, or from a rule, 'is generally accepted as a *good reason*' for criticism or for some other 'hostile' reaction (ibid., pp.54, 88; original emphasis). Where 'our behaviour is challenged we are disposed to justify it by reference to the rule' (ibid., p.136 and compare Baker and Hacker, 1985, pp.155, 159). Perhaps I am labouring these points but I am doing so much less than Hart and the reason is that they serve later to undermine Hart's 'foundations of a legal system'.

'There is some obscurity,' says Harris, 'as to what ... the concept of internal point of view stands for' (1980, p.108). The question has become one of fervent jurisprudential debate in which 'internal' is conceived as internal to the person following the rule. This line of enquiry, however, is comprehensively frustrated by Hart. The internal aspect or point of view, he says, cannot be equated with approval of or moral support for the rule; nor with feelings of pressure or compulsion to follow it; nor with 'beliefs, fears and motives', nor indeed with mental experience at all (Hart, 1961, pp.56, 81, 86, 198-9, 243). To ask what the element of the internal 'stands for', to seek correspondences to it in terms of mental processes is to ignore Hart's whole orientation in linguistic philosophy. I will not go over the ground again except to say that the subtlety and diversity of use and context which Hart draws on in identifying the internal aspect are lost by reducing them in terms of mental processes (see for example, Wittgenstein, 1968, paras. 303-4). What such a reduction misses in particular is the social dimension of the internal aspect of rules. Hart constantly identifies the internal aspect in terms of 'demands for conformity made upon others', of a 'standard to be followed by the group as a whole', of 'a social group [which] accepts' the rules 'and uses them as guides to conduct' (1961, pp.55-6, 86, 99). The acceptance of the rule is manifested in such use (ibid., p.99). For 'the subtle kind of positivism' that is linguistic philosophy this use and the capabilities involved in it comprise the factual correspondences to the internal aspect (Pears, 1971, pp.104, 172). As these points about the social dimension are crucial for the rest of my analysis of *The Concept of Law*, I will consider them a little more extensively.

Hart has a strange footnote supporting his conception of the internal aspect of rules. He refers to two works for 'similar views' to his own (1961, p.242). The first is Winch, *The Idea of a Social Science and its Relation to Philosophy* (1958). Hart's internal aspect closely corresponds to ideas of Winch which in turn closely correspond to those of Wittgenstein. The second work is Piddington, 'Malinowski's Theory of Needs' (1957), an essay which would stand almost completely opposed to Winch's. Hart finds particularly significant, as we shall see, the small area of agreement which these works share. For Winch, a rule is a standard reflectively applied and this is an essentially human activity. An animal cannot reflectively apply a rule. It acts out of ingrained habit (Winch, 1958, pp.57-60). For Piddington, culture entails the resort to 'normative standards or values ... crystallized in a system of symbols which enables individuals to evaluate the behaviour of others, irrespective of whether they are or are not themselves affected or involved'; and culture is distinctive of 'man's life as a social animal', something which does not characterise the lives of other animals (1957, pp.36-8). Thus, for Hart, unless we take

account of the internal aspect of rules 'we cannot properly understand the whole distinctive style of human thought, speech, and
action which is involved in the existence of rules and which constitutes the normative structure of society' (1961, p.86).

This all involves certain human skills and capacities (see for
example ibid., p.120). It entails understanding a rule as well as the
calculation, organisation and other techniques used in following it
(Baker and Hacker, 1985, pp.155, 159–63). Whether or not
Wittgenstein would see all this as exclusively human (see Hirst and
Woolley, 1982, p.81), he did regard human behaviour as separable
from animal behaviour and as characterised by the following of rules
(Wittgenstein, 1968, para. 25). Even 'if a lion could talk, we could
not understand him', speaking, as he would, internally from within
his distinct form of life (ibid., p.223).[1] I will return to the internal
aspect of rules when testing Hart's 'foundations of a legal system'.

Hart now begins to introduce, beside the internal aspect, another
requirement for the existence of legal rules: they must be somehow
involved with officials. The origin of this requirement in Hart's
account, apart from mere invocation, has puzzled acute observers
(for example, Moles, 1987, pp.90–1). Hart does 'suppose' a legislator,
Rex, and his successors, and '[i]n explaining the continuity of law-
making power through a changing succession of individual legisla-
tors, it is natural to use the expressions "rule of succession", "title",
"right to succeed", and "right to make law"' (1961, pp.51–53). What
seems to be Hart's mode of argument here can be best approached
through an example. Hart considers, as we saw, that these usages of
'right' and 'rule' cannot be accommodated by the Austinian notion
of occasional and discontinuous commands or 'orders backed by
threats'. Something better has to be found to sustain, for instance,
the element of continuity involved in a rule and Hart locates this in
the official world.

Such a line of argument, however, merely identifies a deficiency in
one idea of law. It does not identify the official as the only way of
making good the deficiency. The existence of Rex as the origin of
the official world is merely given in Hart's original supposition and
this was an invented example to aid presentation. Nor, it would
seem, does Hart claim that an official element in 'right' and 'rule' is
necessarily presupposed by such usage. Despite Rex's fictional beginnings, Hart continues to insinuate Rex into his account until he is
able to write of 'law-making, law-identifying and law-applying operations' being matters for 'the officials or experts of the system' as
opposed to 'the mass of the population' or 'the ordinary citizen'
(ibid., pp.59–60). He then proceeds to secure this divide in his 'fresh
start', his discovery of 'law as the union of primary and secondary
rules' (ibid., p.77).

The Primal Scene
This 'fresh start' for jurisprudence is also a fresh start for Hart. Having relied on linguistic philosophy to make his case, Hart now unceremoniously jettisons it and pursues a radically opposed perspective. He does, however, maintain a semblance of continuity by invoking a type of argument which has similarities to the mode that gave us Rex and the official world. As we saw, a view of law bearing an uncertain relation to that of John Austin was found to be deficient because it did not accommodate 'the idea of a rule, without which we cannot hope to elucidate even the most elementary forms of law' (ibid., p.78). Now the slippage occurs. From the conclusion that a conception of law must include the idea of a rule, Hart moves towards confining law to rules. Rules provide 'the elements of law' and the foundations of a legal system (ibid., pp.89, 97). The vaunted union of primary and secondary rules – the 'fresh start' which we consider shortly – is 'the heart of' or is 'at the centre of a legal system' (ibid., pp.95–6). Such a 'union may be justly regarded as the "essence" of law' (ibid., p.151).

Those distancing quotes around 'essence' and the resort to building and biological metaphors relating law and rules do perhaps evidence a residual reluctance simply to equate law with rules. This reluctance is an attenuated tribute to Hart's previous reliance on linguistic philosophy. As a linguistic philosopher, Hart would not seek the essence of law. He would not seek out what it is since for linguistic philosophy and for Hart that, as we saw, was a misconceived quest. Yet it is a quest on which Hart now embarks. He bases the quest on the arbitrary and continuous reduction of law to a matter of rules (see also Hart, 1987, pp.37–8). Moreover, he simply asserts that for the existence of such rules we need only look to other rules, for it is 'a very familiar chain of reasoning' that '[i]f the question is raised whether some suggested rule is legally valid, we must in order to answer the question use a criterion of validity provided by some other rule' (1961, p.103). This stunning familiarity and Hart's confining of 'law' to rules, controversial as they have proved in Western jurisprudence, would be spectacularly alien to other major legal systems (see Geertz, 1983, Chapter 8). So much for the claimed universality of Hart's concept of law.

Nonetheless Hart confidently locates his fresh start for jurisprudence in a speculative universal history of early humanity. There Hart is witness to a primal scene in which law as the union of primary and secondary rules is conceived.[2] This myth of origin begins with a type of 'simple tribal society', 'a small community closely knit by ties of kinship, common sentiment, and belief and placed in a stable environment' (Hart, 1961, pp.59, 89). This society has only primary rules of obligation whereby 'human beings are required to do or abstain from certain actions, whether they wish to or not' (ibid., pp.78–9). The primary rules are in Hart's view similar to custom. The imperative of social control means that they 'are in fact always found in primitive societies' where they have to be widely accepted in their internal aspect in order to be effective (ibid., p.89). Societies with only primary rules eventually appreciate the inadequacies of such an Adamic simplicity and thus provide Hart with the components of his concept of law. In that state there would be no way of settling 'what the [primary] rules are or ... the precise scope of some given rule' (ibid., p.90). The resulting uncertainty is cured by a rule of recognition providing 'conclusive identification of primary rules' in some authoritative, written form (ibid., p.92). Again, 'there will be no means, in such a society, of deliberately adapting the rules to changing circumstances, either by eliminating old rules or introducing new ones' (ibid., p.90). The resulting *static* quality of the regime of primary rules' is cured by the introduction of 'rules of change' empowering 'an individual or body of persons to introduce new primary rules ... and to eliminate old rules' (ibid., p.93; original emphasis). Finally, there would be 'the *inefficiency* of the diffuse social pressures by which the rules are maintained' which would be cured by 'rules of adjudication ... identifying the individuals who are to adjudicate' and identifying 'the procedure to be followed' (ibid., pp.91, 94; original emphasis).

> [T]he remedy for each defect might, in itself, be considered a step from the pre-legal into the legal world; since each remedy brings with it many elements that permeate law: certainly all three remedies together are enough to convert the regime of primary rules into what is indisputably a legal system ... If we stand back and consider the structure which has resulted from the combination of primary rules of obligation with the secondary rules of recognition, change and adjudication, it is plain that we have here not only the heart of a legal system, but a most powerful tool for the analysis of much that has puzzled both the jurist and the political theorist. (ibid., pp.91, 95)[3]

Whatever else this antique story may be, it is not linguistic philosophy. It is, for a start, an elaboration of Hart's arbitrary and essentialist confining of law to rules. But Hart's retreat from linguistic philosophy goes much further. Like those whom he has castigated for doing so, Hart now searches explicitly for what law is, for what state of affairs law corresponds to. He is not now looking to use and context. If we explore his sources, the knowledge that enables him to present this primal scene, we can then readily grasp the gulf between it and linguistic philosophy.

Hart's acknowledged source derives from the social anthropology of the twentieth century. Although he veers between the assertion that some, if 'few', societies have existed without secondary rules and the assertion that such a state was 'never perhaps fully realized in any actual community', Hart does rely on anthropological 'studies of the nearest approximations to this state' (ibid., pp.90, 244). Like much legal anthropology, these studies are concerned with the existence of so-called law in so-called primitive or savage societies. They share with Hart the technique of bringing a pre-existing conception of law to bear on the world, a conception corresponding to one type of Western law which claims to maintain or to restore social order. The world then obliges by confirming that this idea of law is universally real. Anthropology has often provided tales of transition not unlike Hart's, covering the development of societies from a primitive state and the distinctive genesis of law in this development when public or official organisation emerges out of diffuse social norms (see, for example, Hoebel, 1954 and Newman, 1983).

Origins for such tales can also be found in Hart's second source, the evolutionary history of the nineteenth century. This source is not explicitly invoked but it pervades Hart's account. The evolutionary history of law is essentialist in that it requires 'the conceptual establishment of an entity [law in our case] that is progressing or evolving' (Bock, 1979, p.71). With this way of thinking, the entity is sustained despite the process of change by presenting transition as a step from one ordered state containing the entity to another – from the primitive to the modern, and so on. The transition is always one from the simple to the complex, from the unified to the diverse. In the process, the entity becomes increasingly distinct and differentiated, but differentiation is always accompanied by a continued social integration, an encompassing order which law itself sustains. The entity in evolving responds to and overcomes the inadequacies of its prior form. It is conceptually viewed in its latest achieved stage and its universal history is told from that vantage point, a recounting of how the entity came to be as it is.

The parallels between this sort of story and Hart's account need not be laboured. Hart's mythic society at first has only primary rules which are 'a primitive or a rudimentary form of law' and which 'we are accustomed to contrast with a developed legal system' (1961, pp.84, 209). So Hart discerns, sometimes explicitly 'in the history of law' or 'as a matter of history', that societies have 'seen the advantages' of changing to more complex forms, that they have 'progressed to the point where' law and morality 'are distinguished as different forms of social control', and that with the introduction of secondary rules they 'step' from primitive or rudimentary law into a fully 'legal world', 'a step forward as important to society as the invention of the wheel' (ibid., pp.41, 91-2, 95, 118).

In the jumble of sources for Hart's story of the primal scene, none is so pervasive as the philosophy of the Enlightenment, usually seen as centred around the eighteenth century. I will consider it in some detail in its relation to Hart's account and I will extract a fundamental opposition between Hart's reliance on Enlightenment thought and his reliance on linguistic philosophy. I will then set Hart's reliance on linguistic philosophy against his account of the primal scene as it draws on all three sources, the anthropological, the evolutionary and the Enlightenment. This disjunction, as we will then see, is at the root of the failure of Hart's climactic attempt to lay 'the foundations of a legal system'.

As with Hart's search for 'the elements of law', the philosophers of the Enlightenment sought the elements of forms in their origins. Numerous stories not dissimilar to Hart's tell of life in a state of nature, or in such variants as the savage state or a state regulated by custom (Meek, 1976). Law as intrinsic to (Western) civilization is contrasted constitutively with the state of nature (Stein, 1980). Law has its origins in the state of nature because its rudiments can be found there and because its existence is a response to the inadequacy of that state. Such inadequacies are viewed by, for example, Locke in much the same way as Hart sees the 'three defects' requiring secondary rules of recognition, change and adjudication (Locke, 1960, para. 124). Even Hart's vaunted discovery of the elements of law as the union of primary and secondary rules is no more novel in this context than it was in the anthropological: the mythic origins of law in the tales of Enlightenment have it emerging when an official dimension operates on the state of nature, when a determining or 'positive' law is separated from and brought to bear on the 'negative ... state which is styled a state of nature', to borrow the terms from Austin's version (1861, pp.122, 124).[4]

As with Hart's story, in the thought of the Enlightenment to account for origins is to establish enduring essence. The correspondence of origin and essence seems to be so obvious in Hart as not to require any explanation. Even in the speculative history that he offers, should there not be an appreciation that things change, that they can become radically different to what they were? Despite its mode of presentation, however, this is not an enquiry into history or into any known state of affairs. Hart, as we saw, is inconsistent on the issue of whether there ever was a society which had only primary rules. Yet such a society is his starting point and the inadequacy of having only primary rules provides the seemingly historical impetus for his elements of law.

For Locke 'it is not at all to be wonder'd, that *History* gives us but very little account of Men, *that lived together in the State of Nature'* (Locke, 1960, para. 101; original emphasis). The answer lies elsewhere. Using Hart's terms for aspects of his primal scene, the answer is 'discoverable by reason' or in 'natural necessity', in 'truisms about human nature', in 'elementary truths concerning human beings' (Hart, 1961, pp.89, 189, 195). In the Enlightenment this was a scientific mode of enquiry which, on the one hand, presupposed and produced constant elements that underlie both the flux of change and the apparent diversity of things, and, on the other, provided their common ground. Thus, Hart's elements of law provide what is common and constant in the diversity of law's manifestations. Given the constant character of these elements an enquiry into origins will reveal them as they are now, and reveal them more readily because in origins we find the elements in their simple forms before the addition of complex and obscuring shapes. Finally, the concern with constant elements in the thought of Enlightenment was a concern with the necessary order of things, with harmony and equilibrium. This concern transfers in Hart's turn to a cohering 'control' as integral to society and law (see, for example, 1961, pp.89, 191). Law is a result of imperatives of order and itself orders. It is *ordo ordinans*, ordering order (Cassirer, 1951, p.240).

We may get some measure of the chasm between this line of thought and Hart's earlier foundational resort to linguistic philosophy by returning to his explicit reliance on Wittgenstein, a reliance which he then found 'peculiarly relevant to the analysis of legal and political terms' (1961, p.234). Instead of looking for a common essence to 'games', Wittgenstein exhorts us to *'look and see* whether there is anything common to all', and if we do that we 'will not see something that is common to *all*, but similarities, relationships, and a whole series of them at that' (Wittgenstein, 1968, para. 66; original emphases). Hart regards this as an instance of Wittgenstein's notion of family resemblances. Like the resemblances between members of a family we do not, if we look and see, find a uniform essence but 'we see a complicated network of similarities overlapping and crisscrossing': 'as in spinning a thread we twist fibre on fibre ... the strength of the thread does not reside in the fact that some one fibre runs throughout its whole length, but in the overlapping of many fibres' (ibid., paras. 66–7).

Elsewhere Wittgenstein contrasted the notion of family resemblances with 'our craving for generality' which he saw as having a source in 'the method of science', a method of a kind I attributed to the Enlightenment:

I mean the method of reducing the explanation of natural phenomena to the smallest possible number of primitive natural laws;

and, in mathematics, of unifying the treatment of different topics by using a generalization. Philosophers constantly see the method of science before their eyes, and are irresistibly tempted to ask and answer questions in the way that science does. This tendency is the real source of metaphysics, and leads the philosopher into complete darkness. I want to say here that it can never be our job to reduce anything to anything ... (Wittgenstein, 1958, p.18)

Thus, if we 'stand back' and consider Hart's story of the primal scene enlightened by its three sources, we do not find a diversity of related ideas of 'law' emerging from its various uses and contexts. Hart seeks and finds elements that constitute a singular and constant essence of law. This idea of law does not come initially from the primal context in which it is supposed to originate. Rather, it comes from a Western conception of law, the terms of which inhabit and shape the whole enquiry. Understandably enough those terms are readily discovered in the enquiry and emerge reinforced from it. In these terms law is intrinsic to social order, it acts on and controls society. It does this determinatively through official performances which emanate from a vantage point of distinct domination, one necessarily separated from the society that is ordered and controlled. All of this bespeaks a peculiar 'western cosmology' (Strathern, 1985, p.128), not, as Hart would have it, a universal history of law.

How does this silent shift from linguistic philosophy to its opposite occur? The answer lies in the nature of the primal scene. It renders the shift unremarkable. All of the inhabitants of the primal scene, from the 'savages' of North America to the colonised of Africa, shared a convenient characteristic which prevented their contributing to linguistic use: they could not speak and thus had to be spoken for. In the imperial mentality which informs Hart's account and its sources, true knowledge is brought by the European to the 'savages' and the colonised. Their reality is thereby known for the first time – known properly and fully both in itself and in the universal order of things. Inadequate local knowledges are infinitely encompassed and given adequacy by European knowledge. Being without a history or a project of their own, the savages and the colonised take their uniform characteristics from the uniform European perception of them. This provides the common ground founding the universal history of 'early man', a ground beyond which only some have progressed. The imperial cast of mind, as Rackett perceives it, neutralised a myriad existences and meanings into a crude, mythical uniformity 'where "whiteness" signifies positivity, identity and certitude, and "blackness" signifies negativity, difference and transgression' (Rackett, 1985, p.195).

To draw out the closer connections between Hart's conception of law and this mythology I will look more specifically at the colonial situation (compare Skillen, 1977, pp.102–7). The stock delusions attending colonial rule permeate Hart's story (see generally Fitzpatrick, 1989). Native society is simple, small and self-contained. It is characterised by uncertainty, stasis, inefficiency, and by a lawless or only incipiently legal condition. The colonists claim to bring a civilisation which will provide many things, among them security and order, incorporation within a dynamic history, efficiency, law and the opportunity for progress by means of social functions becoming differentiated. The natives long for all this in the depth of their being, long for it as their own completion. As the colonial situation presents an administered reality, it is the official who is to bring to fruition the incipient humanity of the native. This account has not been contrived so as to extort a correspondence with Hart's story of the primal scene. The correspondence is exact and I will not elaborate on it.

Let us for a moment be consistent on Hart's behalf and invoke the use and the context provided by the colonised. If we give a local habitation, a finitude to his imperial observation of the mute primitive, we do not find inadequate and impoverished precursors of Western law but subtle, complex and elegant modes of regulation that bear no relation to the constrained conceptions of law as rules and social control that Hart imposes on the situation (see for example Strathern, 1985). The uses and the contexts of the colonised would, that is, undermine the categories on which Hart's enquiry is founded. They would in their plenitude ultimately resist reduction to a uniform, imperial representation. Winch begins his book on social science and philosophy, the work on which Hart draws and which largely corresponds to his position as a linguistic philosopher, with a guiding quotation that in part reads: 'it is unjust to give any action a different name from that which it used to bear in its own times and amongst its own people' (1958). To that Lyotard could add that 'to place oneself in the position of enunciator of the universal prescription is ... absolute injustice' (in Lyotard and Thebaud, 1985, p.99).

At this stage, then, we have two Harts: the linguistic philosopher and the enunciator of the universal. We also have two opposing sets of consequences of this division. With one, we have popular usages, an internal aspect of rules and active, reflective subjects, all of which are at the very foundation of Hart's analysis. With the other, there is the dominance of official determinations, a dominance finally emerging as universal necessity in that natural history of law which Hart finds in the primal scene. It is at this point of cavernous difference that Hart presents a resolved picture of 'the foundations of a legal system', the 'buckle' holding together 'the whole of his normative legal theory' (Cotterrell, 1989, p.100).

The Apotheosis of the Official

These foundations of a legal system mark the triumph of one side of Hart's duality – that is, the triumph of official determinations. The other side is reduced to the internal aspect of rules, presumably as a result of confining his enquiry to law as a matter of rules. Hart effects the triumph of official determinations by making the internal aspect necessary only for them. Such a resolution is reached through an astonishing compression of contradictions. After having based both his criticism of previous ideas of law and the lineaments of his alternative on the necessity for rules to have an internal aspect, Hart proceeds to deny that necessity. Although previously he wrote that the internal aspect cannot be envisaged in terms of individual mental states, he now treats of its presence and absence in terms of individual mental states. And despite having thus subordinated the internal aspect to individual mentality, Hart posits the possibility of a society in which that mentality eliminates the internal aspect for 'the ordinary citizen'. This is a strange society. It is a society without social relations, one which Hart bolsters with desperate metaphor rather than sociolinguistic or sociological observation. It is a society which lacks attributes which Hart elsewhere in *The Concept of Law* considers necessary for the existence of any society. And the contradictions multiply.

I will now provide a more extensive but not exhaustive guide to these contradictions after outlining the so-called foundations of the legal system. There are for Hart:

> two minimum conditions necessary and sufficient for the exis-
> tence of a legal system. On the one hand those rules of behaviour
> which are valid according to the system's ultimate criteria of valid-
> ity must be generally obeyed, and, on the other hand, its rules of
> recognition specifying the criteria of legal validity and its rules of
> change and adjudication must be effectively accepted as common
> public standards of official behaviour by its officials. The first con-
> dition is the only one which private citizens *need* satisfy: they may
> obey each 'for his part only' and from any motive whatever;
> though in a healthy society they will in fact often accept these
> rules as common standards of behaviour and acknowledge an obli-
> gation to obey them ... (1961, p.113; original emphasis)

For 'the ordinary citizen' to have this 'merely personal concern with rules':

> He need not think of his conforming behaviour as 'right', 'correct',
> or 'obligatory'. His attitude, in other words, need not have any of
> that critical character which is involved whenever social rules are

accepted and types of conduct are treated as general standards. He need not, though he may, share the internal point of view accepting the rules as standards for all to whom they apply. Instead, he may think of the rule only as something demanding action from *him* under threat of penalty ... (ibid., p.112; original emphasis)

I will look first at what this account does to that internal aspect of rules which I considered in detail earlier. We saw that for Hart the operation of legal rules necessarily involved an internal aspect. This is entailed in people's '*use* [of] the rules as standards for the appraisal of their own and others' behaviour' (ibid., p.96; original emphasis). The internal aspect has an integral social dimension. Not only do people use rules to evaluate the conduct of others as well as their own but along with Hart we must conceive of the internal aspect in terms of the social group accepting the rules, of 'the way in which the group regards its own behaviour' (ibid., pp.88, 99). The internal aspect is inseparable from 'the whole distinctive style of human thought, speech, and action which is involved in the existence of rules and which constitutes the normative structure of society' (ibid., p.86). So, for the internal aspect individual 'beliefs, fears and motives' are irrelevant (ibid., p.81). It is not tied to individual attitudes to a rule. 'Hence there is no contradiction in saying of some hardened swindler, and it may often be true, that he had an obligation to pay the rent but felt no pressure to pay when he made off without doing so' (ibid., p.86).

In terms of Hart's analysis thus far and in terms of linguistic philosophy these individual mentalities and the internal aspect are incommensurable. But we now reach a point which takes Hart almost as far from his origins in linguistic philosophy as it is possible to go. He now treats the internal aspect not only as commensurable with but as subordinated to individual mentalities. A person can now follow a rule but opt out of the internal aspect simply by adopting an appropriate mental state. If we are to relate the internal aspect and individual mentalities in terms of subordination, then Beehler's view is irresistible: accepting the rules or, alternatively, obeying them for fear of punishment are contrasts within 'the internal point of view' (1978, p.139). Even if we ignored all this and granted scope for what Hart calls this 'merely personal concern with the rules', such a concern cannot extend to the evaluation of the conduct of others in terms of the internal aspect (1961, p.112). The person who obeys 'for his part only' does not thereby create a rule-less world. Sadists for example might not accept a rule prohibiting assault as long as they conceive of themselves doing the assaulting. On the other hand, for their own security and social life they could not be indifferent on this score to the rule-orientation of others. It would be impossible to go into society without using the rules to evaluate the behaviour of others. It is impossible, in short, to ignore 'the normative structure of society' (ibid., p.86). Yet just such indifference and ignorance would have to typify Hart's always singular person or citizen who always in the singular 'obeys for his part only'.

I hope that it is not necessary to take this much further, but there are a few other points which amplify the incongruence of Hart's position. For one, we may ask what could relate these very 'private citizens' to each other, linking all the citizen isolates who 'obey each "for his part only"' (ibid., p.113). They would have no social bonds. Hart confines them tightly in terms of fear and inertia and has them relating solely and passively to the dictates of officials (ibid., p.112). If they were sentient at all this inertia would have to be complete since there would be no basis on which these citizen isolates could overcome complete inertia and relate to each other. Perhaps they have no relevant or significant sentience. If they do not partake of the internal aspect, perhaps they adopt the external aspect of the outside observer. Yet they cannot do this because they are not outside observers and Hart would only go so far on this score as to say that the 'external point of view may very nearly reproduce the way in which the rules function in the lives of certain members of the group, namely those who reject its rules and are only concerned with them when and because they judge that unpleasant consequences are likely to follow violation' (ibid., p.88).

If neither the external nor the internal aspect is involved in following a rule in such terms, then what is? Hart's ultimate answer seems to be no aspect at all. For a society made up of such people would be 'deplorably sheeplike' and 'the sheep might end up in the slaughter-house' (ibid., p.114). This deplorably tired metaphor is apt in that Hart does see the internal aspect of rules as 'distinctive ... of human thought, speech and action' (ibid., p.86). The uncharacteristically lurid metaphor is clearly meant to bludgeon us with obviousness and thus discourage further enquiry. But how would such an inhuman society operate? What exact mechanisms of stimulus–response, what minutely regulated but inexorable appetites would take the place of the critical, reflective human that Hart previously saw as intrinsic to the internal aspect? Hart does not pursue the point, nor is it worth pursuing. It stands opposed to much else in his book: his assertion of humanity as integral to the following of rules; his extensive criticism of other theorists for 'treating all rules as directives only to officials' since this does not take account of the active and reflective ways 'in which these are spoken of, thought of, and actually used in social life' (ibid., p.78). It contradicts the need, if law is to exist, for 'multitudes of individuals' to be able to understand conduct required of them as it is prescribed in general rules (ibid., p.121). And it opposes Hart's finding a minimum content of law involved in the very existence of society, a minimum content whereby people have to relate to each other in 'mutual forbearance and compromise', have to 'co-operate' and have to make and sustain promises (ibid., pp.189–93) – all of which entails an internal aspect of rules widely disseminated in society.

Why then, ultimately, this unpropitious resort to the society of sheep? In attacking existing positivist theories of various kinds, Hart located an internal aspect of rules and in this he endowed the populace with a critical reflective attitude, with abilities to act on and evaluate standards of behaviour, with the capacity to pursue a highly skilled enterprise (see Hirst and Jones, 1987, p.29 and also Baker and Hacker, 1985, pp.155–63). The boar had been released into the vineyard. If the orthodoxy of legal positivism is to be sustained, the populace has to be relegated, in the last instance as it were, to its inert state. The official emerges whole and impregnable to determine, or posit, that which all others must obey. Introduced with the insidious supposition of Rex and his successors, then rendered inevitable by that natural history of the primal scene, the official now becomes the apotheosis of the legal, the only necessarily sentient element in law and hence the only source of the legally positive.

Hart thus effects the separation of the rule from its use and enables it to be treated definitively as so separated. His project culminates in a simple – a very simple – claim to authority. As in the colonial situation, this authority of the official is supreme, coming from outside society and acting upon it. Use and context and the diversity of uses and contexts are ignored. As Césaire says, the rule of the European bourgeoisie has torn up the root of diversity (1955, pp.69–70).

In this deracination of rules the realm of the official is an assumption of pure and complete authority that transcends and determines use and context. We can appreciate this by returning to the disparaged John Austin. Hart's 'two minimum conditions necessary and sufficient for the existence of a legal system' are mocked in their correspondence to Austin's idea of law as expounded in *The Province of Jurisprudence Determined*: 'The matter of jurisprudence is positive law: law, simply and strictly so called: or law set by political superiors to political inferiors,' by superiors to whom 'habitual obedience must be rendered by the *generality* or *bulk* of ... members' of a political society (Austin, 1861, pp.1, 174; original emphasis). But Austin's surreptitious triumph in a sense goes further. He is extensively concerned with the social and moral basis or even the context of this superiority (Moles, 1987). Hart's officials have no constraining context. The only 'need' of official authority is obedience from 'private citizens', although 'in a healthy society' these citizens will 'often accept' the rules produced by officials and not simply obey them (Hart, 1961, pp.112–3). Even this salubrious whimper has no necessary part in a legal system. Hart, in the end, grounds his scheme on an unlimited and unified authority whose existence, apart from speculation about its origins in a primal scene, is merely asserted (Sampford, 1989, pp.35–6, 44–6).

Having thus elevated authority beyond constraint, Hart now vainly seeks to subject it to the essential meaning of rules, meanings as to which there can be 'no doubts' in 'the vast, central areas of the law' (1961, pp.149–50). As we saw, once Hart had simply asserted that law was a matter of rules he could in his fresh start found a concept of law and the elements of law in rules. When he came to tie everything together in the foundations of the legal system, however, Hart discovered that law need only be a matter of official authority. This raises a problem since:

> Hart's legal theory portrays law as a self-regulating system of rules. The rule of recognition and the other secondary rules are seen as governing the entire process of production, interpretation, enforcement, amendment and repeal of rules within the legal system. In contrast to Austin's picture of a legal order as the expression and instrument of all-too-human political power (the power of the sovereign and its delegates), Hart's image of law is that of a system in which rules govern power-holders; in which rules, rather than people, govern. What is, indeed, implied here is an aspect of the deeply resonant political symbol so obviously missing from Austin's jurisprudence – the symbol of the Rule of Law, a 'government of laws and not of men'. (Cotterrell, 1989, p.99)

Hence the resort to essential meaning.

Hart would not go so far as to say that legal rules are always clear and have just to be applied, but for rules to be uncertain and simply subject to human determination is for him a 'nightmare' (Hart, 1983, Chapter 4). Legal rules, he is relieved to find, do have a persistent 'core' of certain meaning but in practice there is also a 'penumbra' of uncertainty where officials have discretion in applying them. What Hart is saying here, astonishing as it may sound, is that in considering the meaning of a rule there are 'paradigm, clear cases' at the core where there are 'no doubts' (1961, pp.125, 149). Official discretion is confined to cases of penumbral uncertainty. Then the process involved in that discretion presumably remains of the law because to characterise it 'would be to characterise whatever is specific or peculiar in legal reasoning' (ibid., p.124). Such cases of uncertainty are exceptional. In the result there are 'wide areas of conduct which are successfully controlled *ab initio* by rule', where determinate rules 'guide' officials (ibid., pp.130, 132). In this the official merely draws out of the rule what is latent within it (see Goodrich, 1987, p.56).

Hart thus resorts to the very mode of determining meaning, to 'the bewitchment ... by means of language' (Wittgenstein, 1968, para. 109), which had plagued jurisprudence heretofore and from which he was to liberate us. The meaning of the rule is divorced from its use and context. It lies within to be discerned in an essential, a paradigm core. This is the concern with 'common qualities' which Hart considered so confused and which is the exact antithesis of the perspective in which he initially conceived his project (Hart, 1961, p.234).[5]

Hart's essentialist position is lent superficial plausibility by the presence of some stability in the interpretation of some legal rules. At the same time, this stability is not one that exists apart from officials or that circumscribes their action from without. What is or is not 'clear' for the time being is a product of official judgement. Apart from drawing on what judges do in order to illustrate his argument, Hart does not say how the core is to be distinguished from the penumbra. Nor does he say how a clear meaning can be swept aside by official judgement and replaced by a different meaning, as does happen. Fish puts the matter with characteristic cogency:

> The question is not whether there are in fact plain cases – there surely are – but, rather, of what is their plainness a condition and a property? Hart's answer must be that a plain case is inherently plain, plain in and of itself, plain independently of the interpretive activities it can then be said to direct. But it takes only a little reflection to see that the truth is exactly the reverse. A plaiи case is a case that was once *argued*: that is, its configurations were once in dispute; at a certain point one characterization of its meaning and significance – of its *rule* – was found to be more persuasive than its rivals; and at *that* point the case became settled, became perspicuous, became undoubted, became plain. Plainness, in short is not a property of the case itself – there is no case itself – but of an interpretive history in the course of which one interpretive agenda ... has subdued another. That history is then closed, but it can always be reopened. (Fish, 1989, p.523; original emphasis)

In terms of linguistic philosophy, 'the rules do not provide a fixed point of reference, because they always allow divergent interpretations. What really gives the practices their stability is that we agree in our interpretations of the rules' (Pears, 1971, p.168). Simply, 'there is as much stability as there is' (ibid.).

I will illustrate these points by eliminating the one elaborated example Hart gives of a legal rule with a core of certainty and a penumbra of doubt. For Hart the stakes here are high because this rule is an ultimate rule of recognition, a rule on which in his terms the unity, coherence and very existence of a legal system depends. That is, a legal system is made up of rules and the legal existence or validity of a rule is determined by reference to another rule superior to it in a hierarchy until an ultimate rule of recognition is reached. If there is no core of certainty to the ultimate rule then this edifice is unsupported. There seems, however, to be no risk of this.

The rule Hart chooses is impregnable. It contains 'the English doctrine of the sovereignty of Parliament,' of which 'the formula "Whatever the Queen in Parliament enacts is law" is an adequate expression' (Hart, 1961, pp.144–5). Integral to this rule is 'the principle that no earlier Parliament can preclude its "successors" from repealing its legislation' (ibid., p.145). A later statute will always override an inconsistent earlier one. The rule thus ensures the impossibility of its being dislodged. Add to this the view of Wade and Bradley in their text on constitutional law that 'this doctrine is to be found in all legal systems' (1985, p.71) and Hart's position would seem assured. Nonetheless even for this rule, he says, 'doubts can arise as to its meaning or scope; we can ask what is meant by "enacted by Parliament"' (Hart, 1961, p.145). He then refers to instances where a legislature has changed what is called the manner and form in which legislation is constituted. Parliament may enact that a type of legislation could in future only be passed by a special majority or with the addition of another element such as a referendum. Would that enactment bind later parliaments or would it on the contrary be subject to later legislation inconsistent with it? This, says Hart, is a penumbral area of doubt. Changing the manner and form of legislation may bind future parliaments but:

> if this device were valid, Parliament could achieve by its use very much the same results as those which the accepted doctrine, that Parliament cannot bind its successors, seems to put beyond its power. For though, indeed, the difference between circumscribing the area over which Parliament can legislate, and merely changing the manner and form of legislation, is clear enough in some cases, in effect these categories shade into each other. A statute which, after fixing a minimum wage for engineers, provided that no bill concerning engineers' pay should have effect as law unless confirmed by resolution of the Engineers' Union and went on to entrench this provision, might indeed secure all that, in practice, could be done by a statute which fixed the wage 'for ever', and then crudely prohibited its repeal altogether. Yet an argument,

which lawyers would recognize as having some force, can be made to show that although the latter would be ineffective under the present rule of continuing parliamentary sovereignty, the former would not. (ibid., p.147)

In other words, the core and the penumbra cannot be distinguished. Or, rather, they can only be distinguished by the mysterious invocation of a way 'which lawyers would recognize', by resort to 'whatever is specific or peculiar in legal reasoning' (ibid., p.124). This is simply 'the language of legal faith' (Goodrich, 1987, Chapter 3). It is also the language of ultimately unquestionable legal authority.

This is enough to dispose of the matter but I would add that even the enduring core of the rule which Hart identifies does not exist. Hart speaks of 'the English doctrine of the sovereignty of Parliament' with the blithe chauvinism that typifies these pronouncements. In Scotland, the courts would see parliamentary sovereignty as indeed a peculiarly English doctrine (*MacCormick* v. *Lord Advocate*, 1953 SC 396). The reasons given by these courts for denying the sovereignty of parliament would extend to England as well. There is not an ultimate rule of recognition for Britain or for the United Kingdom but at least two competing and contradictory ultimate rules of recognition (Wade and Bradley, 1985, pp.84–7). The contradiction is usually hidden in the texts by disregard or bluster (for example Dicey, 1982, pp.cvi, 24–5). The number of contradictory versions of any such rule, however, has now to be multiplied. Section 2(4) of the European Communities Act 1972 says that 'any enactment passed or to be passed ... shall be construed and have effect subject to' European Community Law. The 'core of certainty' in the rule of recognition would deny effect to such a restriction in the case of legislation yet to be passed. The restriction would be overridden by inconsistent subsequent legislation. But the courts have far from unequivocally upheld such a rule of parliamentary sovereignty. Sometimes they have inclined towards upholding parliamentary sovereignty, sometimes they have inclined towards the dominance of Community Law, and sometimes they have managed to do both at once (see for example *Macarthys Ltd* v. *Smith* [1979] 3 All ER 325 and *R.* v. *Secretary of State for Transport* ex parte *Factortame* [1989] 2 All ER 692). Such basic uncertainty may in Hart's terms be accommodated in what he sees as 'the pathology of a legal system,' 'as a sub-standard, abnormal case containing within it the threat that the legal system will dissolve' (1961, pp.114, 119). As we have seen, however, fundamental irresolution has long been the standard, normal case of the 'legal system' of the so-called United Kingdom.

The Jurisprudence of Authority

'Popular Support For the Law. See *Obedience'*: index to Stone (1966)

Thus Hart fails to qualify the blunt equation of law with official authority. This leaves intact the correspondence between his view of the legal system and that of John Austin. Law is the product of officials or superiors and the populace need only generally obey it. The correspondence should by now occasion no surprise. In retrospect, it is clear that Hart was concerned to operate within and to confirm the idea of law as official authority. This idea would have been overthrown by the reliance on use and the internal aspect of rules introduced with that salutary linguistic philosophy which Hart employed to found his project in opposition to essentialist approaches to law. Therefore when he comes to justify the ways of authority, Hart resorts to such essentialist approaches, whether in the primal scene or in laying the foundations of a legal system or in the search for core meanings.

Linguistic philosophy, however, could not be so readily relegated. It proved to be a dangerous supplement. It served to show that Hart's accounts of the primal scene and of hermetic legal authority were fanciful. His ultimate attempt to find a meaning in legal rules outside of the domination of authority merely confirmed that authority in 'the language of legal faith' (Goodrich, 1987, Chapter 3). It was an exclusive legal knowledge that policed the boundaries of true meaning, identified its core and resolved its penumbral uncertainties. In a sense this is unobjectionable. Lawyers generate meanings understood by lawyers (Winch, 1958). But Hart's prospectus was much more extensive. In harkening to the bewitchment of universal enunciation, perhaps we were all along eavesdropping on the conversations of the converted.

The Concept of Law assumes its proper significance within this domain of 'secularized theology' (Kahn-Freund, 1966, p.126). Here the contradiction between positivist jurisprudence and linguistic philosophy becomes amorphous compatibility (see Cotterrell, 1989, p.244).[6] Having relieved positivist jurisprudence from its defects and critics, linguistic philosophy is, as a matter of some necessity, retained as the semblance of a new approach to positivist jurisprudence. True believers can adequately dismiss possible challenges to this expedient union with proprietary scorn (for example Guest, 1988). Even non-believers have to defer to its ubiquitous influence as the now 'standard position' (Leith, 1988, p.85). Yet the greatness of *The Concept of Law* has been somewhat thrust upon it. It is elevated because it affirms the viability and inevitability of legal authority and because in so doing it confirms the peculiar constraints of legal scholarship. Again Austin is the inescapable ancestor figure. In the formation of modern legal education and of the textbook as the standard of legal scholarship in the late nineteenth century, the impact of Austin's work was basic and pervasive (Stein, 1980, p.86). Law in this setting was and predominantly remains what it was for Austin: positive law. And for Austin as well as Hart positive law is posited law. It exists because of the authority of its origin, of the sovereign or the official positing it (Austin, 1954, p.365). The positive law of 'mature societies' contrasts with a 'negative ... state of nature' and the absence there of law 'properly so called,' much like the productive inadequacies of Hart's primal scene (Austin 1861, p.122). Law is 'set' by the sovereign or the official to 'political inferiors' in 'a state of subjection' or to a populace which in Hart's terms simply obeys (ibid. pp.1, 171). Law is thus distinct and dominant, 'set' beyond any influence but that which its sovereign source chooses to recognise. And 'law' is finally rendered in terms of sovereign authority. *The Concept of Law* is but another way, along with Austin's and many more, of securing this result. As with Hamlet's players and their 'abstracts and brief chronicles of the time' (II, ii), *The Concept* is a performance whose truth lies outside of it.

Conclusion: Purity and Danger

The Concept of Law provides an instance of that dynamic of identity in jurisprudence which I noted at the outset. In maintaining law's authority, jurisprudence operated as 'the lawyer's extraversion,' a turning outward to other knowledges (Stone, 1966, p.16). But the lawyer turns outward so as to turn inward more effectively. So, with Hart's resort to linguistic philosophy, once it was incorporated in jurisprudence, once it had served to overcome a certain local difficulty, linguistic philosophy with its troublesome popular element was rendered inessential. Having admitted such a dangerous supplement into jurisprudence, Hart then had to effect 'the restoration of inner purity ... the entity is [after all] what it is, the outside is out and the inside in' (Derrida, 1977, p.248). At the same time, the incorporation of linguistic philosophy had left a trail of danger, one which pointed inexorably to the radical impurity of what was within and thus undermined Hart's jurisprudence.

This volume is a collection of dangerous supplements. It explores the subversive implications of excluded knowledges for jurisprudence. This is done not just to resist jurisprudence as it stands but to provide perspectives in its renewal. It is also a matter of perspectives in the plural. The collection is set against the characteristic claims to 'universal enunciation' in jurisprudence and to the consequent arrogation of truth in its competing versions or schools. It is also set against the closure of knowledge within these or any other versions of jurisprudence. Thus, when the supplements here bring perspectives from feminism, postmodernism, semiotics and so on to bear on jurisprudence, it is not to displace all that is there, much less to erect yet another version of the truth of the subject. A supplementary jurisprudence would be open, responsive – and unachieved.

At the least, these supplements offer students of jurisprudence some introduction to areas of knowledge which have been of great significance intellectually but which have been marginalised in jurisprudence. Some of these, such as feminism and postmodernism, have hardly been addressed at all. Others are dangerous dimensions of concerns which have figured immensely in jurisprudence, such as Marxism and liberalism. Obviously much else could have been covered, but this collection represents a preference for few and usually quite lengthy chapters. There are several reasons for this. Dangerous supplements cannot be readily reduced in the standard terms of jurisprudence and room is needed for them to be presented adequately. The writers of this collection have tried to make themselves as clear to a general academic audience as the nature of the particular supplement allowed. This has often involved explanations and elaborations beyond that which specialist audiences would consider necessary or even desirable. Finally, we wanted the collection to be as accessible as possible in terms of cost. This meant opting for some overall brevity and agonising decisions about what not to include. We hope there will be other occasions, further dangerous supplements.

Sugarman's chapter sets the scene for what is to follow by establishing the necessity of the supplement historically. He explores the creation, in its institutional and intellectual setting, of a narrow, positivist idea of law which endured as an 'archetype' in jurisprudence (Edgeworth, 1986, p.115). The deep complicities between professional and academic conceptions of law produced an English jurisprudence that was peculiarly constrained, one that protected law from significant engagement with political and social issues. This was done not only by limiting the scope of law in jurisprudence and in legal education generally, but also by extravagantly enlarging it in ways that set law above challenging connections with the political and social. Law became transcendent in its scientific and rational nature and in its imperial mission.

The next two chapters deal with liberalism and Marxism, beliefs already generously accommodated in jurisprudence and, so it would seem, hardly the stuff of supplementation. Yet the instance revealed in Thomson's chapter vividly indicates otherwise. He provides an exposition and critique of Hayek, a liberal thinker who has been enormously influential politically and intellectually and who has long pursued central jurisprudential concerns. The story so far heightens the mystery of why Hayek has been virtually ignored in jurisprudence. In his solution to the mystery, Thomson shows that Hayek's thought fundamentally challenges the constitution of jurisprudence and its 'truth claims' by locating them in the history and politics of market capitalism.

Marxism's compatibility with jurisprudence is a very different if equally intriguing case. Marxism has been accommodated comfortably in jurisprudence by presenting it as versions of the integrity and simplicity of law: law is a distinct component of a superstructure determined by an economic base; or law is relatively autonomous within a somewhat more complex determining structure; or law is an analogue of commodity exchange. Hunt deals with these in his chapter but he does so within a more comprehensive and complex engagement with Marxism in his 'relational theory' of law. This serves to disclose 'the directly political character of law' and reveals law as 'an arena of struggle'. The result is not only a radical challenge to jurisprudence and its limits but also an enriching of its traditional concerns.

The remaining three chapters move from disruptions of the mainstream to matters which jurisprudence has treated as marginal. Smart confronts 'assumptions about universality, objectivity [and] neutrality' in jurisprudence. She shows that 'the foundations on which jurisprudence rest are deeply imbued by a masculine perspective and privilege.' Her 'story of feminist jurisprudence' not only makes out the case but indicates how 'a radical transformation' of jurisprudence can begin. So central for jurisprudence are the issues Smart raises that she can justifiably call for its 'abandonment' if they continue to be ignored – although there is, for her, an aptly unresolved conflict between resisting and renewing jurisprudence.

For Goodrich and Hachamovitch, law and the semiotics of law are inextricable. The language of law, for example, is not simply a means or ornament in its expression. Law cannot be regarded as somehow pure and apart from the varying forms in which it is communicated. We must pursue law 'through its images, through the forms in which it works itself into the nervature of everyday life'. In this pursuit, the jurisprudential claims to reason and objectivity themselves become contingent images and forms. The massive contingency in which Goodrich and Hachamovitch revel is that of Englishness. Law's dependence on nation has been a constant affront to jurisprudential elevations of law beyond such compromising situations. One resolution has been to endow nation with the superordinate qualities of universal reason, and so on, attributed to law. It has been done, not least in terms of Englishness. Englishness itself is fast becoming a major intellectual concern.

Carty's chapter sustains that concern in a postmodern dimension. He avoids the constant and impossible question of what postmodernism is by simply adopting and 'doing' postmodernism in an account of origins of English law, an account which profoundly challenges its modernist pretensions. In particular, an autonomous legal-rational authority is shown to be embedded in that realm of the religious supposedly displaced by a secular and sober law. And being about a matter of Englishness, Carty's analysis reveals further peculiarities of the English on the score of law and nation as well.

The postmodern temper also provides an apt point of conclusion. The supplement resists selective incorporation in jurisprudence, yet it does not offer an alternative orthodoxy or general truth of law in which each particular aspect would be put firmly, at last, in its place. The supplement persists in its danger.

Acknowledgements

Thanks again to Dave Reason who teaches me 'to love the little platoon we belong to in society' (Edmund Burke). And thanks to Vagi Fitzpatrick for the title to this chapter.

Notes

1. Can we, with Winch and others, read off the necessarily social characteristic of a rule from the human ability to follow a rule (see Winch, 1958, pp.32–3)? Wittgenstein, it seems, would not see the following of a rule as necessarily social (Baker and Hacker, 1985, pp.164, 172). There could be a private practice of following a rule in the sense that it is not shared with anyone else. Even so, to count as following a rule practice, if not shared, must be shareable. It must be possible to convey the practice to others and for others to act in accordance with it (ibid., pp.164, 179). Thus some sociality in the sense of a relatedness to others is involved in the idea of a rule. This refinement is probably in excess of what is needed to analyse Hart's contribution, which is concerned with 'social rules' and with legal rules as a type of them (Hart, 1961, p.56). Or we may prefer, with Lévi-Strauss, to look beyond the prison of sociality 'in the brief glance, heavy with patience, serenity and mutual forgiveness, that, through some involuntary understanding, one can sometimes exchange with a cat' (1976, p.544). I am grateful to Dave Reason for the points made in this note.
2. I do not intend the ambiguity about the primal scene to be entirely frivolous. In the Freudian sense, the primal scene in which the child witnesses copulation between the parents can have a disabling effect on the child. Legal positivism, which Hart begins to reconstitute here, disables us by confining the origins of our thought and imagination to that which produces 'law' and 'legal' arguments.

3. Hart devotes little attention to what he calls private secondary rules (1961, p.79), such as those for the making of contracts, except to bring out the inadequacies of ideas of law previous to his own.
4. This was published first in 1832. Particularly in his first six lectures, Austin is constantly concerned with this point of transition. For a similar example from the other end of the period of Enlightenment, see Locke in *The Second Treatise of Government* where the transition is integral to his account of political or civil society (see 1960, paras. 1–21, 87–94, 124).
5. The point could be made summarily in the radical contrast between Hart's case here of the paradigm and Wittgenstein's (Wittgenstein, 1967, para. 1–4, and 1968, para. 50).
6. 'Hart's theory' is for Cotterrell: 'testimony to the appeal, among legal scholars, of a normative legal theory which apparently provides unity and system in legal ideas while doing so in the explicitly "legal common sense" terms of conformity with ordinary legal linguistic usage' (1989, p.244).

References

Austin, J. (1861) *The Province of Jurisprudence Determined* 2nd edn., vol. 1 (London: John Murray).

Austin, J. (1954) *The Province of Jurisprudence Determined and the Uses of the Study of Jurisprudence* (London: Weidenfeld & Nicolson).

Baker, G.P. and Hacker, P.M.S. (1985) *Wittgenstein: Rules, Grammar and Necessity: An Analytical Commentary on the Philosophical Investigations*, vol. 2 (Oxford: Basil Blackwell).

Barnett, H.A. and Yach, D.M. (1985) 'The Teaching of Jurisprudence and Legal Theory in British Universities and Polytechnics', *Legal Studies*, vol. 5, pp.151–71.

Beehler, R. (1978) 'The Concept of Law and the Obligation to Obey', *The American Journal of Jurisprudence*, vol. 25, pp.120–42.

Bock, K. (1979) 'Theories of Progress, Development, Evolution' in T. Bottomore and R. Nisbet (eds) 1979, *A History of Sociological Analysis* (London: Heinemann), pp.39–79.

Cassirer, E. (1951), trans. F.C.A. Koelln and J.P. Pettegrove, *The Philosophy of the Enlightenment* (Boston: Beacon).

Césaire, A. (1955) *Discours sur le Colonialisme* (Paris: Présence Africaine).

Cotterrell, R. (1989) *The Politics of Jurisprudence: A Critical Introduction to Legal Philosophy* (London and Edinburgh: Butterworth).

Derrida, J. (1976), trans. G.C. Spivak, *Of Grammatology* (Baltimore: Johns Hopkins University Press).

Derrida, J. (1977) 'Limited Inc abc ...', *Glyph*, vol. 2, pp.162–254.

Dicey, A.V. (1982) *Introduction to the Study of the Law of the Constitution* (reprint of the 8th edn of 1915) (Indianapolis: Liberty Classics).

Edgeworth, B. (1986) 'Legal Positivism and the Philosophy of Language: A Critique of H.L.A. Hart's "Descriptive Sociology"', *Legal Studies*, vol. 6, issue 2, pp.115–39.

Fish, S. (1989) *Doing What Comes Naturally: Change, Rhetoric, and the Practice of Theory in Literary and Legal Studies* (Oxford: Clarendon).

Fitzpatrick, P. (1989) '"The Desperate Vacuum": Imperialism and Law in the Experience of Enlightenment', *Droit et Société*, vol. 13, pp.347–58.

Geertz, C. (1983) *Local Knowledge: Further Essays in Interpretive Anthropology* (New York: Basic Books).

Goodrich, P. (1987) *Legal Discourse: Studies in Linguistics, Rhetoric and Legal Analysis* (London: Macmillan).

Guest, S. (1988) review of Robert N. Moles' *Definition and Theory in Jurisprudence: A Reassessment of H.L.A. Hart and the Positivist Tradition* and other works, *Law Quarterly Review*, vol. 104, pp.644–50.

Harris, J.W. (1980) *Legal Philosophies* (London: Butterworth).

Hart, H.L.A. (1954a) 'Introduction' to Austin, J. (1954) *The Province of Jurisprudence Determined and The Uses of the Study of Jurisprudence* (London: Weidenfeld & Nicolson), pp.vii–xxi.

Hart, H.L.A. (1954b) 'Definition and Theory in Jurisprudence,' *Law Quarterly Review*, vol. 70, pp.37–60.

Hart, H.L.A. (1961) *The Concept of Law* (Oxford: Oxford University Press).

Hart, H.L.A. (1982) *Essays on Bentham: Studies in Jurisprudence and Political Theory* (Oxford: Clarendon).

Hart, H.L.A. (1983) *Essays in Jurisprudence and Philosophy* (Oxford: Clarendon).

Hart, H.L.A. (1987) 'Comment' in R. Gavison (ed.), *Issues in Contemporary Legal Philosophy: The Influence of H.L.A. Hart* (Oxford: Clarendon), pp.35–42.

Hirst, P. and Jones, P. (1987) 'The Critical Resources of Established Jurisprudence', in P. Fitzpatrick and A. Hunt (eds), *Critical Legal Studies* (Oxford: Basil Blackwell), pp.21–32.

Hirst, P. and Woolley, P. (1982) *Social Relations and Human Attributes* (London: Tavistock).

Hoebel, E.A. (1954) *The Law of Primitive Man: A Study in Comparative Legal Dynamics* (Cambridge, Mass: Harvard University Press).

Kahn-Freund, O. (1966) 'Reflections on Legal Education', *Modern Law Review*, vol. 29, no. 2, pp.121–36.

Leith, P. (1988) 'Common Usage, Certainty and Computing' in P. Leith and P. Ingram (eds), *The Jurisprudence of Orthodoxy: Queen's University Essays on H.L.A. Hart* (London: Routledge), pp.85–116.

Lévi-Strauss, C. (1976) *Tristes Tropiques* (Harmondsworth: Penguin).

Lloyd, D. and Freeman, M.D.A. (1985) *Lloyd's Introduction to Jurisprudence* 5th edn. (London: Stevens).

Locke, J. (1960) 'The Second Treatise of Government' in *Two Treatises of Government* (New York: Cambridge University Press).

Lyotard, J-F. and Thébaud, J.L. (1985) *Just Gaming* (Manchester: Manchester University Press).

MacCormick, N. (1981) *H.L.A. Hart* (London: Edward Arnold).

MacCormick, N. (1987) 'Comment', in R. Gavison (ed.), *Issues in Contemporary Legal Philosophy: The Influence of H.L.A. Hart* (Oxford: Clarendon), pp.104–13.

Meek, R.L. (1976) *Social Science and the Ignoble Savage* (Cambridge: Cambridge University Press).

Moles, R.N. (1987) *Definition and Rule in Legal Theory: A Reassessment of H.L.A. Hart and the Positivist Tradition* (Oxford: Basil Blackwell).

Newman, K.S. (1983) *Law and Economic Organization: A Comparative Study of Preindustrial Societies* (Cambridge: Cambridge University Press).

Pears, D. (1971) *Wittgenstein* (London: Fontana/Collins).

Piddington, R. (1957) 'Malinowski's Theory of Needs', in R. Firth (ed.), *Man and Culture: An Evaluation of the Work of Bronislaw Malinowski* (London: Routledge & Kegan Paul), pp.33–51.

Rackett, T. (1984) 'Racist Social Fantasy and Paranoia' in F. Barker *et al.* (eds), *Europe and its Others: Volume Two* (Colchester: University of Essex), pp.190–200.

Sampford, C. (1989) *The Disorder of Law: A Critique of Legal Theory* (Oxford: Basil Blackwell).

Simmonds, N.E. (1986) *Central Issues in Jurisprudence: Justice, Law and Rights* (London: Sweet & Maxwell).

Skillen, A. (1977) *Ruling Illusions: Philosophy and the Social Order* (Hassocks: Harvester).

Stein, P. (1980) *Legal Evolution: The Story of an Idea* (Cambridge: Cambridge University Press).

Stone, J. (1966) *Social Dimensions of Law and Justice* (London: Stevens).

Strathern, M. (1985) 'Discovering "Social Control"', *Journal of Law and Society*, vol. 12, no. 2, pp.113–34.

Twining, W.L. (1974) 'Some Jobs for Jurisprudence,' *British Journal of Law and Society*, vol. 1, no.1, pp.149–74.

Wade, E.C.S. and Bradley, A.W. (1985) *Constitutional and Administrative Law* 10th edn. (London and New York: Longman).

Winch, P. (1958) *The Idea of a Social Service and its Relation to Philosophy* (London: Routledge & Kegan Paul).

Wittgenstein, L. (1958) 'The Blue Book' in *The Blue and Brown Books* (Oxford: Basil Blackwell).

Wittgenstein, L. (1967), trans. G.E.M. Anscombe, *Remarks on the Foundations of Mathematics* (Oxford: Basil Blackwell).

Wittgenstein, L. (1968), trans. G.E.M. Anscombe, *Philosophical Investigations* (Oxford: Basil Blackwell).

'A Hatred of Disorder': Legal Science, Liberalism and Imperialism[1]

David Sugarman

'Black Letter' Law: the Nature of the Beast

The 'black letter' tradition continues to overshadow the way we teach, write and think about law.[2] Its categories and assumptions are still the standard diet of most first-year law students and they continue to organise law textbooks and casebooks. Stated baldly it assumes that although law may appear to be irrational, chaotic and particularistic, if one digs deep enough and knows what one is looking for, then it will soon become evident that the law is an internally coherent and unified body of rules. This coherence and unity stems from the fact that law is grounded in, and logically derived from, a handful of general principles, and that whole subject areas such as contract and torts are distinguished by some common principles or elements which fix the boundaries of the subject. The exposition and systematisation of these general principles and the techniques required to find and to apply both them and the rules that they underpin, are largely what legal education and scholarship are all about.

The claim that law is unified and coherent is also sustained by a battery of dualisms: common law/statute law, law/politics, law/state, law/morality, legal/empirical, technique/substance, form/substance, means/ends, private law/public law, law/history, law/theory, which make it more tenable to regard law as 'pure' and 'scientific'.

Despite the variety of producers and consumers of legal discourse, it is what the judges say and the supposed needs of the legal profession as narrowly defined, that have had the greatest magnetic pull over the nature and form of legal education and scholarship. Other aspects that are equally important to understanding law, such as legislation, the operation of law in practice, as well as the history, theory, morality and politics of law, are ignored or marginalised.

The 'black letter' tradition is also the bearer of an important political message. The message is that the law (primarily through case law) and the legal profession (centrally, the judiciary) play a major role in protecting individual freedom; and that the rules of contract, torts and constitutional law, for example, confer the maximum freedom on individuals to act as they wish without interference from other individuals or the state. Policing the boundaries within, and between, legal subject areas constitutes a major foundation of the rule of law. In this way, the form as well as the content of the law become synonymous with our very definitions of individual freedom and liberty, and thereby acquire an additional patina of reverence and universality. The world, as pictured within the conceptual categories of legal thought, is basically sound. It is more or less the best that is realisable. In so far as a better world is possible, it would not fundamentally differ from the present.

Like any closed model of rationality, the 'black letter' tradition is shot through with contradictions, omissions and absurdities, which generations of judges and jurists have sought to repress. For instance, the notion of law as resting upon an objective body of principle founders when we consider that the quest for underlying principles must involve a selection from the sum of principles available and, therefore, has a strong evaluative element. Principles are thus inseparable from interpretation and theory which, in turn, are determined by values. Thus, the schizophrenia of the first-year law student: when is it that s/he is supposed to talk about 'law', and when is it that s/he can talk about 'policy'? We are heirs of this schizophrenia.

The specific focus of this essay is the creation, diffusion and reception of the 'black letter' tradition within modern legal education and thought, and its archetype, the textbook. How and why were certain practices and beliefs accounted proper and true? Why did the systematisation, exposition and analysis of legal doctrine become the predominant form of legal education and scholarship? How did jurisprudence come to be constituted in a way that privileged analytical concerns and marginalised social, political and moral ones? Why has the standpoint of jurists tended to resemble (but is not reducible to) that of appeal court judges and elite legal practitioners? And why has it been so difficult to broaden the study of law from within? These are the kinds of questions I hope to address in the remainder of this paper. In particular, the essay attempts to describe how and why the 'black letter' tradition came to predominate in legal education and scholarship during the seminal period of modern legal education and thought, 1850–1907. I shall refer to this as the 'classical period' and the jurists associated with it as the 'classical' jurists. This period is of central importance in understanding the current conjuncture because its constructs and assumptions have dominated English legal education and thought at least until very recently. It is because of the continuing tenacity of these constructs and assumptions that jurisprudence, like so much else in legal education, requires a fundamental rethink. Only by locating the history of jurisprudence within this larger context can we really understand the forces that have tended to produce a disembodied conception of jurisprudence. By situating its development in this way we can see how the problem of jurisprudence is shared by other sub-disciplines within legal scholarship such as contracts, torts, constitutional law, legal history, and so on.

In essence, the argument of my paper is as follows. The first generation of fulltime university law teachers was a relatively small and cohesive community, largely based at Oxford. Its leading lights included Pollock, Anson, Holland, Dicey, Bryce, Salmond and Markby. This community was concerned to establish a distinctive professional identity, one that would enable them to control their work and establish a jurisdictional competence *vis-a-vis* their principal competitors, the legal profession, allied academic disciplines and the state. In effect, the jurisdictional settlement arrived at was one of subordination, where the law dons largely accepted the chaperonage of the legal profession in exchange for control of their own limited sphere. This was reinforced by the way in which jurisprudence took on a character congruent with other new academic disciplines (such as history and economics) and with the ideology of liberalism. In this sense, the battle to ensure that jurists had something to keep to themselves can only be understood in relation to those other institutions and professions who also sought to control the work of law teachers (cf. Abbott, 1986).

The process was a profoundly cultural one. The classical jurists selectively invoked the conventions of the legal profession, of liberalism and of 'science' as a way of seeking to control what was permitted to count as legal education and scholarship (cf. Foucault, 1972; Kuhn, 1970). The conventions of the legal community associated with the 'black letter' tradition were not simply agreements about what constituted legal knowledge and education and the form that they should take. They also had a vital influence on the intellectual practices of law teachers and were a way of controlling behaviour within the juristic community. The classical law dons created a framework for viewing, classifying and explaining their lives. This framework was anchored in the notion of law as a certain body of rules and the cultural authority of judges and lawyers – the rule of law – in liberal ideology.

The history of legal science and legal education parallels that of other disciplines: namely the recurrent effort to achieve more precise denotation, the striving to create a single voice and objective knowledge, and the simultaneous recognition that such a state is unattainable. My story is one of continual sliding between gradations on one side and then on the other, of a hybrid enterprise and of the dilemmas and internal contradictions that this both reflected and generated.

It would be easy to explain the contradictions between what jurists said and did at certain moments and what they said and did at other moments in terms of the largely rhetorical character of the language they used. From this vantage point, the language of 'science', 'the rule of law', and so on, was partly concerned to persuade others, principally the legal profession, the universities and the wider community, while jurists largely did as they pleased. However, the movement to construct a science of law, and the recognition that it could not be, were also manifestations of a search for meaning, self-identity and purpose. In particular, my story is less concerned with shifting values than with shifting strategies to manage the problems posed by the effort to separate law from politics and provide a legitimate province for jurists, judges, lawyers and the state (Sugarman, 1990).

Jurists moved back and forth along the rationality–irrationality spectrum with striking regularity. In part this was because the implications of being a jurist and holding a rationalist conception of legal science led some jurists at some moments to feel uncomfortable. They experienced as many dilemmas constructing relatively rational legal discourses as they did with relatively irrational ones. As in other disciplines, the tensions and problems posed by a science of human conduct, a deductive system of universally applicable propositions and a non-scientific account of human conduct continued to haunt legal scholars. In short, the classical jurists simultaneously assisted in the construction of a liberal legal science and demonstrated that its foundations were built on sand (Sugarman, 1983 and 1986).

These dilemmas were accentuated because legal science and education were at the interface of debates about the universities, the legal profession, science, English society, national identity, cultural leadership and the empire. The effort to create a modern legal science and education was not just an attempt to establish the conventions by which legal knowledge was to be produced. It also sought to resolve the problem of social order.

Disciplines are constituted through the construction of a canonical set of 'great texts', which help to define the conventional boundaries and strategies of the discipline. This paper is part of a larger project which seeks to understand and criticise the founding classics of modern legal science through a contextual analysis. Contextual analysis is employed in the belief that it will illuminate how and why the contingent became an 'invented tradition' and, therefore, 'common sense'; and how the original concerns of our patron saints were 'non-disciplinary' as well as 'disciplinary'. (Cf. Hobsbawm, 1983; Kuklick, 1984; McKeon, 1987.) Telling the story of the formation of modern legal science and education in a different way, and using alternative methods, may suggest alternative disciplinary strategies and help us to broaden the study and teaching of law.

The Centrality of 1850–1907 and the Quest for Professional Legitimacy

The role of English universities in legal education is relatively recent. Traditionally, English lawyers have learnt their law by way of apprenticeship. In essence, from the late seventeenth to the mid-nineteenth century formal professional and university legal education was almost non-existent. No wonder John Austin opined that:

> Turning away from the study of English to the study of Roman law, you escape from the empire of chaos and darkness to a world which seems, by comparison, the region of order and light. (1885, p.58)

It was only during the period 1850–1907 that professional law teachers were appointed to universities in any number. For many of these classical legal scholars, the major intellectual task was to transcend the 'chaos and darkness' of contemporary legal education and scholarship and create a world of 'order and light'. In other words, for many classical law dons, their desired professional legitimacy in the face of sceptical universities and a largely hostile legal profession required the assertion of a special body of expertise which they monopolised. What was this special expertise?

The argument espoused by most classical law dons was that law may appear chaotic but that, in fact, it is internally coherent. This cohesion derives from the fact that law is grounded upon relatively few general principles. The legal scholar was in a unique position to be able to tease out the general principles underlying the law and impart this sense of cohesion through the teaching of general principles and the systematisation of those principles in law textbooks. Such scholars were, therefore, uniquely useful to the profession. They showed that the grubby, disorderly world of the courtroom and law office could be regarded as 'science in action'. The law was ultimately governed by principles akin to the laws of natural science. It was, therefore, worthy of a place in the university firmament. In short, exposition, conceptualisation, systematisation and the analysis of existing legal doctrine became equated with the dominant tasks of legal education and scholarship. Here then was the *raison d'etre* of the new professional jurist and university legal education.

Classical law dons asserted that law was a science. This, however, seems to have meant little more than that law was clear, rational, internally coherent and systematised. The implication that with a bit of juristic assistance lawyers might resemble mathematicians, has its origins in Roman law, Bacon and Savigny. Here was a longstanding 'literary technology'(Shapin, 1984, p.490), a model of the jurist's function, which was enthusiastically embraced. It was enlisted in support of a renewed effort to reduce legal discourse to a more logical form. This, and similar rhetorical devices cited throughout this chapter, were used to assert and sustain the identity and unity of the science, scholarship, education and practice of the law. The classical jurists sought to persuade us that despite its doubters and its long history of equivocal success, a programme of legal science in England was viable and desirable. We can see a process of naming and claiming, of attributing to law certain features associated with reason and science. It was neither new nor was it peculiar to law. It exemplified a wider movement to extend scientific rigour to the moral sciences. The increasing prestige of the natural sciences only accentuated the transmission of metaphors such as 'geometry' and 'mathematics', and thereby similar criteria of relevance and significance, as indeed it did between the natural and human sciences and general culture.

The 'Black Letter' Tradition and its Archetype, the Student Textbook

The circumstances in which the classical jurists found themselves seemed to require textbooks that conceived of the law as unitary and principled and which verged on the dogmatic. Pedagogically, their ultimate aim was simplicity of exposition, orientation and standpoint. They did their best to ignore the exceptions and aberrations; they concentrated upon the principles and 'the general part' of the law. Many student texts were organised in numbered paragraphs or as codes subdivided into numbered rules – though this practice was by no means exclusive to elementary texts. The medium was the message. And the message was essentially about simplicity, and also through simplicity, a celebration of law as general principles, leading cases, judges and lawyers and the autonomy and authority of law. Above all, perhaps, its message was about what the average student and lawyer were assumed to tolerate.

The exposition of law in new student texts was where the classical jurists excelled. Within the space of about 30 years a handful of individuals had transformed the teaching and writing of most of those subjects which then, as now, were regarded as the core of legal education, as well as several non-core subjects such as international law and the conflict of laws. Not surprisingly, 'the most interesting, and perhaps the most important sphere of professorial energy' became the writing of student law texts (Dicey, 1883, p.22).

Dicey was exceptionally frank about the jurists' legislative role in this context. The textbook was a new form of codification. It was through these texts that jurists such as Pothier, Savigny, Kent, Story and Langdell (in his casebooks) had reformed, 'modelled, one might almost say brought into existence, whole departments of law' (ibid., p.24).

The rise of the new professional jurists occurred at a unique juncture. To the extent that the common law had a classificatory system it was rooted in that irrational (in the Weberian sense) body of rules we call the forms of action. This, together with the distinction between common law and equity, constituted the conceptual core of the common law. The collapse of the forms of action, the fusion of law and equity and the unprecedented freedom this afforded textbook writers to reconstitute the common law, was freely admitted by jurists and practitioners alike. Here was an unparalleled opportunity for juristic legislation which was not missed.

Nonetheless, the intellectual, scholarly and educational constraints that inhere in a conception of education and scholarship which elevates exposition, systematisation, conceptualisation and the production of lawyers as traditionally conceived as its essence, will be self-evident. The area that they mapped out for themselves, *vis-a-vis* the legal professions and the universities, resembled a very slender ledge. The ways they further trapped themselves within relatively narrow confines is explored in our next section.

The Narrow Ledge: Juristic Attitudes to Judges, the Legal Profession and Law Reform

Persuading the legal profession and the universities to acknowledge the place of university legal education and scholarship called for tact, circumspection and a sense of balance. The legitimacy of the jurist was of course asserted, but in a way that was not incongruous with the established provinces of the lawyer and the don. Naturally the strategies available to the classical law teachers were undoubtedly limited. Traditionally lawyers had not read law at university. The professions and the judiciary had largely managed without them. Many classical jurists maintained direct links with the profession throughout their scholarly careers. Several had failed in their aspiration to practice. It is probably not too much to say that, in most cases, they saw themselves as lawyers first and foremost. Nearly all were personally acquainted with each other for a considerable number of years. They shared, to a remarkable extent, the same social origins, clubs, universities, the sprinkling of practice and similar politics. It was a group unlikely to produce firebrands.

The law dons sought not to monopolise legal education and scholarship, merely to share it with the profession. What, then, was yielded to the sole competence of the profession? Practitioners were the masters of the relation between law and facts. Law dons were masters of the principles of the law. To assert that law was principled and internally coherent seemed to require that facts and reality were kept at a safe distance.

But if the jurist's *forte* was the content of the law, and in particular the exposition and application of its general or universal principles, how did this differ from what, supposedly, only practice and, above all, the decision of the judges could fashion, namely 'the better opinion' and 'sound judgement'? By claiming the exposition and arrangement of general legal principles as the core of their credentials, the jurists had put themselves in a bind. For these were, after all, the very skills that the traditional oracles of the law – the bar and bench – had claimed for themselves. Even the somewhat narrow province which they asserted as their competence turned out to be problematical.

How could jurists maintain their claim to be the devisers and expositors of legal principles without challenging the traditional orthodoxy that vested law-making: better opinion and sound judgement in the bar and, particularly, in the bench? One way the jurisdiction of the jurist was distinguished from that of the judge, counsel and law reformer was by resort to another ideological buffer-zone of classical legal science: the attempted separation of form from substance. Jurists, by an act of conscious self-limitation, refrained from criticising, let alone meddling, with the content of the law. That was for others. Their skills resided in its formal organisation.

The jurists reserved their ire for the confusion and complexity spawned by increasing legislative regulation. Statute law made the view that law was an 'organic and unified system of rules' much more difficult to maintain (Bryce, 1901, p.865). The increasing girth of the statute book accentuated uncertainty and subverted principle. The impact of legislation made the need for the renovation of the form of law and the articulation of its principles even more urgent. It also encouraged jurists to advocate consolidation and even, though less frequently, codification.

The sharply drawn distinctions between form and substance, and between common law and legislation, were accompanied by four further and interrelated dichotomies which preserved the purity and autonomy of both the common law and legal science, that is, the distinctions between law/politics, law/policy, jurisprudence/principles of legislation and is/ought. These divisions sought to differentiate law from politics, treat the common law as the nucleus of the legal system and elevate the authority of the courts. The distinctions between clarification/legislation and is/ought are associated with the writings of John Austin. It is in his name that it was asserted that jurisprudence and, indeed, the scope of legal education should be devoted to the law as it is rather than as it ought to be (Rumble, 1985, Chapters 3 and 4). Of course Austin himself frequently combined the two. Nonetheless it was not unusual to regard the principles of legislation, 'which discusses the ends or objects of law, and the comparative merits of the different means adopted for attaining them' as something the student should only encounter at an advanced stage of studies. '[It] should certainly come *after* the knowledge of some actual legal system. Indeed, there is much to be said for the plan followed by the University of London, which confines this subject exclusively to those few students who proceed to the higher degree of Doctor of Law' (Clark, 1885, pp. 205–6).

I have already stressed the deference that was normally shown towards the bar and bench, and the desire to be seen to be part of the profession. The new student texts were frequently dedicated to judges and their authors tended to adopt the professionally circumspect view of what was, and was not, appropriate in a work addressed to the profession. Thus Pollock tells us that he felt obliged to withhold a discussion of the wider goals of his books on contract and torts from the body of the text (Pollock, 1895, p.ii). For example, 'It would not be proper to repeat in a practical law-book' those criticisms of the Employers' Liability Act 1880 which he had 'recorded in a separate note to the report of the Royal Commission on Labour' (Pollock, 1895, pp.ix–x).

In this way the new professional law dons uncritically appropriated much from the culture of the common law, many of the mannerisms, etiquette, pedagogy and 'commonsense' of the lawyer. The middle ground that the classical scholars had sought to carve out for themselves, between the profession and the academy, was in substance a very narrow ledge – one which was liable to be overwhelmed at any time by the weight of the culture and narrowly defined interests of the profession.

The Selective Appropriation of Bentham and Austin, and the Suppression of History

Of course significant efforts were made to transcend the 'black letter' tradition. Bentham, for sure, was no mere expositor: 'I choose', he wrote, 'rather to [study the law by concentrating upon] what it might and ought to be than in studying it as it is' (1977, p.310). His science of law transcended the boundaries separating philosophy, politics, economics, social thought and jurisprudence. In his own country, however, this mighty challenge to the inherited tradition of the common law was largely stripped of its radicalising potential. How and why did this happen?

Much of what he wrote was unfinished and much remained (and still remains) unpublished. Other hands tampered with his manuscripts. His ideas were simplified and his radicalism was tempered. Then there are the real difficulties which confront Bentham's readers: the pedantic and obscure style characteristic of his mid- and later writings. Even in this form, however, they excited concern, not least from lawyers. Bentham's abrasive vitriols ridiculed the sacred cows of English society: religion, the monarchy, the landed and the law. Most unsettling of all, perhaps, Bentham sought to expand the province of the jurist while diminishing the role of the judiciary. The response of the profession was twofold: lawyers either mocked and disowned his 'eccentric' and 'impractical' schemes, or adopted his commitment to clarification, systematisation and reform, but in a more guarded, step-by-step fashion.

Other factors also contributed to the attenuation of Bentham's ideas and influence. Consider, for example, John Stuart Mill's discussion of the relationship between Bentham and Austin:

> The untying of intellectual knots; the clearing up of the puzzles arising from complex combinations of ideas confusedly apprehended, and not analysed into their elements; the building up of definite conceptions where only indefinite ones existed ... the disentangling of ... classifications ... and, when disentangled, applying the distinctions (often for the first time) clearly, consistently, and uniformly – these were, of the many characteristics of Mr Austin's work ... those which most especially distinguished him. This untying of knots was not particularly characteristic of Bentham ... The battering ram was of more importance, in Bentham's time, than the builder's trowel ... The urgent thing for Bentham was to assault and demolish ... unreason ... To rescue from among the ruins such valuable materials as had been built in among rubbish, and give them the new and workmanlike shape which fitted them for a better edifice ... was work for which ... Bentham had not time ... Mr Austin's subject was Jurisprudence, Bentham's was Legislation ...
>
> [The] subject of his [Austin's] special labours was theoretically distinct, though subsidiary, ... to [that of Bentham's]. It was what may be called the logic of law, as distinguished from its morality or expediency (Mill, 1838, pp. 440–1).

This passage is illuminating in several respects. It shows how Bentham was safely despatched to a past time when destructive (rather than constructive) work was the order of the day. The present, however, required constructive work. And constructive work was jurisprudence, that is 'the logic of the law, as distinguished from its morality or expediency'. In this way one form of juristic enterprise – the analytical approach associated today with Austin and Oxford – became equated with juristic theorisation. Legal theory and the jurist's *raison d'etre* frequently became coterminous with analytical philosophy and, therefore, estranged from mainstream philosophy and social thought.

Thus Austinian jurisprudence was afforded the same artificial primacy over censorial jurisprudence that form had been accorded over substance. Naturally, expository and censorial jurisprudence so defined were 'theoretically distinct'. Nonetheless, if the province of the jurist (and therefore legal theory) were to transcend the confines of the 'black letter' tradition, the symbiotic or dialectical interaction between these two enterprises required activation and encouragement, rather than partition. In practice, censorial jurisprudence was marginalised; when it was not rendered *ultra vires* it was perpetually postponed.

It was Maine, perhaps, more than any other single jurist who, echoing Mill, recast in a dogmatic and condescending mould the relationship between Bentham and Austin and, thereby, the realm of the jurist:

> Bentham in the main is a writer on legislation. Austin in the main is a writer on jurisprudence. Bentham is chiefly concerned with law as it might be and ought to be. Austin is chiefly concerned with law as it is ... [Those] objects are widely different ... Almost all of his [Bentham's] more important suggestions have been adopted by the English Legislature ... The direct improvement of substantive legal rules belongs not to the theorist of jurisprudence but to the theorist on legislation (Maine, 1885, pp.343–5).

Ironically, it was Bentham himself who exalted definition, precision and systematisation as the hallmarks of a modern legal science. His dream of a complete and comprehensive body of laws was in some respects a continuation of, rather than a decisive break with, a longstanding strand within the history of common law thought (Lieberman, 1985, p.205). The ideal of a 'natural' legal arrangement was at the core of the hegemonic assumptions that sustained both Blackstone and Bentham and it could be used to vindicate a more traditional conception of the jurists' art. It was a common hostility towards natural rights and metaphysics and the subsumption of legal science with scientific rationality which led radical Benthamite and conservative lawyers to be perceived as inhabiting opposite ends of the same spectrum.

Yet it would be wrong to characterise the common law mind as wholly concerned with rationality (in the Weberian sense). Bentham's extreme rationalism could repel as well as attract. To understand the ambivalence that Bentham generated among many lawyers, we must perceive how the common law frame of mind straddled a contradictory field of discourses. A tendency towards scientific rationality was yoked to an irrational belief in the spontaneous, piecemeal, unconscious continuity of the law. The law was a residue of immutable custom. In this aspect of common law culture, Whiggish notions of continuity were allied to a Burkean conservative tradition, with its veneration of age-old institutions. Scientific rationality was forever being mediated, refracted and sustained by an omnipresent irrationality: thereby lies the peculiar rationality of the common law mind. Thus the legal community could, with seeming effortlessness, eulogise the haphazard, particularistic, unsystematic, evolution of the common law – and also trumpet its intrinsic rationalism. As if caught in a magnetic field, English legal thought and education have throughout their history experienced the perpetual pull and push of these competing poles. As a result, the common law mind was forever betwixt and between (Sugarman, 1987). It required a little of history and metaphysics. But it could only continue to maintain its complex equilibrium by keeping history and metaphysics at a safe distance, which usually meant being allied to the present needs of the profession. It was Maitland who brilliantly discerned the ways in which the common law required a pseudo-historical and a psuedo-theoretical tradition as distinct from a fully fledged one (1911). The conceptual categories of the common law were therefore a profound obstacle to the broadening of legal education and scholarship from within.

Other factors hastened the relative neutralisation of Bentham's alternate enterprise. For example, John Stuart Mill's critique of Benthamite utilitarianism undoubtedly sapped Bentham's reputation. In essence, Mill sought to enlarge utilitarianism so that it embraced those features of social and political life that Bentham had allegedly neglected: the historical, the sociological, the broader, moral aspects of human nature and feeling, and the reconciliation of majority rule with the protection of minorities. If this analysis had been applied to the province of jurisprudence then it might possibly have inaugurated an even richer and more subtle juristic canvas than that bequeathed by Bentham. This was not to be. Curiously, Mill spared utilitarian legal theory the censure and reappraisal that characterised his critique of Benthamite social and political thought. Legal theory was treated differently from other moral sciences.

The narrowing of Bentham was also advanced by one of his most dedicated followers, John Austin. Austin was not unsympathetic to censorial jurisprudence but the bulk of his energies were expended upon expository (analytical) jurisprudence. For many, therefore, Austin legitimated the conflation of analytical jurisprudence with legal theory, and the narrowing of the jurists' province to the exposition, systematisation and analysis of concepts and principles. Austin replaced Bentham as 'the true founder of the Science of Law', and 'the spokesman of his generation' (Amos, 1874, p.4). Thus Buckland recalled that in his youth 'Jurisprudence meant ... Austin. He was a religion' (1945, p.2).

It would, however, be wrong to assume that Austin swept all before him. For instance, his static and unhistorical deductions were tellingly ridiculed by Maine, Bryce and Pollock. Nonetheless Austin's legal critics did not fundamentally challenge the juristic enterprise he symbolised. For all their efforts to historicise the province of jurisprudence, their central concerns were essentially orthodox and Austinian. The quest for fundamental legal notions and their clarification and arrangement was, at best, relativised rather than repudiated.

What happened to Bentham was also to befall Austin. Friends and foe alike tended to narrow his ideas. His best known work, *The Province of Jurisprudence Determined*, was intended as a tentative preface to his larger *Lectures on Jurisprudence*. But over thirty years separated their publication. The *Lectures*, reconstructed by Austin's widow from his notes, only appeared in 1863. Few commentators read the *Province*, the *Lectures* and his *The Uses of the Study of Jurisprudence* together. It was Austin's avowedly narrower and preliminary *Province* which received most attention.

Sarah Austin tells us that her husband, 'had long meditated a book embracing a far wider field' (Austin, 1879, Vol. I, p.16). Its subject was to be the principles and relations of jurisprudence and ethics. 'I intend', wrote Austin, 'to show the relations of positive morality and law' (ibid., p.18). This book never materialised. He left behind him a body of work which did not fully reflect his juristic ambitions. Nonetheless, Austin's *Lectures* were deemed too elaborate for most readers. They were substantially abridged into popular student editions. It was through these truncated versions that most students experienced Austin and jurisprudence. His discussion of the bearing of morality on law and the relationship between positive law, divine law and utility were expunged from these editions. Above all, Austinian jurisprudence was taken as the most sophisticated defence of the common law credo that the law of the land was the measure of justice. In analytical jurisprudence, as in historical jurisprudence, there was a tendency to equate the good with the existent: the law (and English society) had become normative concepts.

Maine's influential critique of Austin had done much to license this narrowing. For instance, Maine cautioned readers of Austin that 'the most serious blemish in the "Province of Jurisprudence Determined" was Austin's discussion of the relation between the law of God, the law of nature and the theory of utility' (1885, p.369). Maine could barely conceal his irritation at the incursion of metaphysics (or, worse still, natural law) in an avowedly jurisprudential treatise. The

> identification, which is their object ... is quite gratuitous and valueless for any purpose ... I much doubt whether such an enquiry would have seemed called for in a treatise like Austin's. Taken at its best, it is a discussion belonging not to the philosophy of law, but to the philosophy of legislation. The jurist, properly so called, has nothing to do with any ideal standard of laws or morals. (ibid., p.370).

Just how narrowly Austin and jurisprudence could be interpreted is evidenced by the dictum of Austin's most successful editor, Jethro Brown:

> Justice as a concept in jurisprudence, is conforming to law – if not conformity to established rules of law, or to the spirit of law in its totality, then according to a law which the judges make and apply retrospectively. (1916, p.181)

This interpretation of Austin was fortified by the most successful jurisprudence textbook of the classical period, Holland's *Jurisprudence*. Holland's text applied classical legal scholarship's enthusiasm for systematisation, conceptualisation and exposition in a manner which was dogmatic, narrow and pedantic. On Holland's death, a colleague summed up his achievements thus:

> He [Holland] once referred to himself as 'impelled by a ... morbid hatred of disorder'; and it is true that the whole bent of his mind was towards orderliness and simplification ... [Holland's text was] ... perhaps the most successful book on jurisprudence ever written. [It appeared in thirteen editions during the author's long lifetime.] Substantially Holland's doctrine was that of Austin, but he made it less vulnerable by discarding many of Austin's crudities and inconsistencies, and was more persuasive because he wrote in a style which, though sometimes slightly pedantic ... is far more attractive than that of Austin; and in all essentials he maintained the same doctrine through the forty-four years of the book's successive editions ... It is indicative of his serene confidence in the strength of the position he had adopted that in the ... [last] edition he

hardly refers to any criticism more recent than that of Sir Henry Maine. (Brierly, 1926, p.476)

The last edition of Holland's *Jurisprudence* was published in 1924. He defined jurisprudence as a 'formal science of positive law'. The function of his book was 'to set forth and explain those comparatively few and simple ideas which underlie the infinite variety of legal rules' (1924, p.1). By the end of the classical period, legal theory, legal history, private law and public law were dominated by similar criteria of relevance, which simultaneously served to separate them from one another, while recasting them in an analogous fashion.

Anti-metaphysics, the Ideology of Advocacy and the Moral Void

Bentham's offensive against natural rights and natural law – aided and abetted by Hume and Austin – was also used to exalt analytical jurisprudence and marginalise a jurisprudence concerned with morality and justice. Bentham's attack on discussions of rights reflected his more general aversion to the semantic confusions and 'lying fictions' of eighteenth-century legal and political discourse. Clarity of thought, and a sensitivity to the ends and interests served by the law, necessitated a strong dose of demystification. From this perspective ideas of rights and allied abstractions were vacuous, a form of false consciousness that inhibited rational progress. All rights were ultimately derived from and subject to an omnipotent sovereign.

Thus, coexisting with the democratic and anti-statist language of Bentham's *oeuvre* were those voices that were profoundly statist and authoritarian. It was the latter elements that appealed to a diverse constituency: from those officials seeking to administer colonial India to liberal and socialist critics of *laissez-faire* individualism (Burrow, 1966, Chapter 8; Stokes, 1959). The notion that it was the law of the land, and not metaphysics, which embodied the principal criterion of justice distinguished the English polity from its Continental and American counterparts. Moreover, England had no entrenched constitution and supreme court. So English legal and political commentators tended to be more particularistic, less abstract and less grounded in constitutional exegesis than was the case in the Continent and the United States. The relative decline of natural law and natural rights talk within English jurisprudence and political culture made it more difficult for jurists and those at the margins of society to imagine and champion what rights ought to exist (Rodgers, 1987, Chapters 1, 2).

The language of rights can sustain both a conservative defence of the status quo and new and critical elements within law and society.

In England, however, its radical potential was largely sapped. Questions of morality and justice were becoming neutralised and privatised. Ethical values were increasingly located in the private sphere of the family. They were alien to economic, political and legal questions and to the everyday world of the workplace. This tendency was also evident in other aspects of English culture, notably the attenuation of the critical dimension within Christianity (Berger, 1969). All this paralleled and legitimated a modern conception of the lawyers' ideology of advocacy: namely the obligation to be blind to the moral implications of their work (Luban, 1988; Simon, 1978). At its crudest, the lawyer is pre-eminently concerned with winning the case rather than establishing the truth. Here, then, lurked a discourse which sustained a chill, mechanical view of the law and life, one that, at bottom, absolved opportunism and selfishness.

Languages of Reciprocity and Conflict

Thus in the period 1850–1907 we can detect the constitution of a common consciousness – some sort of practical agreement about the underlying form of classical legal thought and the respective provinces of the juristic elite and the legal elite. This consensus was largely shared by and constructed in collaboration with their American and German counterparts. In this sense it was a truly international enterprise.

However, the ideological hegemony of the 'black letter' tradition is not satisfactorily portrayed in terms resembling familiar models of one-dimensional control in which all sense of struggle or contradiction is lost. Far from desiring to convey an impression of stasis, I want to stress the reciprocal and symbiotic nature of the relationship between the respective elites within legal education and thought and the legal profession. It was a relationship whose boundaries were constantly being probed.

While classical law teachers often thought of themselves as 'barristers without portfolio' they were far from being marionettes. Bryce, Pollock and Maitland lamented that English lawyers seemed peculiarly uninterested in, and scornful towards, jurisprudence, legal history, comparative law and Roman law. So it was beyond the confines of Lincoln's Inn, the Temple and Westminster Hall – to Germany, principally, and also to America, as well as to Roman law – that classical jurists turned for their models and their inspiration and erudition. To some extent this happened as early as the 1820s, although it probably reached its apogee during the period 1880–1914. It is an interesting quirk of history that at the same period when Germany's highly systematised Pandectist model of law was being appropriated by law teachers in England, it was under attack in Germany. The 'free' and 'interests' schools of thought associated with the jurist Ihering criticised the Pandectist's elevation of systematisation as an end in itself. This critique prefigured many of the American Legal Realist criticisms of legal formalism and 'mechanical jurisprudence'.

The real and substantial achievements that were effected by English scholars in Roman law, legal science and legal history would have been almost inconceivable without the impressive historical and legal scholarship of Germany. Nonetheless, the impact of German and American thought on English legal science was ultimately double-edged (Stein, 1980, pp.61–7, 87–8). It was both historical and anti-empirical. Its association of law with mathematics rendered the former as a suprahistorical reified logic, while its obsession with systematisation, internal coherence, legal reasoning, textual scholarship and the form of the law was likely to reinforce rather than subvert the 'black letter' tendencies within England's legal community. Continuity and consensus were inferred rather than demonstrated. Ultimately its politics (sustained, in part, by a strong, reassuring evolutionist strain) were complaisant and conservative.

Other factors also explain the anti-historical tendencies of some legal scholarship. History's corrosive message of contingency challenged fundamentalist creeds. Thus, for some jurists the issue became how to circumscribe the influence of history within legal education and thought. Frederick Harrison, Professor of Jurisprudence at the Inns of Court, expressed this concern when he warned that:

It would lead to the utmost confusion of thought ... if we come to regard historical explanations as the substantial or independent part of jurisprudence. From history we always get ideas of ... constant development, of instability. But in law, at any rate for the purposes of the practical lawyer, what we need are ideas of fixity, of uniformity ... [It] would be a real evil if our scientific education gave a bent to the student's mind out of harmony with the practical wants of the profession.

There is ... another inconvenience in the historical way of regarding law. The ... history of legal change is not ... very often determined by purely internal causes. That is to say, that purely juristic considerations or motives ... only partly decide the form which any chapter of law shall take ... All this is very often most alien to the scientific aspect of law.

What is the practical conclusion to which I point? ... [The] business of the lawyer is with the solidarity of [the law] ... [The] essential thing is to know how symmetrical, how wise, how scientifically right [the law] ultimately became ...

It is so great a strain upon the mind to build up and retrace the conception of a great body of titles reducible to abstract and symmetrical classification, and capable of statement as a set of consistent principles – and this is what I take jurisprudence to be – that we are perpetually in danger of giving to law a literary instead of a scientific character, and of slipping in our thoughts from what the law is into speculating upon the coincidences which made it what it once was. (Harrison, 1879, pp.115–16).

Perish the thought!

The legitimate territory of the jurist was problematic. In other words, the identity and standpoint of the jurist were subject to a pattern of struggle: of confrontation and riposte, action and reaction, dispute and resolution. One of the clearest examples of this was the juristic response to the House of Lords' decision in *Derry v. Peek*.[3] The directors of a tramway company stated in the prospectus that they had the right to use steam power: in fact, they knew that they had no such right, but they expected to secure it. The Court of Appeal held that the absence of reasonable grounds for believing a statement to be accurate is sufficient to ground liability for fraud. However, the House of Lords reversed this decision.

Pollock had welcomed the Court of Appeal's decision and waged war against the decision of the House of Lords. Even before it was fully reported, he published a substantial critique of their lordships' decision: 'The purpose of this paper is to show that the grounds assigned to *Derry v. Peek*, ... are erroneous in law, and ought to be disregarded by every tribunal which is at liberty to disregard them' (1889, p.410).

His remarks did not go unchallenged. In the next issue of the *Law Quarterly Review* Pollock's colleague at Oxford, Anson, not only defended the decision of the House of Lords, but admonished Pollock's critical tone: 'I cannot think it desirable', he wrote, 'that an appeal should be addressed to all courts ... to disregard a decision of the House of Lords if they can, to elude it if they cannot'(1890, p.72).

In a footnote Pollock inserted to Anson's essay, he rather lamely explained that his call to disregard or elude the decision of the House of Lords was directed chiefly at American courts! (Anson, 1890, p.72 n.73) Pollock continued to use all the strategies of counsel to denigrate the decision.

It is of course extremely difficult to measure the impact of Pollock's condemnation of *Derry v. Peek*. As the decision itself makes clear, the judiciary were by no means unanimous on the role of equity and negligence-based liability in this area. Parliament, with exceptional speed, limited the impact of the ruling in the Directors Liability Act of 1890. What can be claimed is that the history of *Derry v. Peek*, and several other leading cases, illustrates the complex and symbiotic relationship between judicial and juristic law-making – a creative partnership that has received insufficient attention to date. The subsequent history of *Derry v. Peek* bears this out. In 1914 the Lord Chancellor, Viscount Haldane, decided (in spite of the House being bound by its own decisions) that the decision should be further restricted.[4] Haldane in fact consulted with Pollock on the ways this might be done (Howe, 1961, Vol. 1, p.215). Taking a broader view of the classical period, however, it was Anson rather than Pollock who seemed to represent the dominant view of the permissible scope of juristic criticism.

Upholding and Prolonging the 'Black Letter' Tradition

Austinism also reflected and possibly sustained the slow rise of legal formalism, as the dominant mode of judicial discourse, which parallelled the rise of classical legal education and science.[5] The rise of legal formalism must have appeared to some jurists and lawyers as if the judiciary had endorsed vulgar Austinism. It was as if their lordships had adopted the somewhat circumscribed definition of the legitimate criticism of the judiciary which Anson had espoused in connection with juristic commentaries. In other words, both academia and the bench adopted parallel discourses which rendered criticism more, rather than less, difficult.

A further feature of this unseasonable climate was the translation of that dimension of Hobbes, Locke and Blackstone which elevated the judiciary as the guardians of individual freedom into the language of classical legal thought. This found its most influential expression in Dicey's *An Introduction to the Study of the Law of the Constitution* (1885). Dicey argued that the preservation of the rule of law was dependent upon the guaranteed autonomy of the judiciary. This sought to reconcile the sovereignty of parliament and the rule of law. Thus, to contradict or criticise the decisions of the courts came close to impugning the rule of law. In effect, Dicey had posited the maintenance of the judiciary's authority as the highest value in the legal universe (Sugarman, 1983). In an increasingly democratic society, the legitimacy of the state was, in part, articulated through its claims to judicial independence and the rule of law. Arguably, the English state became increasingly dependent upon an autonomous legal profession and legal system in order to legitimise itself. In this way, the legal profession and legal system constituted the state. One consequence of this was that the state was, therefore, extremely reluctant to interfere in what was perceived as the province of the profession. Codification and the reform of the legal profession (notably the bar) and of legal education all suffered as a result.

But if we are to understand the dominance and tenacity of the 'black letter' tradition, we must also consider the metamorphosis of university education in England and the renaissance in the professional education of lawyers. The great university reform movement of 1850–1914 forced Oxford and Cambridge to become secular institutions. Within Oxbridge the dons were divided about the purpose of education. By 1914 a particular conception of education had emerged victorious. This idea rested upon the following beliefs: firstly, that teaching rather than research was the primary aim of the university; secondly, that regular and extensive examinations constituted the major means of assessing undergraduates; finally, that the job of the university was to provide a 'liberal education'. However, the notion of a liberal education was somewhat narrow, 'exactness within a narrow range', as Sir John Seeley described it (quoted in Sanderson, 1975, p.7). It aimed not at breadth but at highly specialised excellence. Clearly this definition of education was unlikely to encourage a broad conception of legal education and thought.

Other aspects of university education at Oxbridge undoubtedly hindered the development of legal education. Until relatively recently classics at Oxford and mathematics at Cambridge dominated the curricula. Nearly all the available scholarships to students were in those fields. As a result the best students tended to read classics or maths. Those reading law had a maximum of two years' legal studies as they were still required initially to immerse themselves in either classics or maths. All this discouraged students, especially good ones, from reading law. In fact in the race between the new disciplines such as the natural sciences, law and history, law lost out in terms of student numbers and the resources it attracted.

Furthermore, the demise of the 'men of letters' tradition and the professionalisation of academic disciplines undoubtedly fragmented scholarship and learning into narrow, divided camps. Professionalisation and examinations encouraged a 'disciplinary tribalism' (Burrow, 1981, p.x) and a strenuous effort to claim the objectivity of the expert specialist.

Oxbridge's importance in law stemmed from the fact that, numerically speaking, it dominated the production of law graduates. Only in the 1950s did London University join it as a significant producer of law graduates. The dominance of Oxbridge and, more recently, London, was further enhanced by their control of the production of law teachers. Thus the form of education and scholarship offered at

Oxbridge and, later, London, are of special importance in explaining the dominance of the 'black letter' tradition.

Most of the London colleges (and certainly those in the provinces) were created in part as a reaction against Oxbridge. They asserted the vocational, professional and technological nature of their education. Provincial law schools were largely the creation of the provincial law societies. With very little state expenditure on higher education, this was the only way provincial universities could establish law schools. As a result, these schools were highly sensitive to the needs of the profession and for many years the bulk of the tuition there centred around preparation for the Law Society's own examinations, rather than for their own law degrees.

Moreover, until the 1960s a significant proportion of law school staff were part-time practitioners, largely unsympathetic towards and untrained in law in any broad sense. The inadequate resources available to higher education, especially in the period prior to the rise of the new universities in the post-Robbins period, meant that even if somebody desired to teach or undertake a broadened conception of legal education and scholarship, the resources available to fund such work were meagre. In short, the dominant tradition of classical legal education and scholarship had the pre-eminent merit of being cheap. Thus there were real fiscal limits on broadening legal education and thought. The actual number of institutions, students and, therefore, teachers of law were relatively small and grew relatively slowly until about 1960. It is only since the 1960s that an enormous expansion in institutions teaching law and, therefore, in law teachers has taken place. Until then this monolithic quality undoubtedly discouraged pluralism in education and thought.

The law textbooks of the classical period, especially when seen in the context of increasing university examinations, lent themselves to what has become the dominant form of legal pedagogy: that law is taught as a simple set of rules; that examinations test the ability to solve legal problems by reference to certain pat answers, and that law texts and teaching are 'vocational' (albeit in a peculiarly narrow and artificial sense) and examination-oriented. However, further impetus for this conception of law, legal education and legal scholarship came from beyond the universities. We must briefly explore the relationship between university and professional education and scholarship.

The testing and training of the legal profession was in a sorry state for most of the nineteenth century. In essence, this left the legal education of most solicitors and barristers in the hands of the private law coaches, the crammers. These are the great, unsung antiheroes of modern legal education and scholarship. Beyond London, Manchester, Liverpool and parts of Yorkshire, the Law Society provided no formal education for articled clerks. Crammers were, therefore, an essential lifeline for most would-be solicitors who worked in the provinces. Crammers also filled the demand for texts specifically designed for examination candidates. They attracted considerable numbers of students – and a high proportion of those excelling in the Law Society's examinations. From 1893, the Law Society started to copy the methods of the pre-eminent crammers, Messrs Gibson and Weldon (Kirk, 1976, Chapter 3).

In sum, until about the mid-1960s most lawyers acquired their conceptions of – and attitudes towards – law, legal scholarship and legal education from crammers, not universities. Moreover, the crammers' pedagogy – their notions of relevance and identity – undoubtedly percolated upwards into the lecture halls of the universities. The new provincial university law schools significantly drew upon the methods of the crammers in their efforts to provide the vocational education required by intending solicitors. They also employed a number of crammers on their staffs. Crammers were also significant both as coaches and as the authors of texts designed for candidates taking the external LL.B of the University of London. Mini-versions of, or notes to, the classic academic texts were produced by law coaches. It was through these 'nutshells' that many lawyers glimpsed Dicey, Pollock and Salmond. The success and tenacity of cramming in both academic and legal education undercut the legitimacy and worth of an academic legal education in the eyes of lawyers and would-be lawyers; it thereby served to intensify the divide between the academic and vocational, theory and practice.

The dominance of the expository tradition was also sustained because of the relative dearth of mediums through which scholarly work could be published. The tiny number of publishers who specialised in law books was preoccupied with the needs of practitioners or intending practitioners. Standard texts by Pollock, Anson, Kenny, Salmond and Dicey, as well as numerous practitioner works, were edited and updated under new hands but largely retained their old form and values. Thus the influence of many classic academic and practitioner works have persisted long after the death of their original authors. Like the forms of action, their authors may be buried but they still rule us from their graves. This practice, together with the existence of only one major academic legal periodical in England throughout the classical period (the *Law Quarterly Review*), surely inhibited innovative scholarship and education.

The 'Black Letter' Tradition as a Solution to the Problem of Social Order

There are many other factors that helped to sustain the 'black letter' tradition and suppress other visions of what legal education and scholarship might become. The reconceptualisation of the law became imperative as fear of socialism and the breakdown of ordered government increased in the final decades of the nineteenth century. The conservative sentiments of 'old liberals' such as Maine, Dicey and Bryce is clearly manifested in their increasing tendency to view the United States as the model constitutional democracy. Dicey defined the political problem of the age as:

> how to form conservative democracies ... to give to constitutions resting on the will of the people the stability and permanence which has hitherto been found only in monarchical or aristocratic states ... The plain truth is that ... the American republic affords the best example of a conservative democracy; and now that England is becoming democratic, respectable Englishmen are beginning to consider whether the constitution of the United States may not afford the means by which ... may be preserved the political conservatism dear and habitual to the governing classes of England. (cited in Tulloch, 1977, pp.834–5)

Moreover:

> There law rather than government held the federation together, judges not politicians were the ultimate arbiters, and litigation had replaced legislation. The prospect of a vast nation run on the lines of a solicitor's office in Lincoln's Inn must have been very satisfying [to Dicey and many of his legal contemporaries]. (Tulloch, 1977, p.837)

Much of the new legal science was also a response to the role of the middle classes in a polity where, because of the extension of the franchise, they had become a minority voice. Within the old universities, figures such as Bryce, Dicey, Sidgwick, Leslie Stephen and T.H. Green asserted a crucial role for the first generation of professional university scholars. These were the 'brains' who would exercise a pivotal position in Britain's new democracy. They would constitute a counterweight to the excesses of majoritarianism. They would also provide the lower and superior orders with the guidance necessary to produce well-ordered reforms (Kent, 1978). From this perspective, the postulates of the classical law dons were an assertion of the cultural authority of the middle classes.

One area where the assertion of cultural authority was most urgent was in the context of Britain's empire. Here the new legal science had a special role to play. English law was exported to the colonies. The attempt to teach English law to an Indian audience persuaded Macaulay, Fitzjames Stephen, Markby and Maine that English law was overly haphazard and that systematisation and rationalisation were essential. Since the rationale for the imposition of a British minority on an Indian majority was, in part, that Britain had brought India the rule of law and therefore a more superior civilisation, the need to refurbish legal thought became imperative (Sugarman, 1983). Generation after generation of colonial administrators, judges and lawyers cut their teeth on the major texts of the new legal science. And as law schools and the lower end of the colonial civil service opened up to the indigenous population, so the influence of the 'black letter' tradition became further extended. The classical law dons were but one of many contributions to what Oxford had to offer to the theory and practice of the empire. They were part of the effort to transform Oxford into a great imperial university, by a more rigorous training for lawyers, scientists and administrators. In short, the new legal scholars were part of a wider intellectual movement seeking to nourish the empire as one of the last lost causes.

One strand of this assertion of world cultural leadership was the association of race (Anglo-Saxonism) with a unique respect for law and order. The effort to trace an unbroken genetic preference for freedom and individual rights, from the Teutonic forests *via* the village communities of Anglo-Saxon England to America, were commonplace (Burrow, 1981, Chapter 5). Notions of racial genius and their messages about racial inferiority touched some of the classical legal scholarship as it did other intellectual work of this period. Bryce, in particular, was preoccupied with the theme of race. *The American Commonwealth* (Bryce, 1888) and his other writings on race, fuelled contemporary notions of the inferiority of the non-Anglo Saxon – especially blacks (MacDougall, 1982).

Perhaps, in some complex way, the tenacity of legal formalism was associated with a wider failure in English culture and social science. One might point to the distrust of theory that permeated so much of English intellectual life. Several commentators have emphasised the continuing strength of positivistic assumptions about society and the nature of science in late Victorian and Edwardian England (Burrow, 1966, Chapter 8). In the classical period, this received sustenance from a work whose influence on the methodology of law and other human sciences can hardly be exaggerated: John Stuart Mill's *A System of Logic*, first published in 1843 (Grey, 1983). Mill's *Logic* and his resuscitation of utilitarianism discouraged a fundamental rethinking of social thought. Throughout and beyond the classical period, evolutionary positivism tended to remain the dominant paradigm in the human sciences. In contrast, there developed in the United States an anti-positivistic doctrine, pragmatism, that stimulated the rethinking of social thought. This in turn consituted one of the important intellectual bases of American sociological jurisprudence and Legal Realism, a philosophy which was severely confined in England.

If the political right – which embraced most classical law teachers – had a clear conception of the theory and politics of law, what of the political left? What is striking is the degree to which the right and left shared many assumptions about law and social theory. 'The most notable English political theorists of the left, the Fabians, were as firmly wedded to positivist as to gradualist attitudes' (Burrow, 1966, p.262). And many of its leading figures espoused a mixture of statism, paternalism and evolutionary positivism, a cocktail unlikely to produce an alternative way of seeing law and society.

Yet if the connections between legal science, nationalism and Darwinism could sometimes appear quite intimate, a further dimension of the project to create a liberal legal science merits attention. For several of the new professional jurists, law became a religious substitute, one of the many secular religions of Victorian England. As nonconformity helped to sustain the university reform movement, so the quest for faith and certainties in an increasingly uncertain world, and the inseparability of spirituality from ordinary life and thoughts about identity, found one of its expressions in the movement to renovate legal science. The influence of Evangelical 'seriousness' and a concern with duty and responsibility continued to be important in late Victorian England. The law helped those with traditional religious beliefs to adapt to the new intellectual forces of the age, such as Darwinism. For agnostics, a vocation in the law might provide the basis for larger aspirations.

Faith and belief in the law and its beneficence were, like the language of religion, evoked by jurist after jurist. The classical jurists sought to reassure their practitioner brothers (and perhaps themselves too) that they shared the faith. Jurists held themselves out as defenders of the faith, encouraging respect for law and order. Above all, they proclaimed and solemnised the miraculous attainments of the high priests of the law, the judges. In this sense, university law schools were akin to seminaries, socialising future generations in the values of the legal community, systematizing the canonical beliefs which bound the sect, but rarely challenging its foundations (cf. Levinson, 1988, Chapter 5). They consecrated its genius in the manner that was representative of the orations of the profession: 'To Our Lady of the Common Law.' Thus Pollock invoked the 'brotherhood that subsists between all true followers of the Common Law' (Pollock, 1895, p.ii).

In these ways, the classical jurists were 'organic intellectuals' whose words, symbols and rituals helped to produce certain beliefs and values about law and society. From this perspective, the law was a 'civil religion' (Bellah, 1970). It was one of a set of interlinked institutions, along with the royal family, the aristocracy, the established church and the armed forces, which helped to create and maintain a particular conception of Englishness: peculiarly private, insular, eccentric, nationalistic and 'down to earth' (Samuel, 1989). The law, like gardening, celebrated a philosophy of passivity.

'We don't like doing things quickly in this country', Frank Gibbons tells his wife, Ethel, in Noel Coward's *This Happy Breed*:

> FRANK It's like gardening. Someone once said we was a nation of gardeners, and they weren't far out. We're used to planting things and watching them grow and looking out for changes in the weather.
> ETHEL You and your gardening!
> FRANK Well it's true – think what a mess there'd be if all the flowers and vegetables and crops came popping up in a minute. That's what all these social reformers are trying to do, trying to alter the way of things all at once. We've got our own way of settling things. It may be slow and it may be a bit dull, but it suits us all right and it always will. (cited in Samuel, 1989, p.xxv)

A Comparative Perspective: America and England

At first blush, it is the differences between the histories of English and American legal education and thought that are most striking, for example, the American Revolution and the abolition of the forms of action in many American states up to a hundred years before England hastened the creation of a national jurisprudence concerned in part with issues of nationalism, economic growth and the values of 'republicanism' (Newmyer, 1985). The more overtly law-centred, lawyer-dominated culture of American society – where important 'political' problems often became 'legal' ones (Tocqueville, 1945), and where constitutional exegesis and a commitment to natural and entrenched 'rights' encouraged more abstract forms of legal and political discourse – made it especially difficult for American jurists and judges to maintain a strict separation between 'law' and 'policy' (Rodgers, 1987).

The Legal Realists, at least in some of their voices, began to take facts seriously; that is, the ways in which the factual context was crucial in understanding cases. They also paid greater attention to the functions served by law and the role of the law as social policy (Schlegel, 1979 and 1980; Twining, 1973; White, 1972).

The destruction of many local bar associations in the Jacksonian era meant that American lawyers were probably less well organised institutionally than their English counterparts and, therefore, more dependent upon law schools for the acquisition of basic legal skills (in part because some large law firms did not want to train apprentices) and professional legitimacy. Then there is the greater diversity within the American legal profession and between different jurisdictions and different law schools, the lack of a divided profession, and easier access to practitioner status, all of which meant that the potential space for experimentation and difference within the profession and within legal education and legal scholarship was greater than in England. Moreover, the ties between American lawyers and business were even closer than in England. For example, American big business employed teams of in-house counsel; and lawyers established a large market for their services in core areas of management and corporate finance. While English lawyers were also significantly involved in business, they appear relatively less so than their American cousins (Sugarman, 1990). In America even more than in England, this made it difficult to sustain the traditional separation of lawyers' 'public' and 'private' roles as the lines of demarcation between the 'public' and the 'private' were regularly and very visibly crossed with ease. This, in turn, meant that the practice of American lawyering blatantly undermined that tenet of legal formalism that lawyering is really only about those distinctively 'legal' tasks separate from 'society', 'business' and 'politics'.

Also significant is the peculiar character of the American state: a state that was relatively weak and fragmented, and whose servants were often so poorly paid that lawyers took on functions which in Europe would have been performed by the state. In contrast to the copious diversity of the American legal order, the English legal system was more coherent and unitary, staffed by a tiny number of appellate judges exclusively drawn from the ranks of the small world of the bar, who literally could and largely did talk to one another. This made it easier for the bar and bench to try to monopolise the construction and refinement of legal principles. It also made it more difficult for English academics to set themselves up as an independent agency. In contrast, American judges were largely elected, relatively more heterodox and often involved in the hurly-burly of politics. Apart from a celebrated few (Story, Holmes, Cardozo, Hand, for instance), American judges smacked less of the priesthood than of the quack healer; and they did not, therefore, generate quite the same degree of deference.

For many American liberal lawyers and law teachers, faith in an autonomous legal order became further discredited as the American judiciary seemed to become more 'formalistic', and struck down progressive and New Deal legislation. Indeed, American sociological jurisprudence and Legal Realism were in part a reaction against this show of partiality. Some striking down of 'socialistic' legislation also occurred in England; and the judiciaries' antipathy towards trade unions was perhaps even more striking than in the United States. Nonetheless, the ensuing outcry did not sustain the same intensity of feeling as in America. An important factor here was that some Realists were directly involved in the New Deal, as advisers, regulators, commissioners, counsel and judges. In England there was no parallel experience; jurists remained very much on the margins of government and administration.

In other words, in America it was easier for law professors to make a living by openly criticising judges than was the case in England. This was unwittingly aided by what became the characteristic form of American legal scholarship and pedagogy, the casebook and Socratic method. Together they tended to emphasise the relative indeterminacy of the common law, and elevated the law teacher to the role of high priest. It was 'Herr Professor' rather than the judges who now took centre-stage. And, to awestruck and bewildered audiences from coast to coast, it was the law professor who showed how it should or should not be done, wherein lay the peculiar rationality of the law, and what it meant to 'think like a lawyer'. Moreover, the cultural barricade separating lawyers from law teachers was less obstructive than in England where, as Gower complained, 'nothing is more nauseating than the patronising air of mock humility usually affected by one of His Majesty's judges when addressing an academic gathering ... It is my submission that English teachers of law suffer from an acute inferiority complex.' (Gower, 1950, p.198; Atiyah, 1987). Jurists seldom felt valued when judges insisted (as they did until very recently) that the only jurists who could be cited in court were those who were deceased – no doubt sustaining the belief that the only good jurist is a dead one! In America, the respect (if not love) afforded law teachers was no doubt assisted by the comparative ease with which leading jurists could actually become the highest judges of the land: Story, Holmes, Cardozo and Frankfurter are cases in point.

At the institutional level, the creation of American law schools was also facilitated by a more liberal regime governing the creation of non-profitmaking bodies, such as law schools and universities. More generally, the expansion of university education occurred more swiftly in the United States, characterised by the growth of large, rich, private universities and their public counterparts. Greater funding for American law schools, Langdell's success at turning legal education into a postgraduate subject taught by fulltime teachers, and the large market for such graduates – one which, crucially, appealed to elite law firms – made English law dons swoon with envy. Moreover, the development of sociology, anthropology and politics in the leading American universities far outstripped that in England where, principally at Oxbridge, sociology and anthropology tended to be kept 'at punt pole's length' from the rest of the academy (Collini, Winch and Burrow, 1983, p.375). Indeed, in America, a close connection was forged early on in a few leading universities between the study of law, economics and politics, with political scientists dominating large areas of the study of law and the constitution.

However, the construction and diffusion of modern legal science and education in America and England share many similarities. As we have seen, the creation of a liberal legal science in America, England and Germany was a cosmopolitan affair; jurists in all three countries borrowed from one another as they sought to create similar legal orders to address kindred socio-political conditions. All three countries shared a longstanding legal culture, a set of collectively held general assumptions about law, polity and society, that most lawyers imbibed. One of these assumptions was that law could and should be reduced to an autonomous body of rules and principles. This aspiration received added impetus in the modern period (Sugarman, 1986). For instance, the codification movement and the influence of German models of the university, the role of the jurist and the nature of legal science, served to heighten the quest for true and universal legal principles. This was especially the case in America (Hoeflich, 1984 and 1988; Smith, 1988, Chapters 3 and 6). From this perspective, Langdell, Corbin and Williston appear as the ultimate Pandectists. In America and England, the opinions of judges as inscribed in the law reports remained at the centre of legal education and thought. Moreover, the parallels between America and England were further heightened by the fact that the decisions of American and English courts in several key areas of private law in the nineteenth century were very similar in form and outcome.

Lawyers on both sides of the Atlantic were obsessed with the need for constitutional restraints on 'hasty and ill-conceived' change; and 'moderation' and 'statesmanship' became key words in the political lexicon (Sugarman, 1983; Collini, Winch and Burrow, Chapter XI). Liberal legal scientists sought to construct a more orderly world; a world that would keep socialists, anarchists and trade unionists at bay, and where the problem of social integration was resolved by conceiving of society largely in terms of contractual relations (Paul, 1960; Wiebe, 1967; Pick, 1989). In this world, civilised societies were governed by laws not people, and judges owed their allegiance to the law and their conception of 'the public interest'. This tended to ratify the rule of judges and lawyers.

From the late nineteenth century to the 1940s, efforts were made to establish Legal Realism and an avowedly 'sociological jurisprudence' in Germany, America and England. However, both were largely defanged of their radicalising potential (Purcell, 1973;

Kalman, 1986; Glasser, 1987). While they represented a 'palace revolution', they 'no more proposed to abandon the basic tenets of Langdellian jurisprudence than the Protestant Reformers of the fifteenth and sixteenth centuries proposed to abandon the basic tenets of Christian theology. These were the ideas that "law was a science" and that there is such a thing as "the one true rule of law".' (Gilmore, 1977, p.87). In America, the Realists' message that all law is politics was 'so arresting that even the realists never dared face it ...' (Kalman, 1986, p.231). And what was true of America was also true of Germany and England.

The Langdellian revolution established the dominant form, content and pedagogy of modern American law in terms that were remarkably similar to those which predominated in England. As Stevens observes, 'The lasting influence of the case-method was to transfer the basis of American legal education from substance to procedure and to make the focus of American legal scholarship – or at least legal theory – increasingly one of process rather than doctrine.' (Stevens, 1983, p.56). Indeed, his more general prognosis is pessimistic and provocative: that despite repeated efforts to break out of its iron cage, legal education was and is unlikely to transcend the profession-orientated forces that have controlled most law schools most of the time (Stevens, 1983. Cf. McAuslan, 1989; Partington, 1988; Sugarman,1985; Wilson,1987).

Legal Science as Political Thought; the Resistance of Legal Education to Change

The basic tenents of legal education and scholarship were constructed, transmitted and diffused in the period 1850–1907. This period was truly the golden age of modern legal scholarship. And it was in this period that academic lawyers, in partnership with the courts, fundamentally reconceptualised the form and content of English law. Here were the true codifiers of modern law. Moreover, juristic categories were a vital ingredient of the educated person's conception of state, society and politics. The law in the cases and on the statute book, distilled and reconstituted in the new student law texts, operated like a language, naming and claiming wider areas of social life, belief, action, intention and subordinating or driving into silence others. For example, legal categories created social identities: school children, women and young persons, the family, ages or kinds of 'responsibility', the public sphere, the private sphere, and so on. The relative deference of the jurists, the largely invisible practices of lawyers and the declatory theory of precedent have tended to obfuscate the role of lawyers, judges and jurists as the translators and creators of one of our most important political and social discourses. Jurists were important wholesalers of ideology. They fitted legal education and scholarship into an overall ordering of society.

After about 1907 a second generation of professional law teachers emerged who were less cosmopolitan and less contextual than their predecessors. In part, the problem was that Pollock, Dicey *et al.* had done such a good job of appearing to make law certain and systematised that 'the task scholars were left with was to monitor the small changes in the law: a new development in eminent domain, a new wrinkle in consideration' (Schlegel, 1984, p.107).

New texts were discouraged. The great intellectual undertakings of the classical period gave way to a narrowing of vision, seeking to learn in greater detail about smaller areas. Of course, this process had its critics and one can certainly detect a number of counter-currents. What is striking, however, is the extent to which these critics and counter-currents were repressed. Why? In addition to those factors enumerated above, it is undoubtedly the case that high staff–student ratios, the elevation of teaching over research, the isolation of legal education and thought within the scholarly community, the hiring of law teachers based on prowess in examinations rather than flair for scholarship, the failure to provide adequate financial support for research, and the legal profession's control over what law schools taught and how they taught and examined it, all inhibited reform from within.

For many students and teachers of law, the assumptions, classifications and pedagogy of the 'black letter' tradition possess a reified logic or inevitability. It is as if the logic and categories of the law make the choices for us. This de-emphasises that they are human constructs embodying political and moral choices. This in turn inhibits attempts to explore alternatives, and even an awareness of the values and assumptions of the 'black letter' tradition. Transcending the 'black letter' tradition requires that we become conscious of the choices that are made for us by its reified logic and categories; that such decisions are inherent in all spheres of human conduct, and that we are capable of making conscious selections without the illusion that those sometimes difficult choices are simply the product of concrete legal rules or categories.

In addition, changing legal education and scholarship pose a fundamental problem to the professional identity of the law teacher. As we have seen, the *raison d'etre* of the legal scientist is bound up in the claim to be part of the legal profession, to share its values and culture and, above all, in a commitment to the notion of law as a certain body of rules. Any effort significantly to reform legal education and scholarship challenges the very professional identity that jurists have worked hard to establish, and the rule of law ideology itself (Schlegel, 1984, pp.103–4). The secular penalties of conversion or unbelief – such as not having one's work and one's aspirations taken seriously – are an important obstacle to decentering the 'black letter' tradition. To challenge the dominant tradition risks being cast out as a pariah, while aspiring to respectability is purchased only at the price of abandoning one's critical edge.[6] This is the tension in legal education, between the professional and academic, the egalitarian and the elitist, the justificatory and the critical, that characterise so much of the history of legal education and thought (Stevens, 1983).

Notes

1. This essay is for Morton J. Horwitz.
2. This essay is a substantially revised and extended version of Sugarman (1986). Readers should refer to that publication for further discussion and references. The present essay is exclusively concerned with the constitution and reproduction of the 'black letter' tradition in legal education and scholarship. As a result, that body of work which transcended this tradition is not addressed. This risks portraying legal education and thought as more monolithic than was actually the case.
   I should like to thank Dick Risk, Léonie Sugarman and Ronnie Warrington for their helpful comments. Discussions with Bob Gordon helped me to understand the history of American lawyers and legal science, although he is not responsible for my cosmic assertions.
3. [1889] 14 AC 337.
4. See *Nocton* v. *Ashburton* [1914] AC 932.
5. A leading example of this tendency towards legal formalism is *London Street Tramway & Co Ltd* v. *LCC* [1898] AC 375. More generally, see Dawson (1968) p.91.
6. One way of rethinking the character of legal education and thought might be to draw upon and transform the deviations and counter-images within liberal legal thought. This would seek to 'integrate into the standard doctrinal arguments the explicit controversies over the right and feasible structure of society' (see Unger, 1983 and 1987).

References

Abbott, A. (1986) 'Jurisdictional Conflicts', *American Bar Foundation Research Journal*, pp.187–224.
Amos, S. (1874) *The Science of Law* (London: King & Co).
Anson, W. R. (1890) *'Derry v. Peek* in the House of Lords' *Law Quarterly Review*, vol. 6, pp.72–9.
Austin, J. (1879) *Lectures on Jurisprudence* (London: John Murray).
Austin, J. (1885) *Lectures in Jurisprudence* (London: John Murray).
Bellah, R. (1970) 'Civil Religion in America', in R. Bellah (ed.) *Beyond Belief* (New York: Harper & Row).

Bentham, J. (1977) *A Comment on the Commentaries and a Fragment on Government* (London: Athlone).

Berger, P. L. (1969) *The Social Reality of Religion* (London: Faber & Faber).

Brierly, J. L. (1926) 'Sir Thomas Erskine Holland', *Law Quarterly Review*, vol. 42, pp.475–8.

Brown, W. J. (1916) 'The Jurisprudence of M. Duguit' *Law Quarterly Review*, vol. 32, pp.168–91.

Bryce, J. (1888) *The American Commonwealth* (London: Macmillan).

Bryce, J. (1901) 'The Academic Study of the Civil Law' in his *Studies in History and Jurisprudence*, Vol.II, pp.860–86.

Buckland, W. W. (1945) *Some Reflections on Jurisprudence* (Cambridge: Cambridge University Press).

Burrow, J. W. (1966) *Evolution and Society* (Cambridge: Cambridge University Press).

Burrow, J. W. (1981) *A Liberal Descent* (Cambridge: Cambridge University Press).

Clark, E. C. (1885) 'Jurisprudence: Its Use and its Place in Legal Education' *Law Quarterly Review*, vol. 1, pp.201–19.

Dawson, J. P. (1968) *The Oracles of the Law* (Ann Arbor: University of Michigan Law School).

Dicey, A. V. (1883) *Can English Law be Taught at the Universities?* (London: Macmillan).

Dicey, A. V. (1885) *An Introduction to the Study of the Law of the Constitution* (London: Macmillan).

Foucault, M. (1972) *The Archeology of Knowledge* (London: Allen Lane).

Grey, T. (1983) 'Langdell's Orthodoxy', *University of Pittsburgh Law Review*, vol.45, pp.9–48.

Harrison, F. (1879) 'The English School of Jurisprudence III', *Fortnightly Review*, vol. 21, pp.114–30.

Holland, T. E. (1924) *The Elements of Jurisprudence* (Oxford: Clarendon).

Howe, M. De Wolfe (ed.) (1961) *Holmes–Pollock Letters* (Cambridge, Mass: Harvard University Press).

Kent, C. (1978) *Brains and Numbers* (Toronto: University of Toronto Press).

Kirk, H. (1976) *Portrait of a Profession* (London: Oyez).

Kuhn, T. S. (1970) *The Structure of Scientific Revolutions* (Chicago: University of Chicago Press).

Levinson, S. (1988) *Constitutional Faith* (Princeton: Princeton University Press).

Lieberman, D. (1985) 'From Bentham to Benthamism', *Historical Journal*, vol. 28, pp.202–19.

Luban, D. (1988) *Lawyers and Justice* (Princeton: Princeton University Press).

MacDougall, H. A. (1982) *Racial Myth in English History* (Hanover: University of New England).

Maine, H. S. (1885) *Lectures on the Early History of Institutions* (London: John Murray).

Maitland, F. W. (1911) *The Collected Papers of Frederic William Maitland*, Vol. I, pp.480–97, (Cambridge: Cambridge University Press).

Mill, J. S. (1838) 'Bentham', *London and Westminster Review*, pp.434–71.

Pollock, F. (1889) *'Derry v. Peek* in the House of Lords', *Law Quarterly Review*, vol. 5, pp.410–18.

Pollock, F. (1895) *The Law of Torts* (London: Stevens).

Rodgers, D. T. (1987) *Contested Truths* (New York: Basic Books).

Rumble, W. E. (1985) *The Thought of John Austin* (London: Athlone).

Samuel, R. (1989) 'Introduction: Exciting to be English' in R. Samuel (ed.), *Patriotism*, Vol. I, pp.xviii–lxvii (London: Routledge).

Sanderson, M. (ed.) (1975) *The Universities in the Nineteenth Century* (London: Macmillan).

Schlegel, J. H. (1984) 'Searching for Archimedes', *Journal of Legal Education*, vol. 34, pp.103–10.

Shapin, S. (1984) 'Pump and Circumstance: Robert Boyle's Literary Technology', *Social Studies of Science*, vol. 14, pp.481–520.

Simon, W. (1978) 'The Ideology of Advocacy', *Wisconsin Law Review*, pp.29–144.

Stein, P. (1980) *Legal Evolution* (Cambridge: Cambridge University Press).

Stevens, R. (1983) *Law School* (Chapel Hill: University of North Carolina Press).

Stokes, E. (1959) *The English Utilitarians and India* (Oxford: Oxford University Press).

Sugarman, D. (1983) 'The Legal Boundaries of Liberty: Dicey, Liberalism and Legal Science', *Modern Law Review*, vol. 46, pp.102–11.

Sugarman, D. (1986) 'Legal Theory, the Common Law Mind and the Making of Textbook Tradition', in W Twining (ed.), *Legal Theory and Common Law* (Oxford: Basil Blackwell), pp.26–61.

Sugarman, D. (1987) 'In the Spirit of Weber: Law, Modernity and "The Pecularities of the English"' (Madison: Institute for Legal Studies Working Paper 2:9).

Sugarman, D. (1990) 'Lawyers and Business in England, 1750–1950', in C. Wilton Siegel (ed.) *Lawyers and Business* (Toronto: Butterworths).

Tulloch, H. A. (1977) 'Changing Attitudes Towards the United States in the 1880s', *Historical Journal*, vol. 20, pp.825–40.

Unger, R. M. (1983) 'The Critical Legal Studies Movement', *Harvard Law Review*, vol. 96, pp.563–690.

Unger, R. M. (1987) *Politics* (Cambridge: Cambridge University Press).

Taking the Right Seriously: The Case of F.A. Hayek

Alan Thomson

'To market to market to buy a fat pig,
home again home again jiggetty jig'. (Traditional)

Introductory

In a book whose contributors would probably broadly see themselves as on the political left, the inclusion of a chapter on the New
Right might indeed seem a dangerous supplement. However, not
only does the influence of the New Right in contemporary politics
suggest that we must take their views seriously, but at least in the
case of their most articulate spokesman, F.A. Hayek, we find a sustained discussion of law which, as one engages with it, reveals its
capacity to threaten the empire of jurisprudence as a domain of true
knowledge. Most importantly, by locating the discussion of law
within a larger context of ideas about reason and social order, and
by demonstrating the inseparability of questions about law from the
practical question of what is the good society (and in particular from
the capitalism versus socialism debate) Hayek perhaps even more
effectively than Marx discloses the ideological nature of jurisprudence's 'truth' about law.

In the first section I make some brief remarks on the nature of
jurisprudence and Hayek's exclusion from it. In the second I describe
what I see as the intellectual and political climate out of which the
New Right has emerged; this I characterise as a climate of increasing
doubt about the capacity of reason to realise progress. In the third
and central section, following a brief description of the liberal world
view generally, I present an exposition of Hayek's 'restatement' of it,
proceeding from an account of his general position to his views on
law and justice in particular. In the fourth section I consider some
critical responses to Hayek, concluding that while he has presented a
remarkably powerful defence of liberal capitalism and the law that
goes with it – namely that it works – his deep scepticism about the
capacity of reason drives him ultimately to a nihilism that, as with
Weber, leaves him powerless in the face of the probem of meaning-

lessness which modernity engenders. In the final section, after a brief comparison of Hayek with Rawls and Nozick, I return to the specific question of jurisprudence and consider the possibility of reconceptualising it as conversations about law.

Jurisprudence and Hayek's Exclusion from it

As a first approximation jurisprudence could be defined as the project of reason in pursuit of universal truths about law and justice. Thus against the study of the contents of legal rules and systems, which are self-evidently historically and culturally variable, jurisprudence asserts a number of claims. Firstly, in promising to reveal through reason a picture of an unchanging and universal unity beneath the manifest changeability of laws, legal institutions and practices, jurisprudence asserts a claim to foundationalism in relation to law similar to the claims of epistemology in relation to the sciences. Secondly, jurisprudence claims that there is a sufficiently discrete and distinct object, 'law in a universal sense', such that its study can constitute the distinct discipline of jurisprudence. Thirdly, at least the currently dominant interpretation of jurisprudence – positivism – despite its recognition that true knowledge can contribute to the realisation of the good society, asserts a claim to value neutrality between different conceptions of the good, and presents itself as a disinterested enquiry.

In the next section I will consider some of the current doubts about the 'modern' ideas of reason, truth and universality upon which *inter alia* jurisprudence is based; however, I think it is revealing of the character of the jurisprudential project to note at this stage that Hayek has generally been excluded from it and to consider why.

Barnett and Yach's study (1985) of jurisprudence teaching carried out several years after the publication of Hayek's three volumes of *Law, Legislation and Liberty*, (1973, 1976 and 1979) showed that, in contrast to Nozick and Rawls (whose writings have many parallels with Hayek's and who scored very highly), Hayek did not receive even a 'brief mention' in any UK jurisprudence course. As Ogus laments in a recent article (1989) much the same is true of scholarly legal literature. While Hayek's absence from the empire of jurisprudence may be partly explained by the combination of the facts that his work generally has only recently received sustained academic attention[1] and that legal theory is rarely in the vanguard of intellectual developments, there are in my view other more significant explanations.

Firstly, because Hayek's discussion of things legal is part of a much larger theoretical project he poses the same difficulty as Marx in that he resists what authors of jurisprudence texts and courses apparently like so much to do, namely to reduce the subject to a list of tidy, contrasting 'theories of law' which can be learnt by students like so many cases. Indeed it is precisely Hayek's argument that a great deal of our current misunderstanding of law, and of much else besides, arises from the emergence of modern disciplinary specialisms (Hayek, 1973, especially p.5). Secondly, Hayek resists the natural law versus positivism dichotomy which is so central to the constitution of contemporary jurisprudence. Thirdly, Hayek resists, either directly or as an unintended consequence, the claims which I have suggested jurisprudence makes. Thus, as we will see, he is deeply sceptical of the claims of theoretical reason to be the way to truth and success, of viewing law in isolation from the social order of which it is part, and of seeing law and justice as anything more than practical adaptations to particular circumstances. Indeed, as I will suggest, Hayek offers us a vision of law – and more generally of a world – without foundations. Most significantly of all, Hayek's own work stands opposed to a conception of knowledge as a disinterested search for truth, for despite making the standard claims to value neutrality Hayek is quite explicit that his 'value orientation' is towards retaining what he conceives as the great benefits of liberal society and market capitalism, and that his jurisprudence is therefore a 'jurisprudence ... of freedom' (1960, p.6).

The more we appreciate that Hayek's jurisprudence can no more be separated from his arguments for capitalism than can Marx's from his arguments against it, and the more we recognise the similarities in Hayek's conclusions with many of those of 'official' jurisprudence, so we are forced to abandon a view of jurisprudence as a disinterested truth. We may engage in the intellectual game of studying Austin, Hart, Rawls and a host of others and say 'so what'; Hayek, like Marx, denies us that alternative, by making quite explicit that the view we have of law matters, in the sense of shaping the basic character of the sort of society in which we live.

Finally on the exclusion of Hayek from the ranks of jurisprudential worthies one might mention the important, if less respectable, fact that jurisprudence teachers and writers generally see themselves, in comparison with their more 'black letter' colleagues, as superior intellectuals – and intellectuals not only put a high value on reason but, as Hayek himself has argued (1949), tend to be sympathetic to socialism. Thus they tend to avoid confronting Hayek's scepticism of reason and theory, and preserve their academic empire, by dismissing him as a mere polemicist of what to many are extreme and distasteful political values. Perhaps for them this is just as well for, as we will see, Hayek argues that rather than jurisprudence revealing the foundational truth about law, it is law which is the real foundation of jurisprudence.

The Doubt of Reason and the Emergence of the New Right

When the history of the closing decades of the twentieth century comes to be written it will surely be presented as an era of doubt, a profound doubt in which the only present certainty is the absence of certainty. Most importantly, the confident faith in universal reason which has been the history of Western civilisation since the eighteenth century Enlightenment, expressed in the belief in the project of reason both to rationally identify and to rationally realise progress, has in different ways been radically challenged. At an intellectual level the rejection of philosophy as capable of providing either a foundational epistimology or a universalist ethics, the recognition of the relativity of the truth claims of science, the growing awareness of the inseparability of power and knowledge and of our inability to grasp the world in words, are all expressions of this doubt about the project of reason.[2]

At the level of politics and policies this project has equally provoked a deep scepticism. It is as though the immense rapidity of change – technological, cultural and social – that characterises modernity has so shortened the circuits between confident hopes and their pessimistic disillusion that hope and disillusion collapse into each other to reveal progress itself as the master illusion. Thus as the twentieth century ends we are witnessing the collapse of the most ambitious political project of reason: the creation of a whole society, socialist society, based on what reason could anticipate. Similarly the earlier confident faith in science and technology has increasingly given place to a recognition that scientific 'progress' endangers the very conditions of human life.

For a while many Western intellectuals could cling to the view that it was capitalism, perceived as a sort of bastard child of the Enlightenment, which distorted the emancipatory potential of progress through reason. Increasingly, however, we are being forced to realise that it is reason itself, with its claims to universalism, which is the prime suspect in the crime of domination, thereby severing the links which the Enlightenment had sought to establish between reason, progress and freedom.

While Hayek clearly participates in these doubts (for example his critique of socialism is essentially an elaboration of the view that attempts to use reason to design progress are not only doomed to failure, but are inevitably destructive of individual freedom), he does not relinquish all faith in reason. Rather he argues that by adopting a more modest view of the capacity of reason, and a minimum universalism,[3] it may be possible to recover the Enlightenment's potential and reconnect reason, progress and freedom.

Important though the grand doubts about reason may ultimately be, it is the more pragmatic expression of these doubts in recent Western politics which provide the immediate origins of the New Right with whom Hayek is identified.[4] In particular, at the end of the 1960s the confident belief in the capacity of rational planning to bring forth the good society began to crumble in the face of evidence of its failure to realise either economic success or a significant increase in social justice. For example in Britain the so-called 'consensus' politics of the postwar period – characterised by the triple commitment to a mixed economy combining the free market with Keynesian intervention, the welfare state supplementing market provision with state provision and a recognition of the formal role of organised labour in the formation of public policy – by the early 1970s was obviously in severe trouble. Economic controls seemed incapable of stabilising the recurrent crises of 'stop–go' capitalism; inflation and unemployment were uncontrollably rising; talk of a crisis in the welfare state was commonplace, and many perceived an impending crisis of ungovernability resulting from the growing power and activism of organised labour.[5]

While there were many different diagnoses for this state of affairs, one lesson that many drew from it was that rational state planning and provision was a good deal less effective and desirable than had been believed, and that if more immediate confirmation of the failure of planning was required one had only to look to high-rise slums, urban decay and the dramatic failures of Eastern European command economies. It was this climate out of which the so-called New Right emerged in the late 1960s, and which created its three principal targets, economic intervention in the market, the welfare state and the power of trade unions, against all of which Hayek had polemicised two decades before in the *Road to Serfdom* (1944).

Although the New Right is a cloth of many colours, perhaps its most distinctive feature is a general agreement that Western civilisation, which is generally seen to include the fact that it is capitalist, is both uniquely valuable *and* in a state of decay, because it has lost something which it once possessed. In my view it is this emphasis on the past which distinguishes the New Right from those left postmodernists who, while equally doubting the 'modern' faith in progress through reason (so clear in Marxism) nevertheless endorse the Marxists' commitment to the necessity of liberation from the constraints of the past – but with universal reason now appearing as one of those constraints. Thus, while postmodernists are united in seeking to anticipate the 'post' modern, the New Right are united in seeking to recover a lost or forgotten civilisation, though differing on how to identify what it is that must be recovered.

On this side of the Atlantic undoubtedly the most practically influential strand of New Right thinking is that which is usually called 'neoliberalism', to distinguish it from 'neoconservatism', and it is with neoliberalism that Hayek, along with Milton Friedman and bodies like the Institute of Economic Affairs and the Adam Smith Institute, is usually associated. The animating ideas of neoliberalism are, firstly, that economic success is being denied because we are losing the understanding that we once had of how the market works and, secondly, that individual freedom is threatened in so far as we fail to appreciate the necessary connection between freedom at large and market or economic freedom. Thus its prime attack is directed on government, particularly in its wrongheaded attempts to manage economies directly in the name of efficiency and to engineer outcomes in the name of social justice, welfare or democracy. These attempts, it is argued, both tend to destroy individual freedom and initiative, and to deny the economic success upon which the welfare of all depends. Neoliberals see the means of countering these tendencies in measures to restore the free market and market values, particularly entrepreneurial values and ideas of individual responsibility; to 'roll back the state', particularly in its role of monopoly service provider; to restrict welfare to narrowly targeted groups; to restrict trade union power, and to reduce the sphere of politicised activity generally: messages which are all clear in the rhetoric if not fully in the reality of Thatcherism.

While this analysis makes clear that neoliberals wish to restrict greatly the role of deliberate reason in the form of rational planning and state provision, I suggest that reason still has an important part to play in their scheme of things. Thus it is reason which enables us to understand and cultivate the 'natural wisdom' which the market embodies, and it is reason which enables us to identify the conditions in which individual freedom will flourish. To anticipate a criticism that can be particularly directed at Hayek, neoliberals rely on a strong view of the capacity of reason to reveal the very weak and limited capacity of reason to shape the world.

In comparison to the neoliberals' continuing faith in reason (albeit a reason that is critically aware of its own limits) the other main strand of the New Right, neoconservatism,[6] displays a much greater suspicion of reason, leading some to see it as a species of irrationalism. Though neoconservatism takes many very different forms, they all share a belief in the overriding importance of traditions and traditional values, coupled with the view that they are today being eroded and must as a matter of urgency be recovered. While the essential image is that we are losing something of great value, something more substantial than merely a form of understanding, different authors identify differently what that something is. Typical neoconservative themes are that order and authority are under threat in our contemporary individualistic and hedonistic culture; that moral standards and individual responsibility are being eroded in the unprincipled, permissive and irreligious society; that family life is challenged by feminism and the takeover of family functions by the welfare state; that national pride is being threatened by defeatist and pacifist attitudes, and that our cultural heritage is being destroyed by a new class of leftist intellectuals and experts.

While much of neoconservatism is crudely reactionary, it is I think possible to identify a more or less coherent and distinctive position which neoconservatives are attempting to revive. The basis of that position is the recognition that human life and rationality are necessarily contextual, and that that context is only marginally open to rational criticism and reform. Thus what is seen as giving meaning, value and identity to individuals is predominantly the background of institutions, practices and values in which they find themselves. Against the liberal stress on the primacy of *independence*, conservatives stress the *dependence* of individuals on their society and culture, not because they have chosen them but because they precede individuals logically and historically; and against the liberal emphasis on individual freedom and rights conservatives thematise individual duties, structures of authority, the precedence of morality and above all the wisdom of the constituted order. Most importantly (since for conservatives individuals and reason are primarily the product, not the source, of this order) our capacity through reason to penetrate the order of which we are necessarily a part must remain severely limited. Furthermore, since we cannot stand outside the traditions that make us what we are, change must be restricted, and then only in accordance with existing traditions, otherwise we risk a radical social collapse and a disabling anomie engendered by the experience of rootlessness. This is of course what American conservative commentators in particular believe is happening to Western society, namely that it is undergoing a spiritual and cultural crisis.[7] While there is much in conservative thought which harks back to a *gemeinschaft* notion of community, for most it is capitalism which has now become the tradition we must preserve and cherish, and it is this that gives them a common cause with neoliberals.

While as I indicated earlier Hayek is popularly identified with the neo-liberal strand of the New Right, most of his perceptive critics stress the strongly conservative elements in his views, particularly in his later writings,[8] for example in the importance he attaches to social order and preserving moral traditions, and in his rejection of an idea of reason sufficiently independent of its social context to be able to evaluate that context as a whole. Indeed, many critics see in Hayek an unresolved tension between liberalism and conservatism or between rationalism and irrationalism.[9] While I will return later to this point, my purpose in this section has simply been to sketch the background and climate in which Hayek's writings have recently been received with a new interest.

Hayek's 'Conservative Liberalism'[10]

The Liberal Heritage
Despite evidence of a growing conservatism in Hayek's thought it is by seeing him first and foremost as a liberal that we can begin to appreciate his contribution. As the subtitle to *Law, Legislation and Liberty* (1973, 1976 and 1979), *a new statement of the liberal principles of justice and political economy*, indicates, Hayek's concern is to recover a distinctively liberal understanding of the world and to restate it for modern conditions.

While liberalism is a diffuse and historically changing tradition rather than a particular theory, it is, I believe, possible to character-ise it by reference to four distinctive concerns. Firstly there is an emphasis on individual freedom, conceived primarily as a private space which is free from interference, particularly by the state. Secondly it displays a concern with allowing individuals to choose their own ends and values and to pursue their own version of the 'good', thus rendering both desire and virtue strictly private matters. This leads to a conception of the good society as one in which the sphere of the public is restricted to the modest task of coordinating the pursuits of individuals through a thin idea of the right rather than insisting on any stronger idea of the common good. Thirdly liberals share a wish to keep things open for change and improve-ment; thus they typically restrict themselves to indicating the condi-tions for progress rather than identifying that in which it consists. Finally, revealing their essential individualism, liberals are deeply concerned about the threat that any form of collectivity or collective thinking poses to individual autonomy, for in liberalism the individ-ual appears prior both ontologically and morally to society.[11]

Except (as we shall see) in relation to the ontological priority of the individual, Hayek is passionately committed to liberalism as I have identified it. He does argue, however, that there are 'true' and 'false' versions of liberalism, which are primarily distinguished by their attitude to reason. More generally Hayek argues – and this is the first of his great dichotomies – that there are 'true' and 'false' views on the capacity of reason. The 'false' view, which Hayek calls Constructivist Rationalism, is based on the view that 'human institu-tions will serve human purposes only if they have been deliberately designed for these purposes' (1973, p.8), from which it follows that 'man's reason alone should enable him to construct society anew' (ibid., p.10). This exaggerated view of the capacity of reason which

Hayek traces back to Descartes' radical doubt of all but demonstrable truths (Descartes 1960, especially pp.50 ff.) in Hayek's view is the fatal conceit which threatens, particularly in the form of socialism, to destroy both individual freedom and the possibility of progress.

Against this view that we should only be guided by our deliberate reason, and which is based on the assumption that the mind-stuff of reason has some independent existence, Hayek argues that the 'true' view of reason, which he calls Evolutionary Rationalism, is that reason is no more than 'an adaptation to the natural and social surroundings' (1973, p.17), which can therefore give us only a limited understanding of those surroundings. Drawing particularly on David Hume and Adam Smith,[12] Hayek argues that most of what is valuable to mankind – such as language, law, morality, the market, property, justice and reason itself – has not been the product of deliberate rational design but has simply grown and evolved because it has proved useful. Given that on this view reason cannot establish an Archimedean part outside the system of which it is a part, reason is never adequate to design or plan the system as a whole, but must restrict itself to gaining insight into that on which our success depends and, on the basis of such insights, to suggest marginal improvements within that system.

For Hayek then the utility of reason is maximised not by seeking to bring the world under conscious rational control but rather by recognising the limitations of reason. True liberalism is that which understands this, and it is this liberalism, in which law has a crucial part, that Hayek seeks to recover.

Of Ignorance, Knowledge, Minds and Markets

Reflecting the importance Hayek attaches to recognising the limits of conscious reason, one way of conveying the distinctive character of his restatement of liberalism is to see it as an attempt to understand how, despite man's irremediable and constitutional ignorance, progress is still possible. The essence of Hayek's answer is that progress is possible if we acknowledge that on which our progress thus far has depended, namely those institutions such as property, individual freedom, justice and the market which have spontaneously arisen in response to human ignorance. Hayek's concern is then to reconstruct hypothetically the way these typically liberal institutions could have spontaneously arisen to overcome the limitations of ignorance, thereby enabling him to ground liberal values in a social theory.

The starting point and model for all Hayek's thought is the market. Though he was initially trained in law and political philosophy, the early and major part of Hayek's working life was in economics, more particularly as it was understood by the Austrian school of economics founded by Carl Menger. Above all what this inspired in Hayek was a deep sense of wonder at the 'natural' miracle of the market, a wonder akin to that which we feel when we contemplate the undesigned and fragile beauty of a flower or a snow crystal lying in our hand. For Hayek the beauty of the market, which he sees as equally fragile and equally easily crushed, consists not only in its ability without conscious design to coordinate a multitude of individual actions, but most importantly in its capacity to utilise for the benefit of all the fragmented knowledges which individuals separately possess, and to do so to an infinitely greater extent than any imaginary master planner could possibly do. The market then for Hayek is primarily conceived as a discovery procedure in which through the signals provided by prices we discover both what we want, and where and how our particular skills and knowledges can be most usefully directed. Furthermore Hayek argues that the market is superior to planning not only because of its infinitely greater capacity to process information, but also because many of the 'facts' which planners would need to know (such as consumer preferences or entrepreneurial skills and knowledges) not being facts given to the market, but products of its operation, simply cannot be acquired without actual markets involving competition between real flesh and blood rivals.

Hayek's reflections on how the market achieves what no rational mind could ever achieve not only provokes the larger question with which I began this section, of how ignorant people could produce such progress, indeed produce a great civilisation,[13] but also suggests to Hayek the solutions, namely competition and rules that maintain patterns. Before we can begin to understand this, however, it is necessary to say something about Hayek's view of knowledge.

Hayek's epistemology[14] is based upon the Kantian view that knowledge of the world is not given to us directly by the senses but is a construction of the mind, in the sense that it is a product of mental processes or categories. Since Hayek conceives these processes or categories as ordering or patterning processes he argues that we can only know particulars in relation to other particulars in terms of abstract orders or patterns. This leads Hayek to argue that in practice, while we may have considerable knowledge of the general orders or patterns which these particulars form, we will rarely have sufficient knowledge to predict particular outcomes.

This image of the mind as an invisible hand generating an orderly whole out of particulars, without being able to predict particulars, clearly draws on Hayek's idea of the market. This is further reflected in two other features of his concept of the mind. In the first place he conceives mental processes as constituted by rules, just as the market is made possible by individuals following rules; as we will see, rule-following is the central feature of his theory of social order in general.[15] Secondly, mirroring the view that the patterns or orders that markets form are never static, Hayek argues – contrary to Kant – that the mental categories are not given a priori but evolve with society. Put simply, for Hayek mind and reason, like the market, are adaptations to circumstances, producing order without design through following rules. It is this model, as we will see, which underlies the general social theory in which, as I have suggested, he seeks to ground liberal values.

Finally, before we proceed to outline that theory one further important point must be made about Hayek's ideas of knowledge as they were suggested to him by his reflection on the market, for that point constitutes a crucial component of his answer to the question of how ignorant people could produce a great civilisation. The point is simply that although he considers the amount of theoretical knowledge which can be put in propositional form to be extremely limited, being restricted to knowledge of general and abstract patterns, there is for Hayek an enormous store of practical knowledge, or 'know how', which is tacitly embodied in inherited practices, rules and institutions. It is this knowledge, whose model is the tool which is gradually adapted over time and so tacitly embodies the wisdom of generations, which for Hayek provides the explanation for the miracle of the market and the key to the greatness of our civilisation. For Hayek law, justice and individual freedom, properly conceived, are just such tools; only by submitting to their superior wisdom and not to the knowledge of theorists will the possibility of progress be retained.

The Spontaneous Order and Cultural Evolution
The idea that we owe most of what we have achieved not to conscious design but – literally more than we can ever know – to practices which have simply grown is perhaps Hayek's central claim. This finds expression in the two central concepts of his social theory, 'the spontaneous order' and 'cultural evolution'.

The key insight which leads Hayek to the idea of the spontaneous order, and which is clearly derived from his idea of the market, is that order (in the sense of a predictable pattern) is not necessarily the product of orders (in the sense of commands), but can come about simply as a result of the elements of an order acting according to the same rules. Drawing from examples of such spontaneous orders in nature, with which he wishes to associate spontaneous orders in society, Hayek argues that there is a categorical distinction between two types of social order, the spontaneous or 'grown' order, for which he reserves the enthralling term *Cosmos*, and the 'made' order which he calls 'organisation' or *Taxis*. The thrust of his argument is that while deliberately made orders or organisations – of which government is the most important example – may have a certain role to play, they are generally greatly inferior to spontaneous orders and must be contained within an overall spontaneous order or *Cosmos* if the possibility of progress is to be retained.

Taking language as an example of a spontaneous order, and an army as an example of an organisation to have in mind, four crucial distinctions can be made between these two types of order. Firstly, while organisations serve the particular purpose for which they were set up, spontaneous orders merely provide the means to serve the separate purposes of those who constitute them. Secondly, while in an organisation individuals are more or less specifically commanded to perform particular tasks, in spontaneous orders order results from following general rules alone. Thirdly (as is particularly clear in the case of the rules of language), in a spontaneous order, unlike an organisation, it does not matter if individuals do not 'know' *what* the rules are, as long as they know *how* to follow them.[16] Fourthly, unlike organisations we can only know spontaneous orders in terms of the general and abstract patterns their elements form and consequently the knowledge we can have of spontaneous orders will rarely enable us to predict particular outcomes; this is the basis of Hayek's argument against interfering with the spontaneous order of the market, as well as being founded, as we have seen, on his theory of the mind.

For Hayek it is because spontaneous orders possess these features that they are particularly attractive to those sharing the typically liberal concerns outlined above. By relying on general rules rather than more restrictive particular commands, spontaneous orders maintain individual freedom; not being designed for a purpose they do not involve imposing a common purpose on individuals, and because they only maintain a general and abstract pattern rather than a specific pattern of particulars they are more flexible and hence more open to progress. Furthermore, by allowing a greater utilisation of individual knowledges, as we have seen in relation to the market order, they are more likely to be conducive of success.

Although recognising these potential benefits of spontaneous orders Hayek makes clear that only if the rules are 'right' will the actions of individuals, guided only by such rules, spontaneously generate a beneficial order. It is to specify what 'right' means in this context that Hayek introduces the second central concept of his social theory, that of cultural evolution, of which, as we will see, his theory of law and justice is largely a particular elaboration. The basic claim expressed in the concept of cultural evolution is that there is generally good reason to believe that the rules and other institutions that have survived are the 'right' ones. To sustain this claim Hayek argues that there is a natural selection process, similar to that which Darwin identified for biological evolution, operating at group level to ensure that those cultural rules and institutions which are most beneficial will survive; that is to say that groups using such rules and institutions will succeed in competition with other groups. Though Hayek does not go quite so far as saying that we can simply rely on natural evolution to ensure beneficial spontaneous orders will prevail (it is precisely his argument that today orders such as the market are under threat if we do not consciously support them), he gets close to arguing that nature knows best.

Space does not permit more than the briefest critical comments on Hayek's central concepts of the spontaneous orders and cultural evolution; four queries must suffice. Can one sufficiently distinguish the resulting order from the rules and institutions that maintain it so as to make the distinction between spontaneous orders and organisations coherent? Does Hayek enable us to reach a determinate answer on when organisations are to be preferred to spontaneous orders? What is the criterion of success operating at group level, and what mechanism will ensure individual actions will be guided by group success? Finally, and more generally, what reason have we to believe that our actual legal and moral rules are the result of fair competition rather than merely reflecting class and other forms of power? In short one might suggest that there are severe problems in translating the appearance of the market into a general social theory, just as one might suggest there are in translating it into a theory of the mind.[17]

Freedom for Progress

If the spontaneous order is the central concept of Hayek's social theory, individual freedom appears as the central concept of his political theory. Furthermore, both ideas give expression to what I suggest is his most fundamental concern, progress, conceived as keeping the world unknown and unpredictable.

Hayek presents two powerful and related arguments about freedom. He argues both for a particular concept of freedom and that freedom must be treated as the overriding value in the strong sense not only of being superior to other values such as equality and democracy but also in the sense that it should not be traded with such values.[18]

In defining freedom as the absence of coercion, with coercion conceived as situations where 'one man's actions are made to serve another man's will, not for his own, but for the other's purpose' (1960, p.133), Hayek clearly adopts a strictly negative conception of freedom which identifies it with non-restriction of choice, in contrast to positive definitions of freedom which view it as entailing a real power or ability to act as one chooses.[19] Furthermore the only obstacle which for Hayek constitutes a restriction on freedom is intentional human conduct and not, for example, natural obstacles.[20] This is important as the thrust of his argument is that since the results of the spontaneous order of the market are not intentionally planned by anyone, economic coercion can be no more conceived as a restriction of freedom than natural obstacles are. Clearly what Hayek is most concerned about is eliminating relations of personal dependence. Thus he argues that provided the state acts only through general rules whose effects on particular individuals are unknown, it will not generally be acting coercively. In sum, Hayek adopts an eighteenth-century agenda in seeing freedom as dependence only on an impersonal order.

While one can criticise this idea of freedom as unduly restricted and unrealistic,[21] it is important to see why Hayek adopts it by looking at his arguments for treating freedom as the primary value. Hayek does not, I would suggest, treat freedom as an end in itself;[22] rather he sees freedom as valuable for what it achieves. For Hayek that is, as always, progress in the face of ignorance. As he puts it, 'the case for individual freedom rests chiefly on the recognition of the inevitable ignorance of all' (1960, p.29). The most important of the various strands of this argument from ignorance is that freedom enables individuals to use their own knowledges for their own purposes, thereby making such knowledge available for the benefit of all. In other words what is most important about freedom to Hayek is its capacity to stimulate and utilise new knowledges. Only by giving an uncompromising priority to freedom and refusing to treat it as divisible (precisely because we do not know what it will be used for) will, Hayek argues, the future be kept open for progress.

This I think takes us to the very heart of Hayek: his commitment to progress. While he gives us no clear definition of what he means by progress beyond saying it is 'the cumulative growth of knowledge and power over nature' (1960, p.41), he makes it clear that is is neither movement to a known objective nor a gain in any measurable quantity such as human happiness. Indeed he admits that progress often 'makes us sadder men' (1960, p.41). Rather, for Hayek progress is a journey into the unknown, in which we are to value 'movement for movement's sake' because it is in the nature of things that they change and evolve in directions which we cannot anticipate. What preoccupies Hayek, as revealed in the importance he attaches to ignorance and in his abhorrence of all that would seek to render the world predictable, is the thought that the human species, whose peculiar destiny is to increase its power over the world by acquiring knowledge, may be able to use that power to withdraw itself from the process of evolution and thus from nature. Seen in this light the appeal of the market to Hayek resides in the fact that it is a means of allowing the process of 'natural' selection to continue.

While one might then see Hayek's objections to Constructivist Rationalism, to planning and to organisations as expressions of a deep-seated fear that by rendering the world predictable we eliminate chance and thus a real future, the irony is that Hayek cannot see progress in any other terms than a gain in human mastery of the world. He is therefore forced to confront the fact that it is progress itself which comes to threaten the possibility of progress. It is then no surprise that, as many commentators have noted, Hayek is unable to resolve the tensions between rationalism and irrationalism. In using reason to fight reason Hayek reveals himself, like Weber, as locked into the dialectic of the Enlightenment, unable to renounce reason but equally unable to accept a world based upon it.

Hayek's Law of Success
If I have succeeded in conveying the nature of Hayek's position both generally and in its relation to the New Right, then his views on law and justice can be dealt with relatively briefly, for these – and by implication many of those which are shared by official jurisprudence – are, I would suggest, implicit in his overall political and theoretical enterprise, an enterprise that could be summarised as an attempt to answer the question, 'what is necessary to keep the world safe for market capitalism?' Given as I have hinted that for Hayek it is rules which constitute the crucial device discovered by people which has enabled them to succeed in the absence of explicit knowledge, it comes as no surprise to discover that law plays a central part in his answer to that question, and that his primary concern in relation to law is to identify the characteristics that legal rules must have if the possibility of progress, as he conceives it, is to be retained.

In his earlier writings,[23] in which the rationalist elements are more apparent, that essentially takes the form of identifying, under the label the 'rule of law', the criteria which law *must* satisfy if it is to preserve individual freedom and hence the possibility of progress. More recently, as more conservative ideas such as the theory of cultural evolution have come to the fore, Hayek's emphasis has moved to attempting to characterise, under the label *Nomos*, those features which law *will* necessarily have if it has spontaneously evolved and therefore proved its worth. Despite these differences of approach, however, the basic conceptual device remains the same: a dichotomy, mirroring the earlier true/false dichotomies we have discussed, between in this case 'true' law, (rule of law or *Nomos*) and 'false' law (commands or *Thesis*). Furthermore his substantive conclusions on what are the characteristics which 'true' law should have, and will have if it has spontaneously evolved, have remained essentially unchanged; most importantly that 'true' law has the form of general and abstract rules of just conduct.

In terms of what I have suggested is one of the central constitutive distinctions of contemporary jurisprudence (that between natural law and positivism), Hayek then occupies an awkward straddling position. On the one hand, against positivists, he argues that 'true' or 'real' law is not simply that which has been created in the formally correct way. On the other hand, in opposition to many versions of natural law, he states that it is not the content of law but the formal characteristics it must possess, and will possess if it is allowed to develop naturally, which distinguishes 'true' law from that which is merely law in a positive sense.[24]

Clearly what underlies Hayek's search for 'true' law is a concern to identify a form of law which will combine what appear to him to be two critical requirements. The first is the typically liberal requirement that it will allow individuals to pursue their own purposes and idea of the good rather than being merely the instrument to realise a common purpose, or an idea of the common good imposed upon them. The other is that it will create a coordination of individual actions while allowing individuals to use their separate knowledges to the full. In short Hayek wants to identify the form of law which will do what we have seen he believes the market achieves, namely 'coordination without command'[25] and freedom without coercion. Furthermore, just as we cannot tell in advance what are the particular beneficial results as opposed to the general character of the resulting order which the operation of the market will achieve, neither in Hayek's view can we identify in advance the particular content of law which will be beneficial, but only its general characteristics.

Hayek's specification of what these characteristics are is based on two fundamental insights: that there is a categorical distinction between rules and commands[26] in that, unlike commands, the particular effects of general rules are more or less unpredictable; and that rules are primarily guides to conduct rather than the means of telling people what to do. The essence of Hayek's argument is that if government is restricted to operate only through general and abstract rules which apply equally to all, since their particular effects will be unknowable, government will be unable to use law to direct people to its ends, thereby leaving individuals free to pursue their own ends, and utilise their own knowledges in doing so. Moreover if those rules are clear, certain and non-retrospective then they will be reliable guides on the basis of which individuals can plan, so increasing the chances of success of any randomly chosen individual.[27] In other words, generality, equal applicability to all and certainty, which in Hayek's view are the characteristics of Rule of Law type law, will simultaneously provide for both freedom and individual success. Thus, flowing from his view that freedom is the condition in which we are dependent only on an impersonal order, Hayek's idea of the rule of law is an attempt to spell out what characteristics law must have if it is to be an impersonal order, rather than an instrument of personal will.

While in his earlier writings 'true' law conceived as the Rule of Law Law is essentially seen as a rational device to achieve such an impersonal order, with the 'evolutionist turn' (Gray 1984, p.135) in his thought he goes further and seeks to naturalise this device by attempting to demonstrate that 'true' law, which he now calls *Nomos*, will naturally arise from human actions without conscious design, thereby assimilating such law, along with market forces, into the category of natural obstacles, which as such, cannot properly be considered a coercive restriction of individual freedom, but rather a necessary condition of it.

Drawing from his view that the wondrous success of the market arises from the ability of men to follow rules, which as we have seen is reflected in his view of the mind and reason as essentially matters of rule-following, Hayek argues more generally that the essential nature of man is that he is a rule-following animal (rather than for example an egotist) and that he owes most of his achievements precisely to this fact. Most importantly it is the recognition of this relation between rules and success which is the basis of his argument that rules can emerge naturally, that is to say without rulers. For Hayek the model for all rules, including articulated moral and legal rules with an explicit ought content, are the rules of technical know how, such as how to hold a hammer to put in a nail successfully. Just as such technical rules will be naturally selected because they work, without anyone imposing them or even necessarily being able to articulate them as rules or explain why they work, he argues that the rules that are effective in maintaining a successful social order will be similarly naturally selected.

In the earlier stages of human development, Hayek argues that little distinction was in fact drawn between merely technical rules and conventional rules of social behaviour, and that this distinction only became significant when social regularities came to be articulated *as* rules. However, he argues that even when a distinctive category of social rules with an ought content does emerge in an articulate form, the source of the ought in the final analysis remains the technical criterion of success. By insisting that there is no categorical distinction between technical or instrumental rules and normative rules Hayek then follows Marx in reducing the whole domain of normative discourse to the instrumental.[28] However, at this stage what is important to see is that by viewing social rules as technical rules Hayek is able to develop an account of the origin and development of legal rules which does not have to assume the existence of law-makers, as for example do most versions of legal positivism.

Against the view that law is necessarily the creation of law-makers Hayek maintains that law can be and, until around the eighteenth century when the false constructivist view emerged predominantly was, a product not of design but of discovery, a discovery consisting of two stages. The first was when in living together people unconsciously discovered, in the sense of chancing upon, the fact that by all sticking to regular practices the chance of individual success was increased, because it enabled individuals to form more or less reliable expectations of, and thereby count on, the behaviour of others. In other words the societies which were most successful, and therefore survived in intergroup competition, were those in which their members, whether conscious of it or not, followed rules in fact that served to maximise order in the sense of security of expectations (this being for Hayek the vital condition for individual and thus group success). The second stage of the discovery of law, and the only one which most theories of law take account of, consists of articulating the regularities of practice as rules and attaching specific sanctions to them.

In Hayek's view the history of law until modern times, when people began falsely to believe that law could be made,[29] was essentially one in which law merely gave expression to those rules, already embodied in practices, upon which people in fact depended for success in their everyday lives. Essentially then what Hayek is arguing is that 'true' law is the articulation as rules of practices that have proved their worth; by ignoring this, and believing that we can make law whatever we like, we imperil our chances of success, progress and even our very survival. Put simply 'true' law or *Nomos* is the legal expression of the spontaneous order of actions or *Cosmos*, which thus provides the critical device for evaluating actual legal rules.

Although this leads Hayek to the view that the primary task in relation to law is the essentially practical (lawyer's) job of trying to discover which rules will serve the spontaneous order in the sense of maximising the overall fulfilment of expectations, he does believe it is possible theoretically to identify certain general characteristics which law will have if it has emerged spontaneously, and which must be preserved if it is to continue to perform its role of fulfilling expectations.

Firstly, in the absence of an agreed common purpose – which Hayek considers only possible in relatively small and homogenous groups – rules which serve the particular purposes of some could not emerge spontaneously from the separate actions of individuals. Thus the law of *Nomos*, which serves the spontaneous order as a whole, will necessarily consist of general purposeless rules of conduct. This idea that our collective success depends upon *not* directing society to a particular end by rules having particular purposes, but on having only general and purposeless rules, is for Hayek the first great discovery which has made civilisation possible.

Secondly, since individual success depends on secure expectations, one of the key features of the rules of successful societies will be that these rules are such that they can operate as useful guides to individual action. In addition to pointing to elements like clarity and certainty as necessary features of such rules, Hayek argues that the single most important device which people have tumbled upon to maximise the security of their expectations, and hence their chances of success, is that of the 'protected domain' or private property in an extended sense. Quite simply, says Hayek, the discovery that rules which take the form of demarcating the protected domain or private space of each individual will 'maximise the possibility of expectations in general being fulfilled' (1973, p.107) is the second great discovery of human evolution.

Thirdly, since as we have seen the success of a society for Hayek depends largely upon its ability to develop and utilise individual knowledges, the rules of successful societies will take the form of rules which provide for the equal maximal freedom from coercion for all, because only such rules will allow for the unknown contributions of unknown individuals on which success and progress depend. The discovery that for success rules should promote individual freedom, and be just in the sense of applying equally to all, is for Hayek the third great discovery.

To summarise, Hayek argues that those features of law, which he earlier identified as the rule of law, are the natural adaptations to circumstances, particularly to the circumstance of ignorance, of successful societies. Furthermore, while we have reason enough to identify the functions they serve and to reconstruct hypothetically how they could have arisen, and thus to argue rationally for their preservation, they cannot properly be considered the product of deliberate reason. Adopting this view of 'true' law as merely an adaptation to circumstances, which preserves the spontaneous order on which our success depends, leads Hayek to a number of more particular conclusions and prescriptions.

One is a clear view of what the process of law-making should primarily be and indeed, in his view, was in the common law until relatively recently; that is, an attempt to discover the rules which will sustain a consistent order of actions which maximise the overall fulfilment of individual expectations. Most importantly this means that the judge and the legislator should recognise that because they

are operating within a going order, which is maintained by the existing rules, they are never free to criticise and redesign the whole
system, but are limited to an immanent criticism of parts within the
whole, and are therefore free only to make marginal improvements.
While Hayek sees a close approximation to this ideal in the judicial
process where the judge takes as his task that of finding the rule that
consistently fits in with all the other existing rules, he does not deny
the possibility of, and at times the necessity of, occasional deliberate
legislative improvements. For instance he argues that such deliberate
rational legislative intervention may be required where judicial
developments lead to a dead end or, more revealingly, where the
non-generalisable interests of the judiciary, such as class interests,
have been read into the law.[30] This suggests a fundamental tension
and indeterminacy in Hayek's thought between the conservative
who asks us to recognise the superior wisdom of the evolved rules,
practices and institutions, and the liberal rationalist who believes in
the possibility of rational improvement.

Additionally, and this is the core of his criticism of modern law,
Hayek argues that increasingly today 'true' law or *Nomos* is being
overwhelmed, particularly in socialist and social democratic regimes,
by the type of law he calls *Thesis,* which is law only in name and by
virtue of being enacted in the formally correct way. Such *Thesis* type
law, which Hayek sees as the basis of the theorisations of legal positivists, is almost entirely legislative in origin, and typically consists
of instrumental government measures which seek to achieve particular predetermined purposes. In short, *Thesis* and positivism are the
respective legal and jurisprudential expressions of planning, and the
languages of an organisation, just as *Nomos* is the expression of the
market and the language of a spontaneous order. Not only, says
Hayek, does *Thesis,* as a species of command as opposed to rules,
threaten individual freedom (because it inevitably departs from the
rule of law restrictions) but, like all instruments of planning, to the
extent that it ignores the reality of the spontaneous order, it is frequently unsuccessful. Although Hayek does not deny that there is
quite an extensive role for *Thesis,* just as he does not deny that there
is a place for organisations, his main concern is to show that by
failing to recognise the fundamental distinctions between *Nomos*
and *Thesis,* and the types of social order they express and maintain,
Thesis will become not the subservient but the dominant partner, so
transforming society into a total organisation, with the result that
both freedom and success will be denied.

Although, as described in the next section, the pursuit of the false
god of social justice is in Hayek's view the major source of this dangerous tendency, it is made institutionally possible by virtue of constitutional arrangements which allow a 'false' view of democracy to

prevail. Thus Hayek argues that the original and 'true' idea of democracy, which meant that the power of government should be limited by public opinion, is today obscured by the 'false' view that democracy means the unlimited power of the majority to make law whatever it likes. So for example the doctrine of parliamentary sovereignty, originally conceived as a means of limiting monarchical power, has been interpreted as a principle of virtually unlimited government. This leads in his view to the subordination of genuine public opinion – which can only mean a consensus on what are the general rules of just conduct available as means to all – to the despotism of majority interests, in which all are made to serve the ends of some.

To restore 'true' democracy, and thus the supremacy of *Nomos* over *Thesis*, Hayek proposes a model constitution whose basic clause would state: 'In normal times ... men could be restrained from doing what they wished, or coerced to do particular things, only in accordance with the recognised rules of just conduct designed to define and protect the individual domain of each' (1979, p.109). Furthermore Hayek proposes the setting up of an additional democratically elected assembly, which would be elected in such a way that its members would be insulated from particular interests, to determine the content of those general rules of just conduct which would act as the limits of government.

In brief the general answer which Hayek gives to the question with which this section began, 'what is necessary to keep the world safe for market capitalism?', is government under the law in its 'true' sense.

Hayek's Justice[31]

Just as Hayek's view of law as an essentially practical matter denies any important role for legal theory, so his views on justice deny the possibility of any more than a very minimal 'theory' of justice; indeed I would suggest Hayek's theory of justice is little more than his theory of law in another form.

Hayek's starting point for his discussion of justice is to distinguish 'true' justice, which he considers is a quality only of intentional conduct, from a 'false' idea of justice, usually called social or distributive justice, which claims to apply to outcomes or states of affairs. Most of Hayek's writing on justice is in fact concerned with attempting to show that this latter idea is merely a dangerous 'mirage', by arguing firstly that it is simply a category mistake to apply justice judgements to unintended results and, secondly, that since social justice has no objective content, it merely becomes the means whereby some are made to serve the purposes of others. The importance of these arguments in relation to Hayek's overall project is twofold. In so far as he views market outcomes as no more the product of deliberate design than for example natural disasters or the results of fairly played games, such outcomes can be considered neither just nor unjust, thereby disposing in one stroke with the most common socialist and social democratic argument in favour of the sort of state intervention which the New Right oppose. Moreover, since outcomes only have a connection with justice if intentionally designed, the search for social justice will necessarily lead to turning society from a spontaneous order into a designed order or organisation, with the consequent loss of freedom and progress which that entails.

In contrast to his extensive attack on the 'false' idea of justice Hayek has comparatively little to say on the 'true' idea of justice, primarily because he considers that our ability to grasp theoretically and put into words what it means is, as with everything else, both extremely limited and much less important than its practical embodiments. What is clear, however, is that Hayek uncompromisingly rejects the view that justice, along with all other values, has a transcendent validity, in favour of a Humean view of justice as an adaptation to circumstances, of which the most important is as always the 'necessary limitation of our factual knowledge' (1973, p.13). Consequently the content of justice is not given, or available to cognition, but is progressively discovered as we learn what justice must mean if successful living together is to be possible. Furthermore, since the nature of reason is such that it can never stand totally apart from the particular social order of which it is a part,[32] even though the circumstance of justice, human ignorance, may be universal, there are no universal substantive rules of justice. Indeed Hayek argues that it is only in a spontaneous order and not for example in a socialist organisation that justice in its true sense has any meaning at all.

Quite simply then the principles of justice are those principles which we call justice, which seek to articulate what has made possible the progress of the spontaneous order thus far. Hayek's general response to this is, as we have seen, the principles of *Nomos* or the rule of law and so, beyond identifying those principles now as principles of justice, Hayek has really only two points to add on the nature of 'true' justice. The first, reflecting his desire to keep the future open, is that the search for justice is essentially an attempt to eliminate injustice rather than to realise a positive idea of justice; the other is that the only useful general test of justice which we can use to identify and eliminate injustice is Kant's test of universalisability, which deems as just only that which we can will as universal law for all. However, while Hayek clearly has a great admiration for Kant's formulation of justice, in my view (contrary to that of several critics),[33] he completely rejects Kant's rational derivation of it. Instead he sees Kant like a great judge, merely articulating as principles what has been discovered, mainly by lawyers, to be useful in practice.[34] In adopting this view of Kant, Hayek rejects the strong view of the foundational role of reason which is at the centre of the Enlightenment project and which, as I have suggested, gives, *inter alia*, jurisprudence its identity. Quite simply for Hayek law is the foundation of jurisprudence and not vice versa.

Some Critical Responses

While my primary purpose in this chapter has been to bring to attention, rather than to criticise, a view that has generally been excluded from 'official jurisprudence', before returning to the relationship of Hayek to that jurisprudence, a brief indication of the ways in which he may be criticised seems to be in order lest he be seen to have it all his own way.

Perhaps the most common criticism of Hayek is that although he has presented a more defensible version of liberalism, particularly by abandoning the idea that both the individual and reason are prior to and independent of society, he has achieved this only by introducing a fatal indeterminacy between conservatism and liberalism, or between rationalism and irrationalism.[35] Thus for example Kukathas in a recent book (1989) argues that Hayek fails to resolve the tension between Kantian rationalism and Humean scepticism because he is unable rationally to identify the proper limits of rationality. This exposes Hayek both to conservative criticism that he still places too much emphasis on the capacity of conscious reason,[36] and to liberal and libertarian criticisms that his stress on the importance of following received traditions, at least in the absence of a theory of individual rights, results in a theory (that of the rule of law) which is too weak to protect individual freedom.[37] Indeed, as several commentators have pointed out, Hayek's conservative social theory, based as it is on the idea of cultural evolution, not only fails to establish and ground the liberal principles which he wishes to defend, but obliges him to accept the possibility of a future society abandoning such principles if that society were to prove to be more successful.[38]

A second line of criticism is that Hayek has overextended the idea of the market in seeking to develop theories of the mind, social order and law based on the market idea of selection according to success.[39] Thus it is argued that while the invisible hand may be plausible in the market, Hayek has failed to specify sufficiently the mechanisms which, in relation to social practices and rules, link individual choices to group success in such a way as to justify the view that the practices and rules which survive will necessarily be beneficial.[40] Furthermore, to the extent that Hayek sees everything in terms of the market, it can be argued that this prevents him being able to provide a defence of the market idea itself.

A third line of criticism is that Hayek exaggerates the extent of human ignorance and in particular our capacity to predict outcomes. Thus it is argued that the outcomes of markets operating with only general rules, at least as they affect certain groups, are often much more foreseeable and remediable by deliberate action than Hayek would allow – thus entitling us to intervene in the market on grounds of justice, even as Hayek defines it.[41] Similarly it is argued that the value of liberty is not so unknowable as Hayek suggests and that, even in terms of generating progress, attempts to realise a more positive version of equal liberty by redistributing financial, educational and political resources may be justified.[42] Certainly, as I have indicated, Hayek's desire to keep the world unpredictable leads him often to deny, as a matter of principle, planning capacities which we do in fact have, and to treat the impossibility of complete planning as an argument against all planning.

Fourthly one might suggest that there is something deeply paradoxical in Hayek's enterprise, which can be summed up in Oakshott's remark that 'it is a plan to resist all planning' (1962, p.21). Certainly in my view Hayek's arguments generally work by relying on that which those arguments seek to deny. For example his arguments in favour of the market and against social justice work on the basis of imagining market outcomes as though they were the product of a designing mastermind to show they are not. In other words, in each of Hayek's central dichotomies what appear as mere supplements – for example planning and organisation as supplements to the market and spontaneous order; *Thesis* as a supplement to *Nomos* – turn out to be very dangerous supplements, for without them Hayek cannot establish the 'true' versions of order and law. At a more practical level this comes out in the paradoxically 'authoritarian nature of his [Hayek's] dedication to liberty' (Crowley, 1987, p.102), an authoritarianism frequently shared by right-wing governments, which insists that our freedom depends upon an uncritical submission to the superior wisdom embodied in received practices and rules. Like the socialists he has devoted his life to criticising, Hayek insists that there is a correct way of seeing the world which is beyond argument.

This brings me to my final criticism of Hayek, which is essentially about the possibility of argument. That criticism may be expressed as the question, 'Is Hayek's vision of the world realistic?', not only in the sense of offering a realistic description of the world of late capitalism, which it certainly is not, or in the sense of identifying what interest could actually lead us to Hayek's world, which it does not,[43] but in the more fundamental sense of whether such a world is a viable human world at all.

What Hayek suppresses, as communitarian critiques emphasise,[44] is that human life, at least as it has been realised so far, has been not only a quest for success, but a search for meaning. That is, by reducing, as I have suggested he does, the normative to the instrumental, Hayek simply writes off the whole sphere of intersubjectivity, the domain of common meaning that arises from communication within a community that is not strategically aimed at success but oriented to understanding.[45] Thus in place of a genuine dialogue, in which we actively and collectively seek to discover what is the common good, Hayek insists that we passively and without argument submit to a view of the common good as consisting of what successful coordination requires. In short Hayek puts questions of meaning and value beyond politics. So while his view that market outcomes have no connection with justice may be an honest description of capitalism, one may wonder with many critics[46] whether human life is possible in a system which *inter alia* distributes quite independently of moral dessert or merit, and therefore whether capitalism can maintain the moral traditions on which, as Hayek admits, it depends.

In the last analysis, Hayek's view that all moral traditions and values such as justice and liberty are merely adaptations to circumstances, leads him to recognise that all that can be said for the system of market capitalism and its law is that it works, in the sense of supporting an increasing population.[47] We may, however, question whether that recognition alone can sustain allegiance to that system, or whether it can or should be allowed to suppress the search for common meaning through talking.

While Hayek, with Weber, recognises that capitalism is the expression of the moral emptiness of the world and the practical realisation of the thought 'that life has no purpose but itself' (Hayek, 1988, p.134), unlike Weber Hayek willingly embraces capitalism because he believes it is true to nature. Indeed Hayek's lifelong hostility to socialism can be seen as an attempt to destroy the last great mystification of the world which, like all salvationist religions, claims to reveal an inherent meaning for human existence. Seen in this light Hayek's work may be viewed as a further stage in the pursuit of the death of God, in which he asks us in the name of progress to stare into the abyss of meaninglessness and to recognise that our only destiny is to participate, like all other life forms, in the process of evolution.

In my view it is this nihilism which confounds Hayek's liberalism and it arises because, in his desire to keep us from knowing our fate and finding an inherent meaning in the world, he ignores the fact that it is in talking to each other, and in reinterpreting our traditions in the light of our experiences, that we create meaning for ourselves. The danger is that in the self-referential world of consumer capitalism, in which all values become subject to the 'logic' of exchange, Hayek's vision of life without meaning is becoming a self-fulfilling prophecy.[48] Certainly the practical effect of the New Right has been increasingly to close off the possibilities of argument and discussion aimed at understanding.

Hayek and Jurisprudence Revisited

Having presented an account of Hayek's views and some criticisms of them we are in a position to return to the issue with which we began, Hayek's exclusion from jurisprudence, beginning with a brief comparison of his views with those of two authors who are certainly not excluded, Rawls and Nozick.

While there are undoubtedly major differences between their respective views, Hayek, Rawls and Nozick all share two central liberal beliefs. One is that the good society is the one in which individuals are free to pursue their own idea of the good within a relatively restricted framework. For Rawls this eventuates in a theory of justice restricted to the basic institutional structure of society (1972); for Nozick in an argument that no more than a minimal state is justified (Nozick, 1974), and for Hayek, as we have seen, in the idea that the government should be restricted by general rules of just conduct. Secondly they share a belief that justice is a purely procedural affair and reject any idea of justice based on dessert or with the realising of any other patterned outcome. Thus all three agree that there is no ground of justice for interfering with market results provided they were justly reached; for Rawls that means within an institutional framework satisfying his two principles of justice, for Nozick steps consistent with rights in a state of nature, and for Hayek by conduct in accordance with the recognised rules of just conduct. Broadly then, while Rawls by virtue of his difference principle goes further in allowing, perhaps even requiring, measures of the type associated with market socialism, all three accept the basic system of liberal market capitalism.

There is however a vital distinction between, on the one hand, Hayek and, on the other, Rawls and Nozick. This is that while Hayek is quite explicit in indicating that his objective is the practical one of identifying the version of law and justice which will keep market capitalism going, Rawls and Nozick present their views as more or less universal truths based on pure reason.[49] Although the openness of Hayek's politics, and hence the practical relevance of his views, as reflected in the way they have been so enthusiastically received by the New Right, goes some way to explaining his comparative exclusion from jurisprudence, more important in my opinion is the fact that Hayek rejects the strong view of the capacity of reason on which Rawls and Nozick rely. Thus in place of Rawls's rational thought experiment about what people would agree upon behind 'the veil of ignorance', or Nozick's effort to deduce rationally in the form of an invisible-hand explanation what sort of state could arise by only legitimate steps, Hayek argues that law and justice are the product of the practical experiment of people who are ignorant in fact, and the result of an actual invisible-hand process.

Set against the abstract theorising of Rawls and Nozick, Hayek's view of law and justice as essentially practical solutions to the problems faced by real living people, seems initially a liberating perspective. In contrast to Rawls's 'original position', in which it only appears that people are allowed to engage in a dialogue about justice (for Rawls tells us what as rational people they *would* agree upon), Hayek appears to allow people actually to participate in the process of determining what law and justice are to mean to them. As I have argued, however, this too is only apparent, for though Hayek allows people's actions unconsciously to inform law and justice, by insisting that we submit to the wisdom of the evolved practices to which those actions give rise, he too closes the space for real dialogue with a monologue that requires us to be silent in the face of reason, admittedly a reason that is practically embodied rather than theoretically expressed. While this, albeit qualified, endorsement of the Enlightenment idea of reason may be a sufficient warrant merely to add Hayek to the list of theorists of law that constitute jurisprudence, in my view that is not to deny that Hayek is a dangerous supplement to jurisprudence, for two principal reasons.

Firstly and most obviously Hayek is a dangerous supplement because reading him opens us to the recognition that jurisprudential 'truths' cannot be divorced from general political and moral positions. More particularly, as we reflect on why Hayek's 'jurisprudence' is disregarded and marginalised we realise that that which is clearly constitutive of *his* jurisprudence, namely that it is inseparable from the argument for liberal market capitalism, is also constitutive of jurisprudence more generally. In short, only by suppressing the hidden agenda of capitalism, and treating the relation of law to capitalism as an optional and supplementary question, can jurisprudence, as the liberal truth about law, claim to be the product of universal reason and to be independent of any particular conception of the good.

Secondly Hayek, by leading us to question not only whether there are any disinterested truths about law, but whether law and justice have anything more than a practical foundation, renders problematic the idea of jurisprudence as an enterprise of theory. While jurisprudence is constituted by establishing a distance between theoretical truth and the practical law which is its object of study, Hayek's jurisprudence collapses that distance by denying both the possibility of a transcendant reason and the superiority of theoretical over practical knowledge. In brief, Hayek threatens to reverse or dissolve the hierarchy of jurisprudence and law that jurisprudence asserts, disclosing jurisprudence not as the superior, privileged and more profound truth about law, but as, at best, merely a systematic expression of what lawyers have discovered works in practice.

In my opinion as we abandon the view that there is any royal route to truth, and forsake the idea that a 'correct' theory of law is possible, there opens up the possibility of seeing different ways of talking about law as so many contributions to a conversation, each of which gives expression, with a certain validity, to different and often contradictory aspects of our experience. In Hayek's liberal law talk, as in liberal discourse generally, we hear the voicing of ourselves as subjects, as agents who act and choose rather than being acted upon. Thus, however conscious we may be of the determinants of our behaviour and thoughts, while at any present moment we experience ourselves as having the freedom to go beyond those determinants, liberal law talk in some accent can never be totally silenced. My criticism then of Hayek and of liberal jurisprudence generally is not that it is simply wrong, but that in turning a potential conversation into a monologue it silences voices that give valid expression to other aspects of our experience; for example the voice, giving expression to our experience of belonging, of being at home in something, or of being part of a community, that is heard in both conservative and left communitarian discourse.

While there are many voices which liberal jurisprudence silences in the name of universal reason, such as those of women and the colonised, perhaps most importantly, as is so clear in Hayek, it seeks to deny the voice of socialism. Although socialism itself, especially Marxist socialism, makes silencing claims to universal truth, it nevertheless in my view gives valid expression to another crucial aspect of our experience: our experience of ourselves as objects, as things acted upon, as limited and constrained by forces beyond our control, making it rightly said of socialism that it is the language of the oppressed. While the experience of ourselves as objects rather than subjects is an aspect of our experience, the voice of socialism, which talks the scientific language of explanation, conditions, causes and things 'social', and which seeks liberation in explaining us to ourselves, will retain a validity. Thus even though one may agree with Hayek, or for that matter with Foucault, that the 'knowledges' of man, of which socialism is one, are powers over man which constitute him as the object of administration, in my view Hayek has no good reason for imposing a conversational rule outlawing talk of things social such as social justice or the social conditions of freedom.

What I am suggesting then is that if jurisprudence has any value at all, other than providing a living for those who do it, it is as one contribution to ordinary conversations about law; conversations which must be actually engaged in, rather than being merely imagined in the court of reason. Furthermore those conversations must allow for the expression of the interests and experiences of actual people, as opposed to excluding them on the basis of a claim to the superiority of theoretical and expert languages such as jurisprudence traditionally conceived. In learning to find ways of talking against Hayek, particularly as we reflect on the real world which the thinking of the New Right supports, we are, I hope, engaging in such a conversation. More generally, to the extent that jurisprudence can open up, rather than close, conversations about the world in which we experience ourselves as participants, then it may have a role to play.

Notes

1. In the last twelve years, in addition to numerous articles, reviews and essays, eight full length books have appeared on Hayek: Barry (1979), Butler (1983), Gray (1984), Hoy (1984), Rowland (1987), Crowley (1987), Gissuarson (1987) and Kukathas (1989).
2. As representative of these tendencies one might mention Rorty (1979), MacIntyre (1980), Kuhn (1970), Lyotard (1984), Derrida (1976) and the writings of M. Foucault generally.
3. Perhaps the author most commonly associated with a 'minimal universalism' today is J. Habermas. See for example White (1988).
4. Generally on the emergence and nature of the New Right see Bosanquet (1983) and Hindess (1987, especially Chapter 8).
5. For a perceptiv account of these changes see Offe (1984, especially Chapter 6).
6. Neoconservatism in this country is perhaps best represented by Roger Scruton and the other contributors to the *Salisbury Review*. See in particular Scruton (1984).
7. See for example Bell (1976) and Kristol (1978). For a perceptive critique of neoconservatism see Habermas (1985).
8. This is most obvious in Hayek (1988).
9. For example Barry (1979), Rowland (1987 and 1988) and Kukathas (1989). For a contrary view see Gissuarson (1987).
10. I am indebted to Gissuarson (1987) for this title.
11. For two recent discussions of liberalism to which the author is particularly indebted see Arblaster (1984) and Gray (1987), and for an excellent discussion of the 'thin' conception of the right in liberalism see Sandel (1982).

12. For a clear expression of Hayek's indebtedness to Hume see Hayek (1963).
13. I am indebted to Gissuarson (1987) for this formulation.
14. The most systematic account of Hayek's epistemology is contained in Hayek (1952).
15. This view is elaborated in Gray (1984, especially pp.21–66).
16. As many commentators have noted, Ryle's distinction between 'knowing how' and 'knowing that' (Ryle, 1945–6) is a crucial one for Hayek.
17. Vanberg (1986) provides a useful discussion of some of these difficulties. See also Rowland (1987, Chapter 3) and Kukathas (1989, Chapter 3).
18. His most systematic discussion of freedom is in Hayek (1960). In more recent writings, especially Hayek (1988), the issue of freedom is revealingly less in evidence.
19. The classic exposition of the distinction between positive and negative conceptions of freedom remains Berlin (1969). For a more recent study indicating the diversity of ideas of freedom see Pelczynski and Gray (1984).
20. Pigou (1944), Watkins (1961) and Hamowy (1978) are among the more interesting critiques of Hayek's conceptions of freedom and coercion.
21. Good examples of such criticism are found in Norman (1982) and Plant (1984 and 1989).
22. On this see in particular Crowley (1987, especially pp.75 ff.) and Crespigny (1976).
23. Particularly Hayek (1944) and (1960).
24. See Barry (1979, pp.77 ff.)
25. I am indebted for this formulation to Gissuarson (1987).
26. See in particular Hayek (1960, Chapter 10).
27. 'The good society is one in which the chances of any one selected at random are likely to be as great as possible' (Hayek, 1976, p.132). This clearly echoes Rawls.
28. On this see in particular Habermas (1979) especially Chapter 3.
29. On this belief in English law see for example Atiyah (1979, pp.91 ff.).
30. Hayek makes these important concessions in Hayek (1973, pp.88–9).
31. Though more fully discussed in (1976) Hayek's views on justice are perhaps most clearly laid out in (1967, Chapter 11).
32. This contrasts with Rawls' view that such distance can be and must be achieved (1972).
33. In particular Gray (1984) and Kukathas (1989).
34. See in particular Hayek (1976, pp.166–7).
35. See for example Barry (1979), Rowland (1987) and Kukathas (1989).
36. For example Scruton (1984), and see Gissuarson (1987, Chapter 3).
37. For example Robbins (1961), Hamowy (1978), Buchanan (1979) and Rothbard (1981). More particularly on the rule of law see Raz (1979) and Waldron (1989).
38. For example Gissuarson (1987), Crowley (1987) and Rowland (1988).

39. See for example Barry (1979).
40. See for example Vanberg (1986) and Gray (1984, Chapter 2).
41. See for example Plant (1984 and 1989).
42. This is the main thrust of Norman (1982).
43. On the issue of getting to the New Right world see Offe (1984, Chapter 6) and Barry (1984).
44. For communitarian critiques on Hayek see in particular Rowland (1987 and 1988), Crowley (1987) and Kukathas (1989, Chapter 3). More generally see MacIntyre (1980), Sandel (1982) and Unger (1975).
45. Habermas is the leading theorist of the idea of a communicatively constituted intersubjectivity. See for example Habermas (1984).
46. For example Kristol (1978) and Plant (1984).
47. On the idea of supporting an increasing population as the measure of success see Hayek (1988, Chapter 8).
48. On consumer capitalism as a self-referential system of signs see the writings of J. Baudrillard, in particular Baudrillard (1988).
49. In his later writings Rawls has drawn back somewhat from his earlier universalist claims arguing that the validity of his theory of justice is restricted to 'democratic society under modern circumstances' (1980).

Further Reading

While the *Constitution of Liberty* (1960) and *Law, Legislation and Liberty* (1973, 1976 and 1979) are the most important of Hayek's writings on law and justice, probably the most accessible introductions are his two essays, 'The Principles of a Liberal Social Order' (1967, Chapter 11) and 'The Confusion of Language in Political Thought' (1978).

Of the general books on Hayek, Barry (1979) is the most comprehensive, Gray (1984) and Kukathas (1989) the most scholarly, and Rowland (1987) and Crowley (1987) the most stimulating.

More specifically on law, Dietze (1977), Barry (1979, Chapter 5), Ogus (1989) and MacCormick (1989) are good introductions.

References

Arblaster, A. (1984) *The Rise and Decline of Western Liberalism* (Oxford: Basil Blackwell).

Atiyah, P. (1979) *The Rise and Fall of Freedom of Contract* (Oxford: Clarendon).

Barnett, H. and Yach, D. (1985) 'The Teaching of Jurisprudence and Legal Theory in British Universities and Polytechnics', *Legal Studies*, vol.5, no.2, pp.151–71.

Barry, N. (1979) *Hayek's Social and Economic Philosophy* (London: Macmillan).

——. (1984) 'Ideas versus Interests: the classical Liberal dilemma' in *Hayek's 'Serfdom' revisited* (London: Institute of Economic Affairs).

Baudrillard, J. (1988) 'Consumer Society', trans. J. Mourrain, in M. Poster (ed.), *Jean Baudrillard: Selected Writings* (Stanford: Stanford University Press) pp.30–56.
Bell, D. (1976) *The Cultural Contradictions of Capitalism* (London: Heinemann).
Berlin, I. (1969) 'Two concepts of Liberty', in *Four Essays on Liberty* (London: Oxford University Press), p.148.
Bosanquet, N. (1983) *After the New Right* (London: Heinemann).
Buchanan, J. (1979) *Freedom in Constitutional Contract* (College Station, Texas: Texas A. & M. University Press).
Butler, E. (1983) *Hayek and his Contribution to the Political and Economic Thought of our Time* (New York: Universe Books).
Crespigny, A. de (1976) 'F.A. Hayek: Freedom for Progress' in A. de Crespigny and K. Minogue (eds), *Contemporary Political Philosophers* (London: Methuen), pp.49–66.
Crowley, B. (1987) *The Self, the Individual and the Community. Liberalism in the political thought of F.A. Hayek and Sidney and Beatrice Webb* (Oxford: Clarendon).
Derrida, J. (1976) *Of Grammatology*, trans. G. Spivak (Baltimore and London: Johns Hopkins University Press).
Descartes, R. (1960) *Discourse on Method*, trans. A. Wollaston (Harmondsworth: Penguin).
Dietze, G. (1977) 'Hayek on the Rule of Law' in F. Machlup (ed.), *Essays on Hayek* (London: Routledge & Kegan Paul), pp.107–46.
Gissuarson, H. (1987) *Hayek's Conservative Liberalism* (New York: Garland).
Gray, J. (1984) *Hayek on Liberty* (Oxford: Basil Blackwell).
——. (1987) *Liberalism* (Milton Keynes: Open University Press).
Habermas, J. (1979) *Communication and the Evolution of Society*, trans. T. McCarthy (London: Heinemann).
——. (1984) *The Theory of Communicative Action*. Vol.1 *Reason and the Rationalisation of Society*, trans. T. McCarthy (London: Heinemann).
——. (1985) 'Neo conservative culture criticism in the United States and West Germany: An intellectual movement in two political cultures' in R. Bernstein (ed.), *Habermas and Modernity* (Oxford: Basil Blackwell), pp.78–94.
Hamowy, R. (1978) 'Law and Liberal Society: F.A. Hayek's Constitution of Liberty', *Journal of Libertarian Studies*, vol.2, no.4, pp.287–97.
Hayek, F.A. (1944) *The Road to Serfdom* (London: Routledge & Kegan Paul).
——. (1949) 'The Intellectuals and Socialism', *University of Chicago Law Review*, vol.16, no.3, pp.178–94. (Reprinted in Hayek [1967], Chapter 12.)
——. (1952) *The Sensory Order: An Inquiry into the Foundations of Theoretical Psychology* (London: Routledge & Kegan Paul).
——. (1960) *The Constitution of Liberty* (London: Routledge & Kegan Paul).
—— (1963) 'The Legal and Political Philosophy of David Hume', *Il Politico*, vol.28, no.14, pp.106–21. (Reprinted in Hayek [1967], Chapter 7.)
——. (1967) *Studies in Philosophy, Politics and Economics* (London: Routledge & Kegan Paul).
——. (1973) *Law, Legislation and Liberty*, Vol.1, *Rules and Order* (London: Routledge & Kegan Paul).

——. (1976) *Law, Legislation and Liberty*, Vol.2, *The Mirage of Social Justice* (London: Routledge & Kegan Paul).

——. (1978) *New Studies in Philosophy, Politics, Economics and the History of Ideas* (London: Routledge & Kegan Paul).

——. (1979) *Law, Legislation and Liberty*, Vol.3, *The Political Order of a Free People* (London: Routledge & Kegan Paul).

——. (1988) *The Fatal Conceit: Errors of Socialism* ed. W. Bartley (London: Routledge & Kegan Paul).

Hindess, B. (1987) *Freedom, Equality and the Market* (London: Tavistock).

Hoy, C. (1984) *A Philosophy of Individual Freedom. The Political Thought of F.A. Hayek* (London: Greenwood).

Kristol, I. (1978) *Two Cheers for Capitalism* (New York: NAL).

Kuhn, T. (1970) *The Structure of Scientific Revolutions* 2nd edn. (Chicago: University of Chicago Press).

Kukathas, C. (1989) *Hayek and Modern Liberalism* (Oxford: Oxford University Press).

Lyotard, J. (1984) *The Postmodern Condition: A Report on Knowledge*, trans. G. Bennington and B. Massumi (Manchester: Manchester University Press).

MacCormick, N. (1989) 'Spontaneous Order and the Rule of Law – Some Problems', *Ratio Iuris*, vol.2, no.1, pp.41–54.

MacIntyre, A. (1980) *After Virtue* (London: Duckworth).

Norman, R. (1982) 'Does equality destroy liberty?' in K. Graham (ed.), *Contemporary Political Philosophy* (Cambridge: Cambridge University Press), pp.83–109.

Nozick, R. (1974) *Anarchy, State and Utopia* (Oxford: Basil Blackwell).

Oakshott, M. (1962) *Rationalism in Politics* (London: Methuen).

Offe, C. (1984) *Contradictions of the Welfare State* (London: Hutchinson).

Ogus, A. (1989) 'Law and Spontaneous Order: Hayek's Contribution to Legal Theory', *Journal of Law and Society*, vol.16, no.4, pp.393–409.

Pelczynski, Z. and Gray, J. (eds), (1984) *Conceptions of Liberty in Political Philosophy* (London: St Martin).

Pigou, A. (1944) 'Review of Hayek, The Road to Serfdom', *Economic Journal*, vol.54, pp.217–19.

Plant, R. (1984) *Equality, Markets and the State* (London: Fabian Tract 494).

——. (1989) 'Socialism, Markets and End States' in J. Le Grand and S. Estrin (eds), *Market Socialism* (Oxford: Clarendon), pp.50–77.

Rawls, J. (1972) *A Theory of Justice* (Oxford: Clarendon).

——. (1980) 'Kantian Constructivism in Moral Theory', *The Journal of Philosophy*, no.77, pp.515–72.

Raz, J. (1979) 'The Rule of Law and its Virtue' in R. Cunningham (ed.), *Liberty and the Rule of Law* (College Station and London: Texas A. & M. University Press), pp.3–21.

Robbins, L. (1961) 'Hayek on Liberty', *Economica*, NS 28, Feb. 1961, pp.66–81.

Rorty, R. (1979) *Philosophy and the Mirror of Nature* (Princeton: Princeton University Press).

Rothbard, M. (1981) 'F.A. Hayek and the concept of coercion' in M. Rothbard (ed.) *The Ethics of Liberty*, Chapter 28. (Atlantic Highlands NJ: Humanities Press).

Ryle, G. (1945–6) 'Knowing How and Knowing That', *Proceedings of the Aristotelean Society*, vol.46, pp.1–16.

Rowland, B. (1987) *Ordered Liberty and the Constitutional Framework. The Politcal Thought of F.A. Hayek* (London: Greenwood).

——. (1988) 'Beyond Hayek's pessimism – Reason, tradition and bounded constructivist rationalism', *British Journal of Political Science*, vol.18, pp.221–41.

Sandel, M. (1982) *Liberalism and the Limits of Justice* (Cambridge: Cambridge University Press).

Scruton, R. (1984) *The Meaning of Conservatism* (London: Macmillan).

Unger, R. (1975) *Knowledge and Politics* (New York: Free Press).

Vanberg, V. (1986) 'Spontaneous Market Order and Social Rules', *Economics and Philosophy*, vol.2, no.1, pp.75–100.

Waldron, J. (1989) 'The Rule of Law in Contemporary Liberal Theory', *Ratio Juris*, vol.2, no.1, pp.79–96.

Watkins, J. (1961) 'Philosophy' in A. Seldon (ed.), *Agenda for a Free Society* (London: Hutchinson), pp.31–49.

White, S. (1988) *The Recent Work of Jurgen Habermas* (Cambridge: Cambridge University Press).

Marxism, Law, Legal Theory and Jurisprudence

Alan Hunt

The Object of Marxist Theory of Law

Theories may be distinguished from one another in two major respects: they ask different questions and they employ different concepts. There are no 'correct' questions or concepts. The questions we ask and the concepts we use are determined by what we decide is 'important' or 'significant' about our object of study.

Marxist theory of law asks: what part, if any, does law play in the reproduction of the structural[1] inequalities of class, race and gender which characterise capitalist societies? If law participates in the reproduction of capitalist relations, through what mechanisms and processes does it realise this effect?

It is not my intention to write a history of the complex and interesting shifts that have occurred as Marxists have attempted to come to grips with the phenomenon of law.[2] Instead I will identify a number of themes which have been developed and have also been reworked into new and variant combinations. On the basis of this review I will, in the section below, present an outline account of a version of Marxist theory of law which seeks both to integrate these major themes with the tradition and to provide a theory adequate to the task of understanding democratic capitalist law.

In summary form the major themes which are present in Marx's own writing and in subsequent Marxist approaches to law are:

1) Law is inescapably political or law is one form of politics.
2) Law and state are closely connected; law exhibits a relative autonomy from the state.
3) Law gives effect to, mirrors or is otherwise expressive of the prevailing economic relations; the legal form replicates the forms of economic relations.
4) Law is always potentially coercive or repressive and manifests the state's monopoly of the means of coercion.
5) The content and procedures of law manifest, directly or indirectly, the interests of the dominant class(es) or the power bloc.

6) Law is ideological; it both exemplifies and provides legitimation for the embedded values of the dominant class(es).

These six themes are present in Marxist writings on law in a variety of different forms and, in particular, with very different degrees of sophistication and complexity. This point can be illustrated by taking theme 5 concerning the connection between law and class interests. In a simple version this finds expression in the claim that law gives effect to the interests of the capitalist class and that it is thus a means or an instrument by means of which the capitalist class imposes its will upon the working class. But this theme is also present in more sophisticated forms which stress that the content of law can be read as an expression of the complex dynamic of class struggle. As such it comes to include legal recognition of the interests of subordinated classes secured through struggle; for example, factory acts and health and safety legislation are advances secured through political struggle.[3]

The same point can be made with regard to theme 2 concerning the connection between law and the state. In crude versions law and the courts are presented as direct and manipulable instruments of state power. In a more sophisticated version this theme can be developed in a way which stresses the conditioning and limiting connection between law and state, emphasising the relative autonomy of the law and the importance of its own internal coherence such that conflicts and disjunctions may manifest themselves between legal power and state power.

The general point being made is that the six themes are not mutually exclusive; rather they frequently overlap and interconnect. No single theme is intrinsically more important than the others, nor is one of them a privileged route to a 'correct' Marxist theorisation of law.

Marxist theory of law has mainly played an oppositional role. Its most frequent manifestations have been directed towards providing a critique of liberal legal thought. The critique is 'oppositional' in the sense that it has been directed at controverting or negating the conventional wisdom of liberal legalism (Hunt 1981, pp.93–7). Thus, for example, in place of the liberal contention that law aspires to neutrality, Marxist theory of law has asserted the claim that in fact it systematically favours dominant economic and political interests. Rather than serving to balance competing interests, law serves to reinforce and legitimate unequal interests. Law does not derive from consensual social values, rather it employs state power to impose class-specific values. The point to be made is that the reversal or negation of conventional wisdom does not by itself generate an adequate alternative theory.

A stage beyond oppositional critique is reached when Marxist theory of law actively introduces alternative themes to the terrain of legal theory. The themes identified above exemplify such a project. Their significance is that they raise issues excluded or ignored in orthodox jurisprudence. Some of these themes simply add to the agenda of jurisprudence; for instance the focus on the connection between law and politics or between law and class interests either adds to or redirects the concerns of jurisprudence. Other Marxist themes have more wide-ranging implications for legal theory. For example the insistence on the ideological nature of law involves an entirely different way of looking at the texts, discourses and practices of law. Such a point of departure disallows a straightforward or positivist acceptance of legal rules and doctrines as the primary reality of law that is taken for granted.[4]

This brings us to an important dimension of Marxist theory of law. It is not a project which occupies the same field or scope as orthodox jurisprudence; its agenda is necessarily different. Thus it cannot simply replace elements within liberal legalism in order to produce an alternative or competing theory. However, this very different character of Marxist theory of law itself raises problems. If it is so radically different in its agenda, methods and concepts then there will be no real possibility of comparing it with liberal legalism. If it forms a different project then it will be unlikely that Marxist theory of law will be able to provide solutions to any of the questions which motivate orthodox jurisprudence. It is to this question that attention will next be directed.

Outline of a Marxist Theory of Law

What follows is an outline of a Marxist theory of law which concentrates on achieving an integrated theoretical structure from the main themes present in its diverse versions. It is not an attempt to offer a precis of Marx's own writings on law; neither Marx nor Engels produced anything that could or should be called a theory of law; law was never a sustained object of their attention, although they did have much to say about law that remains interesting and relevant (Cain and Hunt, 1979).

My account makes no claim to represent a 'correct' interpretation of Marxism. What I do claim is that it provides a comprehensive framework for a Marxist theory of law. The selection of a starting point is the most important step in the development of any theory. Accordingly I propose to offer both an explanation and a defence of the starting point which I have selected, and to indicate how it differs from alternative candidates.

A Relational Theory of Law
The law is a specific form of social relation. It is certainly not a 'thing', nor is it reducible to a set of institutions. Law as a social relation provides the starting point most in keeping with Marxism because the focus on 'people in relations' is what makes Marxism so strongly and distinctively social – more rigorously social than most sociology. In one of many similar passages Marx stated his relational approach in the following terms:

> Society does not consist of individuals, but expresses the sum of interrelations, the relations within which these individuals stand ... To be a slave, to be a citizen are social characteristics, relations between human beings A & B. Human being A, as such, is not a slave. He is a slave in and through society (1973, p.265).

It is important to stress that Marx does not abolish or ignore the individual. What he does do is to avoid adopting a theoretical humanism which starts from the individual endowed only with native capacities and will (Robinson Crusoe is the classic embodiment of such a humanist approach). The relational approach insists that it is only through living life within a complex of relations that individuals come to be formed and to act with purpose and intention. Life within social relations is the general form of the human experience.

In an important and complex sense social relations are objective. My life and your life are located within sets of relations (of work, politics, domestic, and so on) which are gendered, hierarchic, subordinating and empowering in ways which (although we may affect their impact) are set up or pre-date our individual involvement; thus in some important sense they are external or objective. But social relations are not objective in any sense which implies that they are not a lived part of life within a culture, constructed and lived in and through language and forms of consciousness, as well as sets of objective conditions and sets of social practices. This point needs emphasising to explain why a relational starting point is chosen rather than either of two other influential approaches, namely those provided by the concept of 'base and superstructure' and by 'the commodity form' theory of law.

Mapping Relations
The relational approach to law posits relations as the general form of sociality which are exhibited in a general and undifferentiated category of 'social relations'. Each social relation is constituted as a complex of a variety of different types and forms of relations. For example the social relation of the family involves, among others,

economic, sexual, gender, affectual and legal relations. It is not my intention to suggest a full typology of the varieties of social relations. In the context of Marxist theory of law I will limit my account by assuming that only the following varieties are involved: economic, political, legal, class and gender relations; gender relations are included not only as an important category in their own right, but also because they do not form part of the received Marxist tradition. This preliminary classification is posited at a fairly high level of abstraction. Nowhere do there exist 'pure' economic or political relations; workplaces may exhibit predominantly economic relations, but political relations (embodied in the command structure of management or in trade union–employer relations) and gender relations (sexual division of labour) both play their part.

Each and every concrete relation involves a complex of relations; this is made clear if we adopt the terminology of calling a concrete relation a relation-set. The characteristics of each relation-set are identified by the relative predominance of its constituent relations and, in particular, by whether any pattern of dominance exists. Thus the specificity of a relation-set should be specifiable in terms of patterns of interaction between different relations identifying whether they supplement or conflict with each other.

Before leaving these general conceptual considerations something needs to be said about the problem of power. Despite the expenditure of considerable intellectual labour no usable conception of power is available. We can, however, identify some conceptions of power to be avoided; power is not a 'thing', some property capable of being owned, possessed or wielded. Nor is power a zero-sum game, in which each increment on one side is balanced by a diminution on the other. Power is quintessentially relational; power is the capacity of social actors to realise aims in a relation of oppositions and resistances of others. It is preferable not to speak of 'power relations' since this implies that there exist some relations without a power dimension; on the contrary even in affectual relations, relations of personal attachment, the participants can never be entirely free of the power capacity of the wider social relations in which their relationship is located. Thus in every type of relationship particular characteristic forms of power are discernible; hence it makes good sense to speak of economic power (constituted by access to and control of economic resources), political power, etc.

It is, however, important to avoid such an all-inclusive conception of power that power is everything and everywhere. Foucault's accusation that Marxism equated power with the state is unjustified in the light of Marxism's emphasis on non-coercive economic relations as the primary source and location of power in capitalist societies (Foucault, 1980, p.122). But Foucault is helpful in directing our attention to the dispersal and localisation of power. What is missing, and is of special importance in the theorisation of law, is to grasp how the particularistic and localised powers and disciplinary techniques coalesce or are aggregated at the level of institutions and of the state. To make comprehensible law's dispersed effects, its penetration of many and varied social relations, it is important to grasp that these 'local effects' are made possible or are facilitated by the concentration of the legal system and its proximity to the monopolised coercive capacity of the state. While law cannot be reduced to the commands of some political superior or sovereign, it is nevertheless wrong to lose sight of the command capacity of the centralised legal institutions. It is the mutual reinforcement achieved through coercive capacity and ideological legitimacy that is the key to the understanding of legal power.

These brief comments on power lead to the need to stress the distinction between different dimensions of social relations. Power is one of the most important dimensions. Just as the idea of power relations has been resisted so it is proposed that it is better to speak of an 'ideological dimension' than to speak of 'ideological relations' since this implies the existence of non-ideological relations. It is suggested that it is more fruitful to explore the power, ideological and discursive dimensions of social relations, to examine their form and content and to study their interaction.

The proposed conceptual scheme is represented in Figure 1.

Figure 1

RELATIONS	DIMENSIONS OF SOCIAL RELATIONS			
Type of Relation	*Power*	*Institutional*	*Ideological*	*Discursive*
Economic				
Political				
Legal	X	X	X	X
Class				
Gender				

Legal Relations

Legal relations are first and foremost a variety or type of social relation that are identified by a specific set of characteristics that separates them from other types of social relations. Firstly, legal relations are interpellative in the sense that they can only exist through calling into existence or play social actors as 'legal subjects'. The legal subject does not coincide with the natural person; thus until relatively recently women were either not legal subjects or were constrained within a specific legal status which imposed duties while granting few rights. Similarly children are not full legal subjects and, as the present concern with child abuse highlights, it is not self-evident that either parents or the welfare state can be presumed to be capable of representing their interests. The current controversy arising from the abortion debate over the status of the foetus is another instance of this process whereby legal subjects are constructed or refused. It should be noted in passing that there is an important connection between 'legal subject' and 'citizen' which is neither homologous nor opposed and which has important implications for our understanding of politics, democracy and participation.[5]

The most simple instance of the legal subject is that of the adult person recognised by state, courts and other agencies as the bearer of rights, able to initiate litigation and owing enforceable duties to others (such as having to pay taxes, support dependants, and so on). One important consequence of the point that legal subjects are not coextensive with natural persons is that a variety of groups and social aggregates are endowed with legal subjectivity (or, as it is usually termed, 'legal personality'); the corporation as legal subject is probably the most important example. It is also important to emphasise the wide variety of legal statuses into which people and groups are interpellated; 'defendants' in criminal trial may be held in detention, subjected to bail restrictions and debarred from their normal activities. 'Witnesses' are literally interpellated or summoned by being called before a court. Trustees, beneficiaries, agents, owners, and a host of other legal statuses are also summoned into being.

In one important set of instances this legal interpellation is itself *constitutive* of the social relation, as in the case with the formation of a corporate entity or with the creation of a trust. In these and other instances law is performative (where some legal act of speech, writing or signing changes the positions of the parties). Generally this creative role of law does not create a relation *ab initio*, for example to form a legal partnership will probably only serve to formalise an existing economic relationship. It is, however, important to stress that significant actual or potential changes are effected by changing the positions, capacities and obligations of the parties. In a much wider number of other circumstances the legal interpellation does not create a social relation but rather it affects the terms, conditions and limits under which that relationship is lived out and struggled around. It is in order to keep this general primacy of social relations in mind that in elaborating a Marxist theory of law it is desirable to adhere to the methodological injunction; start with the social relationship before proceeding to examine the legal relation involved.

Law and Modes of Regulation

A legal relation always generates a potential mode of regulation; it is 'potential' in the sense that many legal relations may be wholly or largely passive as the legal dimension of the relation may play no part at all in the way the concrete social relation is lived out. One obvious but important illustration of this is the fact that a legal relation often becomes significant only when a dispute or some other problem arises.

Law provides a wide variety of modes of regulating social relations. Generally a different mode is associated with different types of social relations. In many instances this is directly apparent in the conventional classification of types of law; thus criminal law employs different agents (like police) and imposes different sanctions (for instance imprisonment) from those techniques associated with private law (such as the individual initiation of litigation, monetary damages as primary remedy). The concept of a mode of regulation serves to focus attention on law as a continuing set of practices which contributes to the reproduction and transformation of social relations. It is not the frequently idiosyncratic outcomes of litigation which are significant, but rather the permanent processes which serve to normalise and stabilise the dynamic of struggle, conflict and competition which characterises relations within class society.

The major ingredient of a legal mode of regulation is the form which flows from the attribution of rights to interpellated legal subjects. The discourse of rights needs to be understood as consisting of a bundle of rights/duties distributed between legal subjects located within social relations. Both rights and duties embrace a variety of different types of attributions, whose significance is that they not only provide a relatively unified legal discourse which can handle a range of different social relations, but which also overlap with wider normative and moral discourses. This interface of legal and moral rights provides for both the authoritative determinations of rights/ duties in litigation, a meta-discourse which provides legitimation and also a setting for contestation and change in which new or variant claim-rights are articulated and asserted.

The significance of the rights-grounded discourse is that it provides an integrated field within which all forms of social relations can be made subject to a common discursive apparatus. This is not to suggest that rights discourse is or can be fully coherent or free from internal tensions or contradictions. Indeed one of the major contributions of contemporary critical legal studies (CLS) has been to highlight the internal incoherence and contradictions within the discourse of rights. But this critique ignores the significance of rights as providing a comprehensive discursive field. It is worth noting that rights-discourse figures in other forms of dispute handling that are outside litigation, including negotiation and public debate.

Law as a Distributive Mechanism
Law and the legal process have the potential to change the relative positions of legal subjects within social relations; in this basic sense law is a distributive mechanism. Again it is necessary to stress 'potential' since it does not follow that a change in legal capacity necessarily affects positions within concrete social relations. This is particularly obvious where law 'fails', for example, in not achieving an adequate mechanism to enforce child support payments by divorced or deserting fathers. The general process of legal distribution is that interests and claims are transcribed into rights-discourses, and in that process the capacities of legal subjects are confirmed or varied. Law is rarely involved in the direct distribution of resources, but it is a major distributive process in the sense that it operates to vary the relative positions and capacities of the participants in social relations.

The intimate connection between law and politics is revealed clearly when it is recognised that a major instance of this process of affecting capacities is, particularly in our contemporary age of legislation, to alter the boundary between 'political regulation' and 'market' or 'economic regulation'. For instance the existence of legislation governing unfair dismissals from employment expands the sphere of political regulation of economic power. Thus one important dimension of legal regulation is that it regulates the boundaries or spheres of competence of other modes of regulation. This process frequently manifests itself in the never-ending process in which legal discourse invokes and redraws the boundary between the public and the private. The criticism levelled by CLS points to the inability of legal doctrine to sustain a coherent public/private distinction. While valid in its own terms, the inconsistency criticism misses the point that one of the major legal distributive mechanisms is located precisely in the fact that these boundaries are constantly drawn and redrawn.

It is important to emphasise that I do not suggest that the quest for consistency in legal doctrine is unimportant. Engels formulated the issue clearly in his letter to Conrad Schmidt:

In a modern state, law must not only correspond to the general economic conditions and be its expression, but must also be an *internally coherent* expression which does not, owing to internal conflicts, contradict itself. (Cain and Hunt 1979, p.57; Marx 1975, p.399; original emphasis)

Two important points follow. First, it explains why law is rarely if ever the direct instrumental expression of the interests of a dominant class. Second, it is the persistent quest for coherence, rather than its realisation, that is significant. Indeed a necessary tension between competing versions of legal boundaries, such as that between the public and private, ensures the flexibility and responsiveness of law to changing contexts and pressures.

The theoretical framework developed above is intentionally abstract; it is also consistent with a range of different social theories and political perspectives. Its distinctively Marxist character can be developed by returning to the persistent themes and questions which have motivated it. Theories distinguish themselves by the questions they ask and the conceptual tools used in supplying the answers. I take Marxism's central concerns to be: to explain the relations of subordination or domination that characterise particular historical epochs; to account for the persistence and reproduction of these relations, and to identify the conditions for ending these relations and realising emancipated social relations. The method and content of a Marxist theory of law will necessarily be concerned to explore the role of law in these three areas.

Alternative Marxist Approaches to Law

The claim which this essay seeks to support is that the relational theory of law outlined above provides the most fruitful approach to generating a comprehensive and rigorous Marxist jurisprudence. The characteristics of this theory can be further illuminated by contrasting it with two other variants which have been influential in the history of Marxist work on law. I hope to make clear why these alternative routes have not been adopted.

Base-Superstructure Theory
Marx's imagery of base and superstructure distinguishes between 'the economic structure of society', which forms the base or 'real foundation'

on which rises a legal and political superstructure and to which correspond definite forms of social consciousness ... It is not the consciousness of men that determines their being, but, on the contrary, their social being that determines their consciousness. (Marx 1971, p.21)

Law is thus assigned to the 'superstructure' which 'reflects' the 'base' or 'economic structure'. Thus it is the economic structure which determines or has causal priority in determining the character and content of the law (and all other features of the superstructure).

The base-superstructure thesis is problematic in a number of respects. The notion of base-superstructure is a metaphor; it seeks to advance our understanding of social relations by importing an analogy which involves imagery derived from thinking about society as if it were a construction project. Metaphors of many kinds play a major role not only in social theory but in most forms of human thought (including the natural sciences). We probably cannot avoid using them, but it is important to be sensitive to the implications of thinking about one phenomenon in the language and concepts of something quite different.

The base-superstructure metaphor seems to commit Marxism to advocating an economic determinism; the objection to which is that it proposes a causal law (analogous to classical scientific laws) which asserts the causal priority of the economic base over all other dimensions of society in that the former determines or causes the latter. (For a clear and insightful discussion of determination see Williams [1977, pp.83–9].)

There is a 'weaker' or 'softer' version of the idea of determination in which it is conceived as a mechanism whereby limits are set within which variation may be the result of causal forces other than the economic structure. Thus the economic base is pictured as prescribing the boundaries or as setting objective limits for the different elements of the superstructure. This sense of determination is theoretically more attractive because it does not foreclose or predetermine the causal relationship that exists between the different facets of social life.

Marx and Engels both occasionally came close to this softer version of determination. Perhaps its best known formulation is provided by Engels' letter to Bloch (21 September 1890):

According to the materialist conception of history, the *ultimately* determining factor in history is the production and reproduction of real life. Neither Marx nor I have ever asserted more than this ... The economic situation is the basis, but the various elements of the superstructure – political forms of the class struggle and its results, such as constitutions ... juridical forms, and especially the reflections of all these real struggles in the brains of the participants, political, legal, philosophical theories ... also exercise their influence upon the course of the historical struggles and in many cases determine their *form* in particular. There is an interaction of all these elements in which, amid all the endless host of accidents ... the economic movement is finally bound to assert itself. (Marx 1975, pp.394–5; original emphasis)

This version of the determination thesis is usually referred to as the theory of relative autonomy; its central idea is that law and all other elements of the superstructure can and do have causal effects in that they react back upon the economic base which, however, still retains causal priority, but now only 'ultimately'. Marx and Engels also used phrases such as 'in the last instance' and 'in the final analysis' to express this long-run sense of the determination by the economic.

Many Marxist writers on law have been attracted to this softer version of determinism. Its merit is that it retains some sense of the causal weight or importance of the economic order (which forms one of the intuitive appeals of Marx's thought) while at the same time it provides an invitation to explore the intriguing specificity of law.

Despite the undoubted attractions of soft determinism plus relative autonomy I will argue that it cannot provide a satisfactory starting point for Marxist theory of law. In its simplest form my objection is that it says both too much and too little. It says too much in that instead of providing a theoretical starting point it rather imposes a conclusion for each and every piece of investigation, namely that the economic is determinant only in the last instant. But it also says too little because it offers no account of the mechanisms whereby this ultimate or long-run causality is produced.[6]

Commodity Form Theory

A quite different starting point for a Marxist theory of law was employed by the early Soviet jurist Evgeny Pashukanis who, in the 1920s, produced what still remains the most comprehensive Marxist theorisation of law (Beirne and Sharlet, 1980; Pashukanis, 1978).[7] Pashukanis set out to model his theory on the framework that Marx had employed in Volume I of *Capital* which opened with a rigorous but abstract discussion of the concept of commodity. Accordingly Pashukanis chose to elucidate 'the deep interconnection between the legal form and the commodity form' (1978, p.63). His key proposition was that 'the legal relation between subjects is simply the reverse side of the relation between products of labour which have become commodities' (ibid., p.85). In its simplest form Pashukanis viewed the contract as the legal expression of this primary relationship of capitalism, namely the commodity exchange. Commodity exchange and legal contract exist in an homologous relation; they are mutually dependent.

In the discussion of Pashukanis which follows readers will note that, while I will indicate major disagreement with both his substantive theory and the conclusions which he draws, I am keen to hang onto one significant feature of his approach, his relational approach to law. One of his major methodological injunctions is that law should be conceived as a social relation in the same way that Marx understood capital as a social relation (ibid., p.74).

The most succinct evaluation of Pashukanis is that he correctly identified law as a social relation, but he blocked that insight by reducing law to a single and inappropriate relation, the commodity relation. The root source of both his success and his failure was the rather simplistic reading of Marx in general and of *Capital* in particular on which he relied. He treats Marx's opening discussion of the commodity as if Marx was propounding an economic history of capitalism which traced its development from the general growth of 'simple commodity production' (small-scale production by independent producers for the market).[8] Marx was quite explicit that his analysis of commodity relations was deliberately pitched at a high level of abstraction and did not purport to represent a generalised economic history. For Marx the famous chapter on commodities was a means of approaching what he regarded as the most basic relationships constitutive of capitalism: capitalist relations of production. It is for this reason that one of the standard Marxist criticisms of Pashukanis is that he reverses Marx's priority of production relations over exchange relations (commodity relations). Thus in grounding his analysis of legal relations upon the homology with commodity relations Pashukanis either misdirected or skewed his whole subsequent analysis.

That Pashukanis took this wrong turn can be readily explained. The most important feature of his work, both theoretically and politically, is his contention that law is irredeemably bourgeois: law is especially and distinctively associated with the existence of capitalism. If law is bourgeois it follows that for Pashukanis there could be no pre-capitalist law. For him, all medieval law was not a specific feudal law but was a manifestation of the early stages of the development of commodity relations; similarly there could be no post-capitalist law, and the idea of socialist law is thus unnecessary and contradictory.

Without spelling out its details it is possible to indicate the general features of an alternative which rejects Pashukanis's narrow equation of law with capitalism. Such an alternative would view pre-capitalist law as having distinctive characteristics reflecting the set of economic, political and social relations characteristic of feudalism. Similarly post-capitalism or socialism would involve the development of new sets of relationships and these in turn would necessitate new forms of legal relations. For example, socialism would be likely to accord increased importance to a range of semi-autonomous bodies which would operate with a large measure of self-regulation while drawing their resources from public sources; such bodies would require new legal property forms. To recover the general relational orientation proposed by Pashukanis it is necessary to free Marxist theory of law from the narrow focus on commodity relations.

Ideology as Law and Law and Ideology

The following sections will explore the relation between law and key forms of social relations. This section will examine the ideological character of law; it comes first not because of any intention to insert some claim for the primacy of ideology, but for the expository reason that since ideology suffuses the connection between law and social relations some account of this connection is necessary before focusing on particular types of social relations. The next section concentrates on the law-state relation. The subsequent sections concern themselves with the connections between law and economic relations, between law and class relations, and between gender relations and legal relations.

Law is ideological in a double sense which can be expressed in two theses:

1) Law emerges from an existing ideological field in which the norms and values associated with social relations are continuously asserted, proselytised, debated, abandoned, revised and generally struggled over.
2) The law is a major bearer or carrier of ideological messages which, because of the general legitimacy accorded to law, serve to reinforce and legitimate the ideology which the law carries.

In brief: law is ideologically constructed and is itself a significant (and possibly major) bearer of ideology.

The Marxist theory of ideology has been intensively debated (Larrain, 1983; Thompson, 1984; Callinicos, 1987). Without entering fully into this debate a position within it needs to be indicated. Ideology is not falsity (or false consciousness), nor is it a direct expression or 'reflection' of economic interests. Rather ideology is a contested grid of competing frames of reference through which people think and act.

The dominant ideology is the prevailing influence which comes closest to forming the 'commonsense' of the period and thus appearing as natural, normal and right. If we make the simplifying assumption that classes and other social groups have interests[9] then the dominant ideology will rarely, if ever, be simply the expression of the interests of the dominant class. More normally the dominant ideology will embrace some form of accommodation or adjustment to the interests of other participants in the power bloc[10] and will, to some degree, embody some elements of the interests of subordinate classes or groups secured either through earlier struggles or through compromises stemming from efforts to prevent or to deflect struggle; the current phenomena of ruling right-wing parties seeking to embrace green politics is a very visible example of this process. The key project of every dominant ideology is to cement together the social formation under the leadership of the dominant class. It is this process which Gramsci called hegemony (1971).

The content of legal rules provides a major instance of the condensation of ideology. Law has two important attributes as an ideological process. First, it offers a deep authoritative legitimation to the existing social order through the complex interaction whereby it manifests a generalised legitimacy, separated from the substantive content of its constituent rules. Secondly, because of its continuing legitimacy, it is linked to the particular content of its rules; that is, to the substantive values which it incorporates and expresses.

Modern democratic law occupies a position of special importance in contemporary capitalist societies. Law comes to fulfil an increasingly important role in the legitimation of the whole social order. There is a significant sense in which law moves to centre stage in the general hegemonic process. It comes to replace earlier modes of legitimacy as traditional authority (deference, patronage, and so on) and, in particular, religion weaken and decline.

This expanding role of legal ideology exhibits a number of different dimensions. In the first place modern democratic law involves a change in the form of legitimacy itself; it entails a movement towards impersonal, formal or abstract legitimation of social relations in which law becomes increasingly equated with reason. Second, in the crucial and frequently mobilised figure of law and order, the appeal to law is less and less the rule of order as law itself becomes associated with civilisation, peace and security. More and more the legitimation of social order makes appeal to law simply because it is law, and as such provides the grounds for the obligations of obedience by citizens. The third dimension sees law as the embodiment of the bond between citizen and nation, the people-nation, as law both constitutes and expresses the state's sovereignty.

The general thesis of the increasing centrality of legal ideology in modern capitalist societies is subject to an important qualification. It should not be presumed that the identification of some ideological theme justifies an assumption that it necessarily produces this 'ideology effect' in the consciousness and practices of all social agents. It is necessary to recognise that the legitimatory role of law, while real and important, is also fragile and volatile; its effects are not guaranteed nor do they operate in the same way with all classes, movements and social groups. Legal legitimation competes both with rival legitimations (such as utilitarian political legitimation, lifestyle cultures) and with counter-hegemonic ideologies.

The ideological character of law is also manifest with particular clarity in the conceptual apparatus of its substantive content. It is not so much that individual rules of law can or should be read as ideological; ideology cannot necessarily be read off from the form of words in which legal rules are expressed because to do so would fail to pay adequate regard to the specificity of legal rhetoric. Instead, ideological significance is associated with the key conceptual apparatus and the historical transformation of law that can be ascertained by attending to the shifts, recombinations, displacements and redundancies within this conceptual apparatus.

An adequate ideological reading of law would require a detailed historical treatment, but some features can be sketched. Central to the conceptual structure of modern democratic law are the concepts of property, contract and corporation. These ideas are evidence of the general importance of economic relations in providing the general character of capitalist law. Historically the conception of property separates itself from the doctrine of feudal estates and becomes part of a rights-discourse in which its content has land less and less as its presupposition and which becomes more abstract and universal. All economic relations manifesting either use-value or exchange-value become subsumed in a complex set of rights of deployment and of alienation. In this process we can also observe the way in which ideology conceived as a grid produces both a focusing or concentration (on the primacy of property rights as an extension of the individualising process of legal interpellation of subjects), but at the same time the ideological grid obscures significant differences within the field encompassed by the property conception.

Of particular significance is the conflation of the distinction between use-value and exchange-value. Central to the way in which legal conceptions legitimate capitalist property relations is that they annunciate property rights in individually owned consumption goods (use-value) alongside 'capital', investment resources mobilised within the economy and thus not privately consumed. In, understandably, wishing to protect their personal possessions citizens seem enjoined to associate themselves with the protection of all property rights, including those of capital. It is very noticeable that right-wing political discourses about property frequently conflate socialism's critique of capitalist property with an attack on all property. The ideological pay-off is witnessed in the construal of socialism as threatening the most basic interests in the private (or, more accurately, consumption) property of the 'ordinary citizen'.

The universalisation of the property concept is intimately linked to or is even swallowed by contract as the primary expression of the extension and penetration of exchange-relations.[11] However significant is the universalisation of economic relations, epitomised by the property-contract connection, it is important to stress that the full complexity of an ideological reading of law requires attention to the existence of a subsidiary counter-trend. Side by side with the universalisation of contractual relations and the wider process whereby many other relations become swallowed in the embrace of contractualisation, there is a persistent process of differentiation and separation. Of longstanding significance has been the separation of the contract of employment from the majority of legal systems; this attests to the special significance within capitalist relations of production of the capital–labour relation. Similar issues of separation-specialisation are manifested in the changing patterns whereby credit relations have been subject to special legal regulation.

This discussion of legal ideology makes no claim to completeness; it does, however, serve to put in place two major themes: first, the doubly ideological character of law and, second, the need for attention to the historical dynamic whereby the role and significance of legal ideology has expanded with modern democratic law. (For further and fuller discussion of law and ideology see Collins, 1982, Chapter 3; Hunt, 1985b; Poulantzas, 1978, pp.76–93; Sumner, 1979, Chapters 7, 8.)

Law and State

The relational approach highlights the importance of the law–state connection. It seeks to find a way of furthering our grasp of a connection which is close, but within which a significant degree of autonomy and separation of law from the state is manifest. Orthodox jurisprudence tends to be preoccupied with the issue of the identification and legitimation of the boundaries of legal control of individual conduct. Marxists should, although by no means all of them do, recognise that there are important issues and problems addressed within liberal jurisprudence's problematic. But Marxist theory of law needs to start its project by first undertaking a more descriptive or sociological account of the law–state connection. To do this we must distance ourselves from the myth of the unitary state (in which the state is conceived as a hierarchically organised set of institutions coming under the unified control of a sovereign institution such as 'the government' or 'executive') which misinforms both orthodox jurisprudence and much Marxist theory of law. The constitutionally sovereign body often deludes itself that it exercises central control over all state agencies, but this is constitutional fiction, not political fact.

Without embarking on a full investigation of state theory (see Poulantzas 1973; Jessop 1982) it is sufficient for present purposes to stress that the state is an institutional complex whose dynamic emerges from the tensions within and between state institutions. Coexisting and competing projects are pursued by different state agencies. While some are directed towards the cohesion of the state, such as those pursued in the course of the political projects of governments, it is equally common for agencies to operate in such a way as to create spheres of autonomy. The bureaucratic imperatives at work within state institutions frequently favour such functional separation. The legal system has a distinctive project of state unity whose ideological source stems from the theory of sovereignty epitomised by constitutional doctrines of parliamentary sovereignty; such accounts frequently clash with the projects pursued by governments which operate objectively to curtail the sphere of parliamentary competence. The unity of the state is always a project but it is one which is never realised.

The most difficult feature of the law–state relationship to give an account of is the manner in which the state is both within and outside the law. Even more important than the persistent reality and importance of state illegality, is that of the larger sphere of state action which is not unlawful but which is not subject to legal regulation or control. The critical issue is the way in which law marks out its own self-limitations. The ideological core of the modern state lies in the varieties of the idea of a state based on law (Rechtsstaat) epitomised by the constitutional doctrine of the rule of law. This powerful ideological motif coexists with legal renunciation, the self-conscious recognition of arenas of state action with which the courts will not interfere. The standard example is the exclusion of matters of 'national security' from legal scrutiny;[12] similarly concepts of the 'higher interests of the state' are invoked to remove aspects of the operations of the military and police from legal control. It should also be remembered that more 'normal' doctrines, in particular those surrounding legislative sovereignty, lead courts to adopt a self-denying posture in refusing intervention in matters of state policy. It is in this context that we should note the considerable variation in the degree of judicial review of state action which exists between modern capitalist states, and that these mark out real differences in the law–state connection with contemporary capitalist democracies.

It is only within those aspects of state activities that are subject to the possibility of legal control that law is able to play a coordinating and structuring role on the state apparatuses by stipulating boundaries of competence, resolving jurisdictional disputes and laying down procedural mechanisms. This role always remains a possible or potential role for law; the question of whether or not legal intervention actually plays out this role is one of the most interesting questions which denote the significant differences in the juridico-political structures between different state systems.

Legal ideology also pays a significant part in another dimension of the law–state relation in the process whereby diverse social classes, ethnic and regional groups are represented as forming the unity of 'the nation'. The key processes are the interpellation of people as 'citizens' invested with a degree of identity which displaces the separation and opposition of interests. The doctrine of sovereignty represents the unity of people/citizens as a unity of nation and state. This legal-constitutional imagery is supported and reinforced by means of powerful symbolism of flags, anthems, language and infinitely diverse manifestations of chauvinism which divide 'the people' from both internal and external 'others'.

It is within the law–state relationship that the important but difficult question of the relationship between coercion and consent needs to be posed. Marxists have historically stressed the repressive or coercive character of law; they have done so in order to redress the blindness of most liberal jurisprudence which has systematically played down the role of coercion and repression in the modern state. In reacting against the omissions of liberal theory, however, some Marxists have come perilously close to simply reversing liberalism's error by equating law with repression. The really difficult problem is to grasp the way in which repression is present in the course of the 'normal' operation of modern legal systems. One possible explanation along these lines posits a fall-back thesis: normally law operates more or less consensually, but in exceptional moments the repressive face of law is revealed. Such an account emphasises the role of special powers and emergency legislation as providing the means for the legal integration of repression.

The focus on legal exceptionalism is both important and potentially misleading. It draws attention to the capacity of the state to suspend the normal operation of the democratic process. At the same time, it is misleading in that it draws too stark a distinction between normal and exceptional conditions in such a way as to imply the absence of repression in the 'normal' functioning of law. The role of coercion is most apparent with respect to criminal law where participation in the legal process is generally non-voluntary (often following forcible detention) and criminal sanctions, especially imprisonment, are patently coercive.

A wide range of legal procedures are coercive and where they are deployed systematically set up patterns of repression. The role of the courts as debt enforcement agencies, able to order repossession, grant seizure powers to bailiffs and to attach incomes, runs counter to the liberal image of civil law as a mechanism for resolving disputes. Without proliferating examples it is evident that it is important to recognise the role of coercion and repression as a normal condition of the operation of law.

Economic Relations and the Law

A core question for Marxist theory of law is: what part does law play in the production and reproduction of the class relations that are characteristic of capitalist societies? While it is emphasised that there is an interactive connection between economic and legal relations, the focus adopted here will concentrate on the contribution of law to the reproduction of economic relations.

In the first instance a number of key legal relations form part of the conditions of existence for capitalist economic relations without which they could not function or would be able to do so only in a temporary or fragile manner. Law provides and guarantees a *regime of property*. In the discussion of ideology above attention was directed towards the universalisation which characterises the property relations of contemporary capitalism; the trajectory has been away from a unitary regime of individual legal owners exercising direct control over production, epitomised by the classical imagery of the factory owner standing by the gates of 'his' factory, selecting the workforce and organising the productive process. The expansion of the forms of capital, and their complex routes of circulation, requires a regime of property which recognises and protects multiple interests that fall short of an absolute right of ownership.

The development of the modern regime of property has given rise to the recognition of a complex of legal rights which coexist between multiple interests. It is necessary to consider the nature of law's contribution to this modern property regime. One possibility is that law does no more than give retrospective recognition to those economic relations which develop spontaneously in the course of economic change and innovation. If this is the case, law would have no causal significance and, in principle, might even be largely redundant, merely giving formal expression to already existing normative practices.[13]

This view of the legal relation as simply reflecting economic change is misleading; it assumes that informal normative mechanisms operate in the same way and with the same results as legal regulation. Heavily dependent on the idea that all that law adds is a slice of formality (it merely formalises that which already exists), this view ignores the extent to which legal relations have distinctive effects. The most important of these is the extent to which legal relations actually constitute economic relations. The most significant example is the formation of the modern corporation with limited liability; this is a legal creation in the important sense that it is precisely the ability to confer a legal status limiting the liability of participants that makes the relationship not only distinctive, but also a viable vehicle for the cooperation of capital drawn from a range of sources.

There is a more general context in which law, while not creating or constituting an economic relation, makes it possible for a social relation to exist in the complex form necessary to support and sustain its contemporary economic role. There are undisputed connections between the modern commercial contract and the simple act of barter. There is thus a superficial plausibility to the view that law merely reflects the prerequisites of economic life. However, this anthropological extrapolation breaks down in the face of the degree of specialisation of modern exchange relations, which involve a degree of complexity that could not be sustained within informal normative mechanisms. The modern contract must embrace contract planning for a wide range of potential variables. The same consideration affects the expansion of issues embraced in collective agreements between labour and capital, which necessitates a level of detailed specification that cannot be sustained within traditional notions of custom and practice.

It is important to stress the complex interaction that exists between legal and economic relations (Hunt 1988). Some of these features can be briefly indicated. First, for any set of economic relations to operate with any regularity they must do so within conditions of a reasonable and sustainable degree of social peace and security. In general law plays an important but not exclusive role in providing the general condition of personal security that allows us to get on with life in general and to participate in our economic roles as employees, consumers, and so on.

Second, legal doctrines and processes must make provision for the inter-relations of capital, through commercial law, insurance, banking and other financial services. One traditional way of identifying these activities is to speak of the conflict–resolution role of law. But it may be wise to avoid this formulation since it focuses too narrowly on litigation and the courts. It is probably more helpful to think of these mechanisms as background conditions which constitute the framework within which economic relations are conducted, that is as providing a mode of regulation.

Third, as has already been mentioned in the discussion of legal ideology, law provides the central conceptual apparatus of property rights, contract and corporate personality which plays a double role in both constituting a coherent framework for legal doctrine and providing significant components of the ideological discourses of the economy. In speaking of legal ideology it is important to avoid any suggestion that judicial rhetoric does, save in exceptional circumstances, directly enter the field of public debate. This does not imply that legal ideology and judicial rhetoric are unimportant. Their significance is that legal conceptions and frames of reference have come to play an increasingly central part in the public discourses of the media, politics and culture. Conceptions of rights, duties, responsibility, contract, property and the like, are persistent elements in public discourses, and the interpenetration of the legal and non-legal features of these discourses plays a significant part in explaining the reach and purchase of legal conceptions on popular consciousness.

Legal Relations and Class Relations

Another of the core questions for Marxist theory of law is: what contribution, if any, does law make to the reproduction of class relations? 'Class' is a disputed concept within Marxism. Put simply, the controversy centres around the question of whether classes are a strictly economic category, or whether some element of consciousness on the part of class members is involved. To avoid the need to debate this issue I will adopt the strategy of distinguishing between two overlapping conceptions of class, the 'immediate relations of production' and 'general class relations', dealing with each in turn.

Immediate relations of production centre on the connection between labour and capital embodied in the contract of employment. The legal relations of employment exhibit the characteristics of a distinctive form of law which, on the one hand, embodies the general features of contract doctrine (universality and individualisation) and, on the other, comprises a significant specialisation which in most modern legal systems marks off the contract of employment as distinct from other contractual forms. The individualising element of general contract doctrine represents the presupposition of a voluntary relation between formally equal legal subjects, whereas the specialisation of the contract of employment allocates distinctive sets of rights and duties to employer and employee. It is this combination of identity and difference which demonstrates the practical and ideological significance of the legal relation of employment. It constructs an apparent coherence within a framework which both denies and confirms the underlying inequality of the labour relation.

The regulation of the contract of employment, perhaps more than any other field of law, reveals the directly political character of law; labour law epitomises an integrated field of law and politics. This politicisation is apparent if we consider the legal response to trade unions as the distinctive form of organisation of labour in capitalist economies. There are two salient consequences of the development of trade unions. The first provides one of the most important illustrations of the way in which law expresses the historically changing balance of forces between labour and capital. From periods of simple illegality to times when legislation imposed recognition of trade unions upon employers, the content of the law has expressed the complex and shifting balance of forces. The second feature reveals the tension within legal doctrine. The classical individualistic core of contract doctrine presumes that the bargain is struck between individual employee and employer; yet the economic reality increasingly strips these parties of any significant role in determining the content of the labour contract, because the locus of bargaining has shifted to the collective agreement between trade union and employer. The complexity of labour law doctrine manifests the unstable tension between the form of law and its substantive content.

Aside from providing a basis for understanding the complex development of legal doctrine, this framework for analysis also discloses the difficulties associated with working out a political practice in this central arena of class relations. One illustration should indicate the complexity of political strategy in this field. The legislation of the British Conservative government since 1979 has been explicitly directed at weakening the position of the trade unions and reversing the gains made by organised labour since 1945. One important feature has been the imposition of legal controls over the internal procedures and democracy of trade unions; an example of this was the imposition of ballots prior to strike action. These proposals were bitterly resisted by the majority of unions on the grounds that the legislation infringed the self-governing autonomy of the unions. However the imposition of ballots has had the paradoxical effect of providing increased legitimacy for strike decisions taken after ballots. It is thus arguable that from the outset trade unions should have moved prior to legislation to incorporate ballots and other mechanisms which increase membership participation into their own procedures.[14]

Turning the role of law with respect to general class relations involves a shift of attention to the wider impact of law upon the broad pattern of social inequality and subordination (though it is important to stress that focus on 'class' does not exhaust the forms of inequality/subordination). Two general theses will be defended:

1) The aggregate effects of law in modern democratic societies work to the systematic disadvantage of the least advantaged social classes and groups.
2) The content, procedures and practice of law constitute an *arena of struggle* within which the relative positions and advantages of social classes are changed over time as a result of the interplay of struggles within the legal arena and those outside it.

The important point to be stressed is that these two theses are neither incompatible nor contradictory; they are both true at one and the same time. The first thesis, that law disadvantages the disadvantaged, operates at all levels of legal processes. I will assume that these unequal consequences are either self-evident or so well-evidenced in empirical studies as not to require support here. Substantive inequalities disadvantaging the working class (and other subordinate groups or classes) are embedded in the content of legal rules. The procedures of law, the discretion of legal agents (in particular the police), the remedies and sanctions of law, the accessibility of legal representation and many other dimensions all manifest unequal social effects. In order to produce a complete analysis of law's capacity to participate in and to reinforce the reproduction of social inequality it would be necessary to trace the detailed interaction between the different processes involved and, at the same time, to provide an analysis of the ideological effects and resonances of these processes.

The second thesis, about law as an arena of struggle, involves the outlines of an account of the historical trajectory of law as providing evidence of shifts and changes that are to be understood by reference to the play of social interests (material, symbolic and ideological) within a field of social struggle of which law and legal relations are a component. The class analysis of legal doctrine requires some means of registering and establishing the connection between economic interests and the categories of legal doctrine.

An adequate theory of the dynamics of law and class needs to focus on how interests and claims are translated and transformed through the discourses of law. It is here that Marxist theory of law must come directly into contact with the concerns of liberal jurisprudence about the nature of judicial reasoning. Yet this does not involve a simple adoption of jurisprudence's problematic.

The difficulty to be confronted in developing a Marxist approach to judicial law-making is to avoid any assumption of the direct transposing of social interests into legal rights. Rather it needs to attend to the manner in which social interests are translated into rights-claims, and the degree of 'fit' between those claims and the prevailing form of law expressed in existing legal rights. Analysis of this type generates hypotheses such as: claims capable of translation into a discourse of individual rights and those interests congruent with existing rights categories are more likely to succeed than claims not matching these characteristics. This line of enquiry is fuelled by empirical evidence which suggests that different social movements of the disadvantaged meet with markedly different success when pursuing social change through law. The exploration of such issues fits well with the general concern of Marxism that its theory should be able to generate political strategy.

Gender Relations and Legal Relations

The connection between legal and gender relations exhibits an interesting paradox in that it is marked by both persistence and variability. The persistence is to be found in the near universality of gender inequality being expressed and reinforced through legal rules and procedures, while the form and content of that inequality exhibit great variation in the forms of disadvantage which law inscribes in the relations between women and men and between particular categories of women.

Marxist theory has exhibited considerable difficulties in coming to grips with gender relations. Marxism played a historically progressive role in its early recognition of the persistence of the subordination of women. It sought to provide a general historical explanation of the origins of oppression through focusing on the connection between property relations and unequal gender relations (Engels 1970). On the other hand Marxism's tendency to accord priority to economic relations has persistently submerged the specificity of gender relations under the general primacy accorded to class relations. This tension attests either to an as yet incomplete theoretical project of understanding the interconnection between gender and class – a project which has been taken up by socialist feminism. Or, alternatively, it may be that Marxism is incapable of resolving this theoretical tension – a conclusion pressed by radical feminism.

The uncertain condition of Marxism with respect to gender seriously handicaps the capacity of Marxist theory of law to offer a developed account of the connection between gender relations and legal relations. The comments that follow should therefore be regarded as very tentative. They are motivated by an attempt to understand the paradox referred to above concerning the persistence and variability of the law–gender connection.

One route to making sense of this paradox stresses the importance of a continuing attempt to identify the origins of the subordination of women. The significance of the quest for the origins of oppression stems from the suggestion that whatever these originating circumstances may have been, subsequently the oppression of women has been ideologically reproduced and has persisted beyond the socioeconomic conditions that generated it. The emphasis on the ideological reproduction of the subordination of women has two important consequences. First it suggests that it is precisely this ideological reproduction which is the reason for the very diversity of the legal forms this oppression has taken. Second it suggests the political conclusion that the primary arena of the struggle against oppression is ideological and revolves around the multiple and complex processes through which gender difference is socially constructed. This emphasis on ideology should not be understood as denying or marginalising the role of economic and political struggles; rather it suggests that material issues around, for instance, pay equity or child care, are manifestations of the ideological construction of gender.

It follows that the connection between gender relations and legal relations can best be understood as exemplifying a situation in which legal relations are the bearers of ideological determinations, where these legal relations play a significant but prescribed role in their constitution and legitimation. In its simplest form this suggestion is that, with regard to gender, law plays a narrowly ideological role. For example, while the institution of marriage is a legally constituted relation it also exemplifies the role of law as a distributive mechanism assigning differential rights and duties between the parties. Yet the distributed benefits and burdens do not originate in legal doctrine but rather reflect the prevailing ideological construction of gender relations. At the same time the legal form imposes definite limits upon the content that can be borne by the legal rules. The general trend of legal relations towards universalisation produces a pressure towards formal equality. This process is by no means automatic as is witnessed by the resistance from most legal jurisdictions to the recognition of marital rape. This predisposition to favour formal equality, however, suggests that struggles around the legal reform of gender relations are likely to favour those reforms whose content most closely approximates to formal equality. Conversely, legal reform is likely to lend itself less effectively to programmes of affirmative action or substantive equality which conflict with the presuppositions of formal equality.

The tentative nature of these observations on the connection between gender relations and legal relations underlines the absences and uncertainties with which Marxist theory confronts the field of sex–gender relations.

Conclusions

This essay has been concerned to outline a general framework for a Marxist theory of law. There are inevitably issues that have been omitted or passed over. Most significantly I have had almost nothing to say about the history of Marxist work on law, whether of Marx or of more recent Western Marxism. Consequently I have had little to say about how the position which I argue relates to the wider currents and themes within the ever-growing body of Marxist theory. But in default of addressing these issues I do need to make it clear that my position is contestable and would not be acceptable to many shades of opinion within the Marxist tradition.

There is one other omission which I do want, albeit briefly, to comment upon; it concerns the relationship between Marxist theory of law and orthodox jurisprudence. The agendas of Marxist theory and jurisprudence overlap but do not converge. Marxism gives prominence to issues omitted or marginalised within jurisprudence, such as the repressive role of law and its fundamentally political character. In these and other respects Marxism can provide a much needed supplement to jurisprudence by its stress on the rootedness or connectedness of law with social, cultural and economic relations. It provides a powerful source of resistance to the prevalent tendency within orthodox jurisprudence to treat law as disconnected, even autonomous, as being capable of study in and of itself. Marxism further refutes the timeless or ahistorical quality of much liberal jurisprudence. Marxism insists that the role and place of law are always consequences of a concrete and historically specific dynamic of the interaction of institutions and practices.

If Marxism supplements jurisprudence, it should not simply seek to negate or displace orthodox jurisprudence. The pervasive jurisprudential issues – such as the grounds for the obligations of citizens to obey the law, the means of determining the proper limits of state action and the conditions under which it is permissible to restrain the conduct of citizens – are also important questions for Marxism. Not only are these issues important questions within modern capitalist democracies, but history is currently teaching us most forcibly that these issues are ones which should have been on the agenda of Marxism's political project of building socialism. The contemporary revolutions in Eastern Europe hold many important lessons; one of the more important is that the renewal of socialism requires not the withering away of law, but the realisation of a legal order that enhances and guarantees the conditions of political and economic democracy that facilitates democratic participations and restrains bureaucratic and state power.

The implication is that a Marxist approach to law will be concerned not only with characteristically jurisprudential issues, but also with the potential contributions of legal strategies to achieving effective political strategies for the social movements that reflect the Marxist political and ethical commitment to the poor and the oppressed.

Notes

1. The reference to 'structural' inequalities stresses that the most important inequalities of class, race and gender are manifestations of relations which are structural in the sense that they define the general characteristics of a particular form of social life. For example, paid or wage labour and a sexual division of domestic labour are two structural features of modern capitalist societies which go a long way to influence many other features of such societies.
2. Despite the burgeoning literature of Marxist theory of law (MTL) that has appeared since the late 1970s there has as yet been no attempt to trace its historical development.
3. My contention that the themes within MTL exist in more or less sophisticated form marks a significant difference from Hugh Collins' (1982) interesting and stimulating overview and intervention in MTL. He distinguishes between two general approaches, 'crude materialism' (corresponding to theme 3) and 'class instrumentalism' (theme 5). He argues for the rejection of the former and in favour of developing 'a sophisticated version of class instrumentalist theory of law' (1982, p.34). My point is that all or any of the themes I have identified can and do exist in unsatisfactory or 'crude' form or can be developed into more satisfactory 'sophisticated' expressions.
4. To talk about 'the law' in the singular is strictly unsatisfactory because it implies a degree of unity and centralisation which misrepresents the real complexity of the variety of laws, within which 'state law' is generally paramount and which continually seeks to assert control over the diverse forms of law which make up the richness of legal phenomena (legal pluralism).
5. For a discussion of the connection between law, citizenship and politics see Hall and Held, 1989.
6. These brief comments on the relative autonomy thesis take no account of more recent attempts to provide a more rigorous version. For example, Louis Althusser and Etienne Balibar, using the concepts of overdetermination and structural causality, produced a more sophisticated version of relative autonomy theory (Althusser, 1969, pp.87–128; Althusser and Balibar, 1970, pp.216–33; for a criticism of the Althusserian solution see Cutler *et al.* 1977, Vol. I, pp.229–42).
7. Evgeny Pashukanis was a leading figure in Soviet legal circles in the 1920s; his major work *A General Theory of Law and Marxism* was first published in 1924. The clear political message that flowed from his theoretical position was that law was of only transitory significance for the young Soviet republic since as it progressed towards achievement of communism the need for law would wither away. This view sat uncomfortably with the project of developing a specifically 'socialist law' which became an integral part of the state-building activities associated with Stalin's 1936 Constitution. Pashukanis became increasingly isolated and he was liquidated in 1937. His work has recently become available and his reputation rehabilitated in the

Soviet Union. His work remained largely unnoticed in the West until the renaissance of Marxist scholarship in the late 1960s and the emergence of an active debate around MTL in the mid 1970s.

8. That Pashukanis should adopt this position was particularly strange since as a Russian and a Bolshevik of some experience he must have been familiar with Lenin's important early analysis of the development of capitalism in Russia. Lenin's key insight was that capitalist development came about not so much from the development of independent commodity production or the importation of foreign capital, but through the slow but inexorable capitalist transformation of backward, semi-feudal Russian agriculture (Lenin, 1960; Hunt, 1976).

9. The identification of class interests involves a simplification because interests are not pre-ideological and are thus only formed in the context of an ideological framework which influences the content of the apparently objective interests.

10. The concept of power bloc derives from Gramsci and makes the point that no class is entirely homogeneous or ever rules alone, but rather involves the formation of a bloc of a diverse section of the dominant class along with major and minor allies whose interests and ideology must be welded together in a more or less stable set of compromises.

11. A pioneering analysis of the complementarity of property and contract was made by Karl Renner (1949). His work provides an interesting counterpoint to Pashukanis' work discussed above; despite its rather positivistic and functionalist character it deserves more attention than it has received with recent discussions of MTL.

12. It is important to recognise that there is considerable national variation; the British courts have historically been much more prepared to concede large areas of state autonomy from legal scrutiny than have, for example, the US courts.

13. The argument which follows can be read as a criticism of Hugh Collins' 'solution' to the 'legal problem in Marx' which relies on the distinction between 'social rules', reflecting the requirements of the dominant ideology, and 'legal rules', which remain superstructural (Collins, 1982, pp.84–90).

14. That the paradoxical nature of trade union law is not confined to the topic of strike ballots is indicated by the fact that the imposition of direct elections for trade union office, and of membership ballots before a trade union may establish a political fund, has increased membership participation and caused the unions to improve significantly their communication and contact with their members. These examples are good illustrations of the unintended consequences of law, that is where legislative policy results in outcomes at variance with those intentions.

Further Reading

Beirne, P. and Quinney, R. (eds) (1982) *Marxism and Law* (New York: John Wiley).
Cain, M. and Hunt, A, (1979) *Marx and Engels on Law* (London: Academic Press).
Collins, H. (1982) *Marxism and Law* (Oxford: Oxford University Press).
Hall, S. *et al.* (1978) *Policing the Crisis: Mugging, the State, and Law and Order* (London: Macmillan).
Hirst, P. (1979) *On Law and Ideology* (London: Macmillan).
Sumner, C. (1979) *Reading Ideologies: An Investigation into the Marxist Theory of Ideology and Law* (London: Academic Press).

References

Althusser, L. (1969) *For Marx* (Harmondsworth: Penguin).
Althusser, L. and Balibar, E. (1970) *Reading Capital* (London: New Left Books).
Beirne, P. and Sharlet, R. (eds), (1980) *Pashukanis: Selected Writings on Marxism and Law* (London: Academic Press).
Cain, M. and Hunt, A. (1979) *Marx and Engels on Law* (London: Academic Press).
Callinicos, A. (1987) *Making Histories* (Cambridge: Polity Press).
Collins, H. (1982) *Marxism and Law* (Oxford: Oxford University Press).
Cutler, A., Hindess, B., Hirst, P., and Hussain, A. (1977) *Marx's 'Capital' and Capitalism Today*, 2 vols, (London: Routledge & Kegan Paul).
Engels, F. (1970) *The Origin of the Family, Private Property and the State* (London: Lawrence & Wishart).
Foucault, M. (1980) *Power/Knowledge: Selected Interviews and Other Writings*, ed. C. Gordon (Brighton: Harvester Press).
Gramsci, A. (1971) *Selections from the Prison Notebooks of Antonio Gramsci*, ed. Q. Hoare and G. Nowell Smith (London: Lawrence & Wishart).
Hall, S. and Held, D (1989) 'Left and Rights', *Marxism Today*, Vol. 33, pp.16–23.
Hunt, A. (1976) 'Lenin and Sociology', *Sociological Review*, vol. 24, no. 1, pp.5–22.
Hunt, A. (1981) 'The Politics of Law and Justice' in D. Adlam *et al.* (eds), *Law, Politics & Justice: Politics & Power IV* (London: Routledge & Kegan Paul), pp.3–26.
Hunt, A. (1985) 'The Ideology of Law', *Law and Society Review*, vol. 19, no. 1, pp.11–37.
Hunt, A. (1988) 'On Legal Relations and Economic Relations', in R.N. Moles (ed.), *Law and Economics* (Stuttgart: Franz Steiner), pp.57–82.
Jessop, B. (1982) *The Capitalist State* (Oxford: Martin Robertson).
Larrain, J. (1983) *Marxism and Ideology* (London: Macmillan).
Lenin, V.I. (1960) 'The Development of Capitalism in Russia' [1899], in *Lenin Collected Works*, vol. 3 (London: Lawrence & Wishart), pp.23–607.

132   *Dangerous Supplements*

Marx, K. (1971) *A Contribution to the Critique of Political Economy*, ed. M. Dobb (London: Lawrence & Wishart).

Marx, K. (1973) *Grundrisse: Introduction to the Critique of Political Economy* (Harmondsworth: Penguin).

Marx, K. (1975) *Marx-Engels Selected Correspondence* (Moscow: Progress).

Pashukanis, E. (1978) *Law and Marxism*, ed. C. Arthur (London: Ink Links).

Poulantzas, N. (1973) *Political Power and Social Classes* (London: New Left Books).

Poulantzas, N. (1978) *State, Power, Socialism* (London: New Left Books).

Renner, K. (1949) *The Institutions of Private Property and their Social Functions* (London: Routledge & Kegan Paul).

Sumner, C. (1979) *Reading Ideologies* (London: Academic Press).

Thompson, J. (1984) *Studies in the Theory of Ideology* (Oxford: Polity Press).

Williams, R. (1977) *Marxism and Literature* (Oxford: Oxford University Press).

Feminist Jurisprudence

Carol Smart

Introduction

Until quite recently the subject of jurisprudence in law schools has failed to address itself to, or defend itself against, the growing feminist challenge to its orthodoxy. Feminist jurisprudence has not been taken seriously although, as I hope to show here, it poses a very real threat to the complacency of traditional jurisprudential thinking. One small indication that this neglect might be changing can be found in the criticism that Freeman (1987) has directed at the major text on jurisprudence that he co-edits (Lloyd and Freeman, 1985). In his auto-critique he points out that only three of the papers in the extensive collection (over 100 extracts) are by women, and that probably only one could be called a feminist. He rightly admits that this is a failing. However, we should not assume from this that jurisprudence is about to undergo radical transformations. The addition of one or two feminist articles to a major teaching text might indicate that there is such a thing as feminist legal scholarship but it would not transform the subject. Yet this is precisely what feminist jurisprudence wishes to achieve.

I shall argue in this paper that traditional jurisprudence can neither assimilate nor continue to avoid feminist legal scholarship. Feminism has gradually and painstakingly created a fundamental critque of orthodox jurisprudence which insists that all the taken-for-granted assumptions about universality, objectivity and neutrality are swept aside to make room for a completely different conception of law and its underpinnings. Feminist legal scholarship is no longer assuming the stance of a supplicant requesting that the orthodoxy hears the case for women's rights or extends the benefits of objectivity and neutrality to the female legal subject. Rather, feminist work has shown that the foundations on which jurisprudence rest are deeply imbued with a masculine perspective and privilege. Moreover it has become clear that what is required is either a radical transformation or an abandonment of jurisprudence altogether.

This chapter will therefore briefly map the development of feminist jurisprudence from its early conception in the first feminist movement of the nineteenth century. It should then be possible to

133

see how different interpretations of jurisprudence have been favoured at different times, or how certain developments seem to coincide with other developments in specific geopolitical spaces (that is, the USA as compared to Europe). To do this I shall construct certain categories in which the different schools of thought can be located. However, the reader should recognise that this is a device to untangle what might otherwise appear to be a complex web of inter-connections with no beginnings or ends. I shall construct a story of feminist jurisprudence, but there will be other stories that remain to be told and the categorisations I use should not become fixed and rigid.

Tentative Beginnings

Mitchell (1987) has argued that the history of feminist thought and the history of the idea of equality are virtually synonymous. From the seventeenth century onwards, she argues, the notion of equality informed individual feminist demands or, perhaps more accurately, the concept of equality provided the political and conceptual context in which a feminist voice could be constructed. The work of Mary Wollstonecraft (1975, but first published in 1792) is an example of how the growth of liberalism as a philosophy allowed women to make demands for freedom, equality and personhood in the way that disenfranchised men had been able to. As Mitchell argues,

> feminism as a conscious, that is self-conscious, protest movement, arose as part of a revolutionary bourgeois tradition that had equa-lity of mankind as its highest goal. The first expressions of femi-nism were endowed with the strengths of the concept of equality and circumscribed by its limitations. (Mitchell, 1987, p.31)

Perhaps the most significant 'limitation' to which Mitchell refers is the way in which the individual in liberal thought is constructed as a fully autonomous being and as capable of competing on equal terms with others within the parameters of a capitalist economic system. The liberal concept of equality therefore demanded demo-cracy *within* capitalism (and patriarchy) rather than a transformation of the economic and cultural system itself. The broad notion of equality did not become condensed into the narrower and more practically applicable notion of 'equal rights' until the last half of the nineteenth century. Mitchell argues that it was at the point that feminism became an organised political force (a movement rather than a scattering of individuals) that demands were coalesced into demands for equal legal rights. There is a world of difference between the work of early feminists like Mary Wollstonecraft who discussed the subjugation of women in terms of the stunting of women's personalities and talents, the limitations of women's educational horizons, the power of social mores to restrict women's activities and the overwhelmingly stifling effects of sexual morality, and the later work of J.S. Mill and Harriet Taylor (1869) or Caroline Norton (1982), Frances Power Cobbe (1878) or Barbara Leigh Bodichon (1869) who were more interested in specific legal rights. From the middle to the turn of the nineteenth century feminist demands increasingly took the form of narrowly conceived reforms to law or equal rights claims. So while law did not feature in Wollstonecraft's exegesis in the eighteenth century, it became a central focus for later feminists.

We can therefore argue that the nineteenth century marks the beginnings of a feminist jurisprudence, even though such a conceptualisation would have been quite foreign to feminists then. The principles of this jurisprudence were synonymous with the liberal philosophy of equal rights. However, feminist campaigns around law were always grounded in the material restrictions that women encountered, for example bars to entering universities and professions, marriage laws which deprived them of almost all legal rights, or absolute restrictions on political participation. It should also be appreciated that this focus on law was not simply a reflection of the narrow horizons of bourgeois women in the nineteenth century. Law had begun to play a very specific role in the oppression of women in the eighteenth and nineteenth centuries. This period marked a major growth in legislative activity when women's 'disabilities' became codified rather than simply being a matter of common law or practice.

The law could, therefore, be identified as a very real obstacle to women. It formalised their social and economic disabilities and, in many ways, extended and legitimised them. Moreover, as law became the vehicle for extending rights to categories of men, it expressly excluded women. This gave law the appearance of being the source of the 'problem', or at least the potential solution to the problem. Hence feminist campaigns focused on the injustice of law and its denial of basic rights and freedoms to women. It would, however, be erroneous to imagine that all feminist demands of law took the form of equality claims. In fact from the middle of the nineteenth century we can see the emergence of the alternative strategy of making claims based on difference. What we now refer to as the equality/difference debate in feminist analysis of law has a very early precedent in the work of Caroline Norton in the 1860s and later on can be seen in the work of Eleanor Rathbone in the 1920s. Both of these early feminists eschewed equality in favour of demands based on the special position or qualities of women as mothers. Rathbone, who was required to justify her stance by equal rights feminists, argued that the law should reflect the situation in which women find themselves and that women's greatest needs were in the sphere of motherhood, which had nothing to do with questions of equality and equal pay.

A fundamental difference of view was therefore apparent in the first wave of the feminist movement. These two opposing strategies of equality and difference in legal campaigns reflected competing concepts of justice and fairness. One model saw justice epitomised in the desserts law meted out to men and required the same standard for women. The other model took the 'reality' of women's lives as its starting point and argued that law should be moulded to meet existing needs. It is important to recognise, however, that these early feminists were not in the business of constructing models of justice in an abstract way. Few women were to be found in the universities and none in the legal profession. Early feminist thoughts on jurisprudence therefore stemmed directly from campaigning and the largely middle-class background of the women involved. Thus, while later feminist work in this area retains these elements of conflict between equality and difference, the corpus has been significantly altered by the entrance of women into the academy and law schools, and also into politics and law-making. In particular we see the growth of a self-conscious theoretical orientation rather than a reliance on appeals to apparently self-evident notions of justice and fairness. From the 1960s onwards we therefore witness rapid changes to what we can call feminist jurisprudence and it is to these developments I shall now turn.

Feminist Jurisprudence and the Second Wave of the Women's Movement

The second wave of the women's movement began at the end of the 1960s and beginning of the 1970s. Although it has been argued that there has always been a women's movement (Spender, 1983) there is no doubt that this period marked a revival of feminist politics on a wide scale in North America and Europe. The 1960s and 70s were a period of economic and cultural optimism and, in Western 'developed' countries, these decades marked a time of legislative activity which focused on pressing social problems such as divorce, abortion, child benefit, equal pay and sex discrimination, racial discrimination, capital punishment, housing and many other issues (Hall, 1980; Smart, 1984). There developed a strong commitment to radical lawyering in which lawyers were seen as crucial to the battle against injustice and inadequate civil rights and provisions. The identification of social problems met with a variety of legislative responses aimed at relieving the problem, or at least some of its symptoms.

By the end of the 1970s the political climate had changed. Not only were progressive social reforms to become a thing of the past but certain gains were to be challenged. In any case feminists had begun to have renewed doubts about the usefulness of law reform. But by this time they were themselves practising and academic lawyers. It was this combination of factors, most especially in the USA, that provided the foundations for feminist jurisprudence. On the one hand feminists wanted explanations about why law reforms had achieved so little when they seemed to promise so much, and on the other hand feminists had moved into the very heartland of law and legal practice. They had come to know its operations inside and out and were able to identify that it was not only legislation which was the problem, but such accepted elements as legal reasoning, ethics and concepts of justice, objectivity and what MacKinnon (1983) has called the maleness of law. Feminist legal scholarship found itself in a position to challenge fundamentally the traditional premises of law and legal knowledge. This discovery of the limitations of law was not a naive rediscovery of what social scientists claimed already to know, but an insider's discovery which was able to locate with much more subtlety the kind of resistance law could produce in response to threatened changes. So for feminists closely involved in law the emphasis shifted from being one of optimism and campaigning to taking law more seriously as the emphasis of analytical study.

What we might call a self-conscious feminist jurisprudence arose out of this specific historical moment and has really been framed to address questions like 'what is wrong with law?', 'why do rights framed to overcome discrimination against women serve to benefit men?', or 'why do law and legal practice work against the interests of women?' It has very different antecedents to more traditional forms of jurisprudence and, in the main, it is not interested in creating abstract or philosophical models to explain the origins or legitimacy of law. Feminist jurisprudence to date has therefore taken the form of a critique although some feminists are beginning to suggest moral or ethical principles which might replace existing legal principles in an attempt radically to transform the form and content of law.[1]

The development of feminist jurisprudence has not taken the form of a linear and chronological ordering of ideas, but rather a scattered and somewhat tangential set of thoughts, some developing in the USA and others in Europe and Australia, some within the field of civil law and others with a more specific concern with criminal law.

There are key writers who shall be examined in some detail, for instance Tove Stang Dahl (1987), Catharine MacKinnon (1982, 1983, 1987) and Carol Gilligan (1982). However, the movement towards feminist jurisprudence goes much wider than these contributions. For this reason it is perhaps useful to try to group together the feminist work in this field into different categories. Instead of relying on traditional categorisations of radical, socialist, cultural feminism and so on, I propose to use loose groupings based on the focus of the work. The categories I have identified are: the master theory approach; the experiential/epistemological approach; the psychological/modes of reasoning approach, and the social justice/ harm approach. Some authors fit into more than one category and the boundaries between all four inevitably blur under close scrutiny.

The Master Theory Approach

By the master theory approach (or meta-narrative) I mean the attempt to account for everything in relation to one mode of explanation. Thus in the 1970s many scholars insisted that Marxist theories of capital could account for 'everything' worth accounting for. This meant that they argued that racial and sexual oppression either could be explained by reference to class oppression or that these forms of oppression were so insignificant that they did not require explanation. Feminism includes a variant of this approach in the tendency to assume that every significant phenomenon can be accounted for by reference to the operations of patriarchy or the needs of men.

The urge to produce the one theory which would account for the oppression of (all) women became evident in feminist work in the 1970s. It is therefore unsurprising to find that it is a strand in some of the early work on feminist jurisprudence. There are two prime examples of this genre which I shall examine. The first is by Rifkin (1980) which seeks to sketch out for us the whole story of the origins of law and patriarchy, and the second is by MacKinnon (1982, 1983) who has constructed the most precise version of a meta-narrative in feminist legal scholarship and who has set the parameters for later work in the USA and, more recently, elsewhere.

Janet Rifkin's article entitled 'Toward a Theory of Law and Patriarchy' was published in 1980. It marked an important shift away from the established 'sexism and law' paradigm in which feminists would expose exactly how sexist were the legislation, the legal and criminal process, and the judges. Rifkin stood on the threshold of the concept of feminist jurisprudence but did not in fact use the term. Her aim was to provide a framework in which the fundamental connections between culture, patriarchy and law could be revealed. She speaks of law in terms of a paradigm of maleness and this marks a major shift away from the empirically correct, although analytically limited, observation that men make and operate the law. Consequently she achieves a shift of emphasis away from men as biological beings towards the problem of masculinity and masculine values which are cultural constructs rather than biological facts.

Her argument is that patriarchal culture originates at the moment of this exchange, at which point women become property. This is a complex argument which requires some knowledge of structural anthropology. But Rifkin is really using this framework as a device to persuade us that two major developments occurred at the same moment. These developments are firstly, the beginnings of culture which is founded upon patriarchal values (that is, the exchange of women) and secondly, the creation of property whereby women (along with cattle, tools and so on) become a form of commodity or property. Onto this she grafts the familiar idea that law has two main functions, namely the protection of (men's) property and the mystification of the real nature of this patriarchal arrangement (or culture). So while setting law into a cultural context derived from a structuralist school of anthropology, she engages the idea of law as ideology, using ideology as meaning mystification derived from a version of Marxist thought. Law is therefore a distortion of the reality while justifying the subordination and oppression of women and celebrating masculine values. The point that is so interesting about the article is not this rather crude conspiracy thesis as much as her assertion that law is grounded in the oppression of women because it is grounded in culture. Whether or not we accept this account as it stands, Rifkin provides a coherent argument against the prevailing notion that when sexism occurs it is an epiphenomenon which can be dealt with fairly superficially by the introduction of more or different legislation. Here we have an insightful hint as to how difficult the feminist project in law and jurisprudence is going to be. Her assertion that the paradigm of law is a symbol of male authority marks the beginnings of a new mode of conceptualisation.

Catharine MacKinnon's major contribution to this field came in two linked articles published in the US feminist journal *Signs* in 1982 and 1983. Although her work has developed since, these two papers provide the theoretical coherence for her later work (1987). The first article was entitled 'Feminism, Marxism, Method, and the State: An Agenda for Theory'. In this MacKinnon develops a theory of women's oppression which closely parallels Marx's early theory of exploitation and alienation. She argues that 'Sexuality is to feminism what work is to Marxism: that which is most one's own, yet most taken away' (1982, p.515). So, modifying Marxism, she embarks on her own version of the meta-narrative by substituting sex for work (or labour) to produce a compelling framework which takes sexual exploitation as the basis of women's oppression. She is also able to argue that all women have this one thing in common, and that what they have in common is more significant than their differences. She argues that she is constructing a theory of power and, implicitly, it is one which will explain the oppression of all women at all times. So for example she states,

> Feminists do not argue that it means the same to women to be on the bottom in a feudal regime, a capitalist regime, and a socialist regime; the commonality argued is that, despite real changes, bottom is bottom. (ibid., p.523)

Having identified sex as the core of women's oppression and men's power, MacKinnon goes on to argue that men also have the power to define the world (and hence make it real) from their own perspective. This male point of view is taken to be objectivity. In turn this is taken to be the only possible reality: the real truth of things. This male gaze is turned on women to produce them as men wish to define them. This process MacKinnon describes as objectification; women are objectified. This is the defining characteristic of women's sexuality, that is it is objectified by and for men. In constructing this complex argument MacKinnon is making important links between power and knowledge and the power to define. In her theory women are the victims of this process, but feminism can construct its own method of resistance. This method is consciousness-raising by which women can collectively and critically reconstitute 'the meaning of women's social experience, as women live through it' (ibid., p.543). So, while standing inside the reality constructed by the male perspective, women can collectively redefine their experiences and produce an alternative critical and reflexive form of knowledge. MacKinnon does not pursue this in detail but in outline we are provided with the basis of a feminist theory of knowledge to counter what she regards as 'male' epistemology (which passes itself off as objectivity). She constructs feminism in opposition to male power. In her work feminism is what reveals the workings of male power and the extent to which women's experience has been devalued.

In the second article, 'Feminism, Marxism, Method and the State: Toward Feminist Jurisprudence', MacKinnon turns her focus on law which is for her a straightforward extension of the state. She writes, 'As a beginning, I propose that the state is male in the feminist sense. The law sees and treats women the way men see and treat women.' (1983, p.644). She argues that jurisprudence as currently constituted is the institutionalisation of objectivity (that is, a male perspective which is also male power). She explores this argument through the example of rape and the parallel between men's inability to differentiate between rape and intercourse and the law's inability to do so as well. From this starting point MacKinnon is able to elaborate a complex argument which shows that only from a woman's point of view is rape an injury. Because the legal system insists that rape only occurs when a man has a guilty intent, if he does not perceive what he does as being anything other than sex, then neither will the law. Hence as far as the law is concerned she is not violated; there was no injury; she simply had sex. As men have no glimmer of an insight into what women want, MacKinnon goes on to argue, accusations of rape are truly mystifying to them. The point is, however, that the law reflects the male understanding rather than the experience of the woman who has been violated.

What is so important about this analysis is that it reveals the depth of the problem of law. It is clear here that the problem is not going to be successfully tackled without challenging fundamental principles of neutrality, objectivity and meaning (knowledge). The jurisprudence that MacKinnon is moving towards is therefore not concerned with concepts of equality or fairness; instead she is concerned with how male power is exercised in the guise of the neutral and objective standards of law. She does not provide a blueprint for a feminist jurisprudence, rather, in this early article, she aims to expose the maleness of law.

The question that must be asked, however, is how much of an advance is her conclusion that law (including legal reasoning and values) is male on the earlier (vulgar) Marxist analysis that law is bourgeois? Here again we encounter the problem of the master theory. Having identified sexuality as the mainspring of women's oppression, MacKinnon quite logically focuses on rape to make her points about law and jurisprudence. The logic is seamless and the argument extremely powerful. But the same could be said for Marxist analyses which identify the exploitation of labour as the mainspring of class oppression and then point to labour/trade union legislation as proof that law merely reflects (or is synonymous with) the interests of the capitalist class. These arguments assume the unity of the state and the unity of law. They also assume that law is merely an arm of the state and that there exists a coherent set of interests which are always smoothly met. MacKinnon gives us a partial story and attempts to convince us that it is all that needs to be said about law and jurisprudence. She argues that her analysis which identifies the basis of women's oppression (sex), the process by which oppression is achieved (objectification) and the methodology for challenging oppression as well as providing the basis of a new form of knowledge (consciousness-raising) supercedes Marxism as a satisfactory version of events. Yet the claim is too sweeping, not because Marxism cannot be superceded but because the theory deals with race and class only by collapsing them into gender oppression. Just as Marxism has collapsed gender and race into class so MacKinnon's approach gives no room for other oppressions. She falls into the seductive trap of the master theory in attempting to explain everything and the value of her critique of jurisprudence risks becoming lost in the attempt to beat Marxism at a game that it is probably no longer playing (Fryer *et al.*, 1981).

The Experiential/Epistemological Approach
This loose category embraces work which gives priority to women's experience as a basis for jurisprudence and for a new way of knowing. It is committed to the production of a new epistemology which can form a concrete base from which to reject or criticise orthodox or male forms of knowledge, and hence jurisprudence. These ideas are prefigured in MacKinnon's work but are developed differently by other feminists. The two main orientations to be found in this work also coincide with geopolitical variations. Hence the MacKinnon approach is developed in the work of North American legal feminists, while a more social scientific approach has been developed by feminists in Scandinavia. What they have in common is the claim that women's experience must be revealed and communicated in order to transform the form and content of law and prevailing concepts of justice and fairness. While the North Americans rely on the method of consciousness-raising to achieve this, the work of the Institute of Women's Law in Oslo depends on the methods of social scientific research informed by feminism.

Experience, consciousness-raising and epistemology
Lahey (1985) provides an excellent example of the first (North American) approach to feminist jurisprudence. Avoiding any hint of liberalism she argues that 'The struggle for feminist representation in the production of knowledge is ... a political struggle' (p.522). Her paper does not aim for a feminist certainty to replace patriarchal knowledge, nor does it claim that consciousness-raising produces a truth to replace the patriarchal lie. Rather she develops an argument in which conciousness-raising can be seen as a method to produce moments of knowing. She argues against hierarchies of knowledge and is undisturbed that this method produces different knowledges and different subjectivities. For Lahey feminist method is a voyage into ambiguities and uncertainties. Certainty is part of objectivity, which she insists is merely male subjectivity elevated to a realm of universality and neutrality as a consequence of the workings of male power. For her there is no neutral space, knowledge cannot reside outside of politics and one's own point of view.

Lahey does not claim that consciousness-raising is a perfect method either; she sees it as a continuing, imperfect struggle. Her main tenet, however, is that consciousness-raising produces feminist theory, but it is only feminist as long as it remains grounded in women's experience. Theory that is not so grounded but which derives from abstractions, she argues, is dangerous to feminist thinking. Her sphere is therefore small-scale and interpersonal with the requirement for constant reference back to women's experience. This is quite a different approach to the one demonstrated by MacKinnon even though the language deployed is similar. There is no tendency to construct the meta-narrative, the overarching explanation which accounts for everything. Instead Lahey provides uncertainty. She does not try to beat the male theorists at their own game, but alters the parameters of doing theory.

The modest and intentional uncertainty of Lahey's argument is not, however, a defining feature of all feminist work in this field. By the time Wishik's article is published in 1986 certainties are being formed. She states,

> feminist jurisprudential inquiry focuses particularly on the law's role in perpetuating patriarchal hegemony. Such inquiry is feminist in that it is grounded in women's concrete experiences. These experiences are the source of feminism's validity and its method of analysis. Feminist inquiry involves the understanding and application of the personal as political. Feminism's method is consciousness-raising. (1986, p.69)

Gone are the doubts about consciousness-raising as a method, and the problems which might arise in assuming that the concrete experience of all women can be communicated and pressed into a feminist policy are glossed over. That different women may want very different things, indeed things which may be in conflict, does not occur to the author. Here we see a determined zeal overtaking the political sensitivity of earlier writers like Lahey. Why should Wishik assume that all women want to engage in consciousness-raising? What power is exercised in the consciousness-raising process? How can *all* women's experience be represented unless it is, a priori, assumed to be fairly homogeneous?

Wishik continues, 'In addition, feminist jurisprudence can help us envision the world we wish to create – that is, a world without patriarchy. It can also assist us in focusing our deliberations about the nature of that world' (ibid., p.72). This becomes a version of feminist idealism. It is not that the thinking of alternatives is so problematic, rather it is the naivety of the idealist thinking about the nature and significance of law. Here feminist jurisprudence becomes almost a messianic movement and notions of the limits of the ability of law (whether feminist or not) to transform social reality are forgotten.

Scales (1986) takes up and furthers the debate on legal objectivity and its part played in denying the reality of women's experience. In a long article (to which I cannot do justice here) she attempts to substantiate the idea that objectification – and hence objectivity – is the source of women's oppression. She relies on the work of Dinnerstein (1978) and Gilligan (1982) to point out that objectification is part of gender differentiation (the process that boys and girls go through in becoming masculine or feminine) and hence is part of masculine consciousness. So objectivity is not just a stance that law adopted after prolonged consideration, it reflects something much deeper and much more powerful, namely the celebration of masculine existence and consciousness. From this we can see, according to Scales, that objectivity is more than masculine in the cultural sense, it is also masculine in the psychological sense. We can also understand (assuming that we share her faith in the object relations school of psychoanalysis to be found in Dinnerstein's work) why it is a symbolic standard which inspires such a deep commitment.

In arguing that nonetheless we must abandon objectivity, Scales does not mean to advocate the abandonment of standards. What in fact she argues is that our standards must emerge from an evaluation of results and not from an a priori abstract concept which prevails regardless of its results. (For instance equality is a useless standard if it merely treats the unequal as equal; what is needed is equality of outcome.) She goes on to argue that feminism is ideally suited to this approach because it has always been results-oriented and has a methodology which reveals the experience against which legal procedures must be tested. This method is, once again, consciousness-raising. Before discussing Scales' version of this it is perhaps important to note at least one problem in her approach. Being results-oriented is not such a panacea as it might appear. We cannot, even among feminists, assume a consensus over what a good result is. Moreover, results orientation may not be that far removed from what judges do already. The idea that a pure principle is applied regardless of outcome is part of the myth of legal method perpetuated by law. Critics of the legal system have long pointed out that judges come to the decisions which they prefer and then, *post hoc*, read the principles which support their decisions into their interpretation of case law (cf. Sumner, 1979). Therefore pressing for a results orientation alone may achieve very little.

On consciousness-raising Scales states that the experiences which it reveals do not need validation by traditional methods – indeed she suggests they cannot be validated by these criteria. Relying on MacKinnon (1983) she argues that feminism does not need an abstract concept of truth, rather she insists that the expression of experience is all there is. Feminism therefore provides law with what Scales calls 'dramatic eye-witness testimony'. It has the capacity to place what law has regarded as irrelevant or subjective onto the agenda and to use this alternative knowledge as the basis for new standards and principles in law.

Scales therefore provides an argument for the validity of what might be called 'subjugated knowledges' (Gordon, 1980). What is missing, however, is any critical evaluation of the practice of consciousness-raising. It is given the accolade of a method rather than a practice, and in this respect it is claiming a place on the very hierarchy of knowledge it shuns. 'Method' is a term used in scientific or social scientific activity and it therefore seems odd to find it appropriated so unproblematically here. There is also a more fundamental problem than this misappropriation and that is that the denial of truth is insincere. In challenging the idea that only the knowledge that has been produced by so-called objective methods is the truth, this version of feminist jurisprudence claims to abandon truth altogether. Yet implicit in this work is the idea that feminist accounts are more valid than masculinist accounts. Scales argues,

Heretofore, the tried and true scientific strategy of treating non-conforming evidence as mistaken worked in the legal system. But when that evidence keeps turning up, when the experience of women becomes recalcitrant, it will be time to treat that evidence as true'. (1986, p.1402)

Consciousness-raising is therefore seen to produce a more powerful truth, not a variety of truths. In this form feminist jurisprudence, which sets out to deconstruct method and truth, creates its own version of the same problem. It does not challenge the central place of epistemology in social science, it merely asserts that it has a more reliable access to unassailable knowledge.

Experience, social science and law
While North American feminist legal scholars have turned to consciousness-raising as a way of challenging legal orthodoxy and the problem of method, the approach taken by the Institute of Women's Law at Oslo, exemplified in the work of Tove Stang Dahl (1987), adopts a very different approach. Before highlighting the differences, however, it is important to be aware of certain similar premises. Both approaches presume that the basis for restructuring law must be women's experience. Hence both move away from abstract concepts and from law itself to start with women. But there is a basic presumption here, namely that 'women' is not an abstract

concept but a concrete and automatically knowable category. Obviously there is something in this; just as we know a tree when we see one, we know a woman. This, however, is merely an act of recognition based on a constructed typology of physiological difference. It ignores the fact that the definition of gendered existence may vary considerably; furthermore it presumes that experience of a gendered existence is natural. In so doing, this form of feminism mistakes the product of its politics for a pre-cultural reality. By this I mean that it is the gaze of feminism which has produced Woman as a specific and significant category; women (as identified by feminism) do not exist outside this process of recognition. In a similar way other discourses (opposed to feminism) have produced Woman as an insignificant, malign, ignorant, invisible (etc.) category. The problem is that feminism ignores its role in constituting Woman in a particular form at a particular moment in history, and assumes that it discovers a reality which is merely waiting to be emancipated. As Riley (1988) argues,

> There is a wish among several versions of Anglo-American feminism to assert the real underlying unities among women, and of the touchstone of 'women's experience'. It is as if this powerful base could guarantee both the integrity and the survival of militant feminism ...
> Because of its drive towards a political massing together of women, feminism can never wholeheartedly dismantle 'women's experience', however much this category conflates the attributed, the imposed, and the lived, and then sanctifies the resulting melange. (pp.99–100)

The concepts of Woman and of experience are therefore not unproblematic but they form the taken-for-granted basis of this approach to jurisprudence. This would not be an issue if it were admitted that this was a political device or a value position, but the concepts invoked often seem to hold the promise of an unassailable truth with which feminism can defeat not only other politics but also inferior (less truthful) knowledges.

The claim to truth is not a trap that Dahl falls into, however, in spite of her unproblematic use of the terms 'women' and 'experience'. She argues,

> Women-centred policy considerations are the *values* that are accorded special weight in women's law. These values – ideals of the 'good society' – are essential, both in the evaluation of existing law, and as criteria for the structure and methodology of women's law, and even as indicators of reform ideals. The values are thus

used analytically to give substance to the expression women's law, born of the intention to describe, explain and understand women's legal position. (1987, p.83)

Dahl deploys the concept of justice in her approach. This is not an abstract notion, however, but one which, she argues, is based on what women want. Like Scales she appears to reject the idea of the application of principle from on high and her aim is to start with beliefs which are widely held (by women) and from these to construct moral principles. Dahl therefore suggests that we start with the needs and wants of women in general and their opinions about what is fair and just.

This approach differs considerably from the consciousness-raising method. The latter presumes that the basis for law will be a feminist consciousness, while the former is content with women's consciousnesses. Dahl starts where women are, not where feminists are. From this starting point she argues that there are new legal categories which must be constructed, for example money law, birth law, housewives' law and paid-work law. This reorganisation breaks down the traditional categories of law and arranges them on the basis of women's needs. It would, however, be incorrect to assume that Dahl does not herself have an ethical starting point which seems to pre-date her inquiries into what women want. For her the principles of freedom, equality, dignity, integrity, self-determination and self-realisation are paramount. She treats these as unproblematic in the sense that she presumes that there is already a consensus of opinion behind her. She is not wrong in this respect, for these are exactly the concepts implicit in much feminist work which never strays into such philosophical territory. Concepts of integrity and self-determination form the very cornerstone of much feminist work on rape, for example. But the problem is that these are precisely the abstract ideas which she argues women's law eschews. There would therefore seem to be a contradiction between the aspiration to start with women's definitions of morality, justice and so on, and the imposition of a predetermined set of values which are assumed to provide the correct framework for women's law.

There is also another difference between Dahl's approach and the North American (and British) approach, even though on the level of values there may be similarities. Dahl does not locate her analysis within a theory of the state or law. The question of power which is so central to MacKinnon, for example, is missing here. It is implicit in Dahl's work that eventually the state and law will come round to accept that its conceptualisations of justice have been too limited. It would therefore be easy to criticise Dahl's position as a form of liberal feminism but this would be to ignore certain historical and political developments which have occurred in Norway. The state has become much more welfarist and progressively interventionist in Norway than is apparent in the UK or USA in the late 1980s. There appears to be an optimism about law and welfare reforms which has diminished elsewhere. Notwithstanding this fact there is a major disparity between this formulation of feminist jurisprudence, which ignores the problem of power (whether male, state or legal), and most of the other forms discussed in this chapter.

The effects of this difference can be remarked elsewhere. Dahl argues that the way to transform existing law and produce women's law is to bring to bear the methods of social science to the formulation and modification of legislation and legal practice. In other words it is depicted as a process of education. Yet, surprisingly, she is unconcerned with questions of the application by judges of legal logic to decision-making because she maintains that the vast majority of women are not affected by the sort of law that goes on in court or which exercises the minds of judges. Women's lives are affected by administrative law and more mundane regulations which she treats as outside (or beneath) the application of formalistic legal thinking. Her strategy therefore is to leave the 'higher reaches' of law alone. Indeed she does not wish to challenge or interfere with legal method at all. She argues,

> Legal doctrine, i.e., the interpretation of law according to prescribed methodology, should remain the core area of legal science because it is there that lawyers have their own tools and a distinct craft. (1987, p.32)

This would be heresy to MacKinnon and others (myself included) who have precisely argued that it is this 'craft' which is so fundamentally oppressive to women. But Dahl is content to leave it alone as if it occupies a separate sphere and is indeed a neutral tool which is applied when necessary. Yet she is not prepared to ignore the development of legal theory which she identifies as the formulation of statements about the relationship between legal rules and reality. It is here that she sees social science methodology beginning to play a major role, and where empirical studies on the lives of women will provide a corrective to existing theories of law. Hence women's experience will be communicated through the process of research. This will, in turn, produce a 'consequence-oriented' and 'realistic' legal theory. Again these are almost the same terms used by North American feminists (such as results-oriented) but within a very different theoretical context.

There is one further important difference between Dahl's work and that of other feminists in the field (at least outside Norway). This is her adoption of scientific methodology as unproblematical. She argues, 'While politics first and foremost deals with power ... it is the primary duty of science to seek knowledge and understanding, and by means of this to promote action' (ibid., p.23). In saying this she does not exclude the importance of an exchange between the women's movement (politics) and women's studies (science) but while she sees the insights gained from political activity as providing vital directions for feminist research, she regards the fruits of research as providing the best solutions to the problems thus identified. Dahl's work would therefore, in my view, fall directly into that category of work called feminist fabianism. By fabianism here I mean the idea of promoting science as a value-free and superior form of knowledge whose results can be applied to improve society and eradicate social problems. Although this has been social science's main claim to relevance and authenticity during the development of the postwar welfare state, it is now a position which is increasingly regarded as inadequate (not just by the right; see Bauman, 1988). Not only is the clear-cut distinction between politics and knowledge now questioned (not least by feminist scholars) but the idea that retrospective empirical studies provide answers to future problems is also subject to scrutiny (see Smart, 1986 and 1990a).

Dahl's feminist jurisprudence therefore may have the appearance of similarity with other forms but it does espouse a very different political stance. She does however reintroduce ideas of justice which have remained untouched in other feminist works on law (if not philosophy) until quite recently. Yet questions of justice and ethics have become increasingly important to discussions on jurisprudence and we shall return to this theme below.

The Psychological/Modes of Reasoning Approach

The main contribution to this approach is the work of Carol Gilligan (1982). Indeed it is probably fair to state that Gilligan's work launched feminist legal theory down the path of psychology and moral reasoning. Her book, *In a Different Voice*, is a critique of Kolberg's theory of moral development in which he outlines these stages in children. Kolberg used boys in his experiments yet claimed a universality for his results. He therefore failed to recognise the part gender might play in the development of moral reasoning. He elevated the boys' development to a model of development for all children. If girls were to develop differently his study would have failed to notice it. Indeed, as Gilligan points out, traditionally moral philosophers and psychologists have in any case tended to assume that it is only men who develop the highest standards of moral reasoning. Women were rejected, a priori, as having less moral sense and as having less ability to be objective. Hence the way men reason has become *the* way in which reasoning is done.

Gilligan's thesis does not dispute this difference, rather she seeks to re-evaluate what has been rejected in the feminine mode. So she stresses the way that the masculine mode, which she calls the ethic of justice, has been both celebrated and used as the basis of our legal system. This ethic of justice relies on objectivity, rationality and emotional distance. The feminine mode, which she calls the ethic of caring, is based on connectedness, subjective emotion and responsibility for maintaining relationships. The ethic of justice is founded on the idea that everyone should be treated the same, while the ethic of caring means that no one should be hurt.

This work has generated a complete re-evaluation of the concept of justice and objectivity in much feminist work. Gilligan has provided a new 'angle' to the argument that law is male, which is based on psychology rather than philosophy or sociology. Her work also complements the influential work of feminists like Chodorow (1978) and Dinnerstein (1978) who have studied the psycho-social development of girls and boys and have argued that a basic element of masculinity is separateness and individuation, while a fundamental element of femininity is connectedness. These works therefore argue that the problem of maleness and masculine values is located in the psychic development of children.

Because Gilligan's starting point is developmental psychology rather than law or culture, she begins with the way in which boys and girls reason (in the present) and works from there, rather than asking why they reason so differently. In this respect she is close to Dahl, who also starts from the position of where women are. This stance has led to considerable criticism. Scales for example has stated that 'Just as Gilligan's work has the potential to inspire us in historic ways, it could also become the Uncle Tom's Cabin of our century, (1986, p.1381). MacKinnon (1987) is even more scathing in her criticism, arguing that Gilligan merely attempts to give value to the form of femininity that patriarchy has imposed on women. The problem with Gilligan's approach therefore is that it may merely affirm the feminine, rather than promoting the feminist. In using terms like the ethic of caring Gilligan inevitably reaffirms that women are naturally caring – even though this may not be her intention. Moreover her analysis can be used to keep women excluded from the corridors of justice since her version of the way that women reason would seem to be an unacceptable mode.

However, these criticisms are in many ways misguided. All 'knowledge' can be put to reactionary use and Gilligan's work does not carry a special responsibility in this respect. What is useful about her work is the way in which she identifies a hierarchy of moral reasoning and her recognition that there are subjugated modes which could be used to challenge an existing orthodoxy. This is not an entirely new approach. It can be found in work on customary law which, when compared with Western law, is construed as quite inadequate. What Gilligan identifies as male has, therefore, also been identified as Western, imperialist or 'white' thinking (Harding, 1986). Such work locates modes of thinking in their cultural and historical specificity and challenges the orthodoxy of claims to universality and naturalness.

In terms of a specific contribution to feminist jurisprudence, Gilligan suggests that what is needed is a more generative view of human life in which the ethic of justice and the ethic of caring can both be deployed. This is perhaps the weakest part of her thesis, since she assumes that law really does operate by an ethic of justice rather than by making claims to objectivity and neutrality as part of the exercise of power. She also fails to appreciate that what she calls the ethic of caring does already operate in the legal system (Daly, 1989a). These weaknesses perhaps stem from the fact she is a psychologist with little knowledge of law's operations and how (or whether) moral values become transposed into law. Despite this her work has been extremely influential in generating ideas about legal and moral reasoning and in raising debates about what form feminist values might take. It is to this issue I shall now turn.

The Social Justice/Harm Approach
This approach to feminist jurisprudence marks a shift towards the attempt to construct feminist values which could actually be deployed in the practice of law. As noted above, Dahl's work in Norway has also adopted this strategy, but here I want to focus on different contributions from the USA and Australia.

One crucial development in this approach was the attempt to redefine certain social practices as 'harms'. Hence behaviour now labelled sexual harassment has been construed as a harm. Although there is considerable resistance to labelling certain sexualised exchanges as sexual harassment, once so labelled there follows an automatic assumption that some harm has been caused. Another equally important area has been the redefinition of the harm that pornography causes. This has attempted to shift the understanding of the harm away from one of moral harm – in the traditional Christian sense – to one of harm to women – in the feminist sense (MacKinnon, 1987).

Wishik (1986) has called for a global use of the term harm, that is she argues that feminist jurisprudence can identify the harms of patriarchal law and can begin to describe an existence unharmed by patriarchy. This is a very unfocused use of the concept of harm which has little strategic value. West (1988) is more specific in her use of harm in the attempt to build what she calls a reconstructive feminist jurisprudence. She argues that feminists have succeeded in having harms recognised by law only when the harm is made analogous to the deprivation of a right which masculine liberal jurisprudence can comprehend. She is therefore critical of the strategy on sexual harassment which turned it into the infringement of a civil right in order that law could recognise it as an offence. Although there was some 'success' in this strategy it left the problematic rights-based jurisprudence untouched.

Consequently West argues that it is vital to reassess what harms are done to women and what harms the legal system fails or refuses to acknowledge. Here she relies on the work of feminist psychologists (such as Dinnerstein, 1978) to argue that what matters to women is intimacy and connectedness and protection against invasion. However, law protects or values autonomy and individuation and protects against annihilation. Hence law responds to the harm of rape when it entails a good deal of violence (that is, the threat of annihilation). It cannot respond to a rape which is an unwanted invasion. Equally the law cannot recognise the harm of foetal invasion (as West describes unwanted pregnancy) even though it threatens a woman's bodily integrity. This is because it does not threaten her life, only her 'self'. So West concludes that feminist jurisprudence must re-articulate women's rights 'in such a way as to reveal, rather than conceal their origin in women's distinctive existential and material state of being' (p.61). Hence the right to abort should no longer be a right to privacy (as it is currently construed in the USA) but a right to defend against a particular bodily invasion.

These attempts to redefine harm are useful in the way they reveal the acceptedness of the harms which law maintains deserve protection. But they also raise a number of problems. Firstly we can see in West's work a return to the old problem of equality and difference. In a way which is more sophisticated than Gilligan she is rehabilitating the difference approach.

Secondly, in more specific terms, her examples of reframing the basis of current jurisprudence pose a number of difficulties. It would, for example, seem necessary to define all pregnancies as bodily invasions in order for some women to exercise the right to abort. Yet not all women experience their pregnancies in this way. Moreover defining pregnancy in this way may simply encourage greater medical intervention in and control over the pregnant mother. Defining the foetus as separate from the mother may seem helpful in terms of abortion but it has reactionary consequences in terms of the development of foetal rights and the possibilities of prosecuting mothers for harm done to the foetus in utero (Smart,

1990b). Equally, sexual intercourse which is welcomed is not necessarily experienced as a bodily invasion. The problem is that the term invasion, which is used to convey harm, assumes there is a harm regardless of the views or consciousness of the woman involved. This may make it easier for women who are raped or unwillingly pregnant to make claims of the law, but it does not necessarily reflect the 'true subjectivity' of women that West wishes to see reflected in jurisprudence. Rather it elevates a particular (radical) feminist version of women's experience into a norm for all women.

Ultimately, and unfortunately, West's work slides into liberal utopianism which seems to be the pitfall of so much North American feminist jurisprudence. She argues that law provides a way to counter profound power imbalances which, in my view, hugely overstates the power of law to achieve structural change within a capitalist and patriarchal state. She goes on,

> In a utopian world, all forms of life will be recognized, respected and honoured. A perfect legal system will protect against harms sustained by all forms of life, and will recognize life affirming values generated by all forms of being. Feminist jurisprudence must aim to bring this about ... Masculine jurisprudence must become humanist jurisprudence, and humanist jurisprudence must become a jurisprudence unmodified. (1988, p.72)

And, I am tempted to add, pigs must learn to fly.

For a more pragmatic approach it is useful to turn to the work of Adrian Howe on social injury (1987). She borrows the idea from the criminologist Edwin Sutherland who deployed it to extend the use of the concept of crime to include activities like white-collar and company crime which have been regarded as less problematic or damaging than, for example, theft or burglary. Howe uses the term social injury rather than the more typically feminist 'harm' (although the two are related) because she argues that injury is something the law can recognise and which can therefore become actionable. She sees this process as a form of political action rather than idealising a feminist jurisprudence. She acknowledges the differences between women and argues that the idea of redefining injury on the basis of women's experience can still accommodate these differences. But the most significant difference between Howe's work and that of the 'idealist' feminists is that she makes it clear that redefining certain experiences as injuries should not automatically lead to the assumption that legal action – and most particularly criminalisation – is desirable. She holds back from the assumption that there should be an inevitable movement between redefinition and a legal response. In this respect she takes a similar line to Daly (1989b) who is quite categorical that criminalisation (of pornography) is misguided (see also Brants and Kok, 1986). The important feature about Howe's approach is that for her it is the redefinition which is important, not the legal action. Although she concedes that legal sanctions can provide legitimate recognition of a social injury, she does not insist that law should be put in the position of validating or invalidating every harm that women identify. What is not clear, however, is which harms should become actionable and which should not. Howe uses the example of pornography, pointing out that women have different and conflicting views on whether or not it causes a gender-specific harm. She suggests that it should become actionable only if it is 'shown to legitimate "the expropriation of our sexuality" ' (p.433). However, this evades the fundamental problem of whether such a connection could ever be unambiguously shown or universally accepted. It postpones making a decision on the grounds that we may eventually have the full facts which will make the answer obvious. So the problem with Howe's approach is that it does not provide any clear instances of when or how we should use the concept of social injury. Her paper does, however, constitute a major advance over many other forms of feminist jurisprudence in that it does not presume that a recourse to law is necessarily a solution. While exploring the idea of a feminist jurisprudence Howe remains sceptical of law and the power of law to order our existence (even a feminist existence). This brings me to the one question which it has been impossible to pose until now. This is, 'do we really need a feminist jurisprudence?'

A Future for Feminist Jurisprudence?

I have suggested elsewhere that the search for a feminist jurisprudence is like a modern quest for the Holy Grail (Smart, 1989). In the work of authors like West and Wishik, for example, it does seem to take an exaggeratedly idealised form in which feminist jurisprudence becomes the answer to women's oppression. Linked to this is the failure to think critically about what is meant by women's experience which is thought to provide the basis of this feminist vision. Whether it is idealised or not the question that is rarely addressed is whether we really do need a feminist jurisprudence. The strength of the feminist work so far lies in the critique that has been mounted of the foundations of traditional jurisprudence. It challenges all the main assumptions of jurisprudence, except the assumption that we need some form of jurisprudence. This is because the central role of law as an organising principle of everyday life is rarely challenged in the construction of the new jurisprudence.

Taking the problem of women's experience first, I have argued that the terms 'experience' and 'consciousness-raising' have become virtual slogans which are almost meaningless. This is not to argue that feminist policy should divorce itself from the multiplicity of women's different experiences. Instead what is needed is a recognition that knowledge of these experiences will not provide simple answers. This has been well documented, especially by black women who have made it clear that they are critical of the goals and practices of a women's movement which is predominantly white but which proposes to speak for all women. Matsuda (1987) has argued most cogently that radical jurisprudence in the USA does not yet seem to have room for the experiences of ethnic minorities (see also Monture, 1986). The proposal for a feminist jurisprudence therefore already looks suspect in that it is unsure what it might mean for black women (let alone for black men). But the problem is not only to try to find a space for other silenced experiences (although this is difficult enough), rather it lies in what is to be done when different experiences conflict. Muslim women, Afro-Caribbean women, Native women, Jewish women and Irish women may all have very different experiences which cannot easily be collapsed into a single feminist jurisprudence.

The second problem I have identified is perhaps even more serious for feminist legal scholarship. I want to argue that in spite of the value of the critique mounted by feminist jurisprudence, in constructing a new jurisprudence feminists give a renewed legitimacy to the power of law to organise and regulate our lives. For example almost all the feminist work cited above takes issue with law's claim to objectivity and neutrality, claiming that what passes for these qualities is really male subjectivity and interests. But the claim to objectivity and neutrality has always been exactly that – a claim to be refuted, not taken seriously. The law does not operate according to any one set of standards, nor is the law itself a unitary phenomenon which has one direction and purpose. There is no single foundation to jurisprudence and no single outcome to the application of any one principle. In other words it is more complex and less of a conspiracy than the model implied in much of the work on feminist jurisprudence would have us believe. This leads to the question of whether it is sensible to try to impose a unitary standard on law except as an intellectual exercise which reveals the failure of law to be objective and so on. A simplified model of law may be useful in the construction of a critique, but it is a poor basis for a reform strategy. Perhaps even more important is the way in which the search for a feminist jurisprudence retains law as a central focus of feminist strategy. Of course feminists cannot help but respond to the growing influence and intervention by law into new areas of regulation. Maybe the response should be one of resistance rather than calling for more law – even law based on agreed feminist principles. A feminist jurisprudence gives renewed hope that law can be rehabilitated, but the resort to law remains a white middle-class privilege unless there are commensurate fundamental changes elsewhere. And if we could have those fundamental changes we should ask the question why we would still wish to retain such a reliance on law to tackle the oppression of women.

Clearly feminist legal scholarship cannot ignore the way in which traditional jurisprudence is formulated and the way it influences the practice of law. However, it faces formidable problems. The form that it has taken in the 1980s has been defined by the interests largely of white, North American, feminist legal scholars. Although self-critical work is beginning to appear (cf. Kline, 1989), feminist jurisprudence tends to be limited by the very paradigm it seeks to judge. In criticising law for being male it cannot escape the related criticism of promoting a (classless, white) female point of view as the solution. Neither can it escape idealising law as a solution to women's oppression. The question is whether feminist jurisprudence can overcome these conceptual and political problems or whether we need to start from somewhere else fundamentally to challenge the power of law and the heritage of traditional jurisprudence.

Notes

1. Feminist legal scholarship and campaigns during the second wave also focused attention on the question of rights and how to reformulate them in order that women's needs could be better addressed. Although this is an important element in the development of feminist jurisprudence space will not allow me to explore this question here. See Smart 1989, Chapter 7, for a detailed discussion.

References

Bauman, Z. (1988) 'Is there a Postmodern Sociology?', *Theory, Culture and Society*, vol. 5, no. 2/3, pp.217–38.

Bodichon, B. (1869) *A Brief Summary in Plain Language of the Most Important Laws of England Concerning Women* (London: Trubner & Co).

Brants, C. and Kok, E. (1986) 'Penal Sanctions as a Feminist Strategy: a Contradiction in Terms?', *International Journal of the Sociology of Law*, vol. 14, no. 3/4, pp.269–86.

Chodorow, N. (1978) *The Reproduction of Mothering* (London: University of Chicago Press).

Cobbe, F. P. (1878) 'Wife Torture in England', *Contemporary Review*, April, pp.55–87.

Dahl, T. S. (1987) *Women's Law: An Introduction to Feminist Jurisprudence* (Oxford: Oxford University Press).

Daly, K. (1989a) 'Criminal Justice Ideologies and Practices in Different Voices: Some Feminist Questions About Justice', *International Journal of the Sociology of Law*, vol. 17, no. 1, pp.1–18.
——. (1989b) 'New Feminist Definitions of Justice', Conference Proceedings, Institute for Women's Policy Research, Washington, DC.
Dinnerstein, D. (1978) *The Rocking of the Cradle* (London: Souvenir).
Freeman, M. D. A. (1987) 'Feminism and Jurisprudence' in S. McLaughlin (ed.), *Women and the Law* (London: Faculty of Laws, University College London, working paper no. 5).
Fryer, B., Hunt, A., McBarnett, D., and Moorhouse, B., (eds) (1981) *Law, State and Society* (London: Croom Helm).
Gilligan, C. (1982) *In A Different Voice* (London: Harvard University Press).
Gordon, C. (ed.) (1980) *Michel Foucault: Power/Knowledge* (Brighton: Harvester).
Hall, S. (1980) 'Reformism and the Legislation of Consent' in The National Deviancy Conference (ed) *Permissiveness and Control* (London: Macmillan).
Harding, S. (1986) *The Science Question in Feminism* (Milton Keynes: Open University Press).
Howe, A. (1987) '"Social Injury" Revisited: Towards a Feminist Theory of Social Justice', *International Journal of the Sociology of Law*, vol. 15, no. 4, pp.423–38.
Kline, M. (1989) 'Race, Racism and Feminist Legal Theory', *Harvard Women's Law Journal*, vol. 12, pp.115–50.
Lahey, K. (1985) '... until women themselves have told all that they have to tell ...', *Osgoode Hall Law Journal*, vol. 23, no. 3, pp.519–41.
Lord Lloyd of Hampstead and Freeman, M. D. A. (1985) *Lloyd's Introduction to Jurisprudence*, 5th edn (London: Stevens and Sons).
MacKinnon, C. (1982) 'Feminism, Marxism, Method, and the State: An Agenda for Theory', *Signs*, vol. 7, no. 3, pp.515–44.
——. (1983) 'Feminism, Marxism, Method and the State: Toward Feminist Jurisprudence', *Signs*, vol. 8, no. 2, pp.635–58.
——. (1987) *Feminism Unmodified: Discourses on Life and Law* (Cambridge, Mass: Harvard University Press).
Martin, A. (1911) *Mothers in Mean Streets* (London: United Suffragists).
Matsuda, M. (1987) 'Looking to the Bottom: Critical Legal Studies and Reparations', *Harvard Civil Rights/Civil Liberties Law Review*, vol. 22, no. 2, pp.323–99.
Mill, J. S. (1869) *The Subjection of Women* (London: Everyman Library), reprinted 1970.
Mitchell, J. (1987) 'Women and Equality', in Phillips, A. (ed), *Feminism and Equality* (Oxford: Blackwell).
Monture, P. (1986) 'Ka-Nin-Geh-Heh-Gah-E-Sa-Nonh-Yah-Gah', *Canadian Journal of Women and the Law*, vol. 2, no. 1, pp.159–70.
Norton, C. (1982) *Caroline Norton's Defence* (Chicago: Academy Chicago).
Rathbone, E. (1927) *The Disinherited Family* (London: George Allen & Unwin).
Rifkin, J. (1980) 'Toward a Theory of Law and Patriarchy', *Harvard Women's Law Journal*, vol. 3, pp.83–95.

Riley, D. (1988) *Am I That Name?* (London: Macmillan).

Scales, A. C. (1986) 'The Emergence of Feminist Jurisprudence: An Essay', *Yale Law Journal*, vol. 95, pp.1,373–1,403.

Smart, C. (1984) *The Ties That Bind* (London: Routledge & Kegan Paul).

——. (986) 'Feminism and Law: Some Problems of Analysis and Strategy', *International Journal of the Sociology of Law*, vol 14, no. 2, pp.109–23.

——. (1989) *Feminism and the Power of Law* (London: Routledge).

——. (1990a) 'Feminist Approaches to Criminology or Postmodern Woman meets Atavistic Man', in Gelsthorpe, L. and Morris, A. (eds), *Feminist Perspectives in Criminology* (Milton Keynes: Open University Press).

——. (1990b) 'Penetrating Women's Bodies: The Problem of Law and Medical Technology' in Abbott, P. and Wallace, C. (eds), *Gender, Sexuality and Power* (London: Macmillan).

Spender, D. (1983) *There's Always Been A Women's Movement* (London: Pandora).

Sumner, C. (1979) *Reading Ideologies* (London: Academic).

West, R. (1988) 'Jurisprudence and Gender', *University of Chicago Law Review*, vol. 55, no. 1, pp.1–72.

Wishik, H. (1986) 'To Question Everything: The Inquiries of Feminist Jurisprudence', *Berkeley Women's Law Journal*, vol. 1, pp.64–77.

Time out of Mind: An Introduction to the Semiotics of Common Law

Peter Goodrich and Yifat Hachamovitch

And though this law be the peculiar invention of this Nation, and
delivered over from age to age by Tradition, yet may we truly say,
that no human law, written or unwritten, hath more certainty in
the rules and maxims, more coherence in the parts thereof, or
more harmony of reason in it; nay we may confidently aver, that
it doth excell all other laws and is the most excellent form of government; it is so framed and fitted to the nature of this people, as
we may properly say that it is connaturall to the Nation. (Davies,
1615, pp.2b–3a)

Introductory

A semiotics of law studies all the different means by which law is
communicated. One of its principal objects is obviously the language of law. In relation to common law it must thus provide some
account of the paradoxical fact that English law comes clothed not
in the English language but in Latin, French and Middle English, an
archaic form of English itself. The fact that the language of English
law is in many aspects a foreign dialect indicates that it is unlikely to
be widely read outside the profession. The texts of law are thus likely
to have a symbolic rather than an immediately semantic – that is
linguistic – content. The language of law, however, is only one
medium of its transmission. Law is a material presence, a visual
structure of everyday life, a heritable form of repetition which comes
to constitute in a very real sense part of the nature of things. For a
semiotics of law this point is crucial. It is through symbols, its forms
of appearance, its phenomenonality, its emblematisation of persons
and of public space that law makes itself felt as the trace of either a
legitimate or simply a *de facto* sovereign social power. Its traces are
legible in all the surfaces of everyday life; precisely because it is experienced as a system of images, not as a system of rules, law represses,
repeats and institutes life.

The power of law is not simply that of an external or objective
social and administrative force. For a semiotics of law, the legal

order of institutional life is a matter of what is lived, accepted and made familiar through the images and signs, the rituals and sacraments, the liturgies and emblems of law's public presence. Consider first the element of ritual accompanying the legal institution since it first began to travel out of London: through the aura of reverence, the ceremonies of process and the spectacle of trial, law textualises and inscribes a particular map of the social and so also of the legal subjectivity that inhabits it. Its rituals are historical devices of fascination and conversion through which law enchants presence and re-creates its subjects, not through reason but through the imagery of reason, the mythology of reason, through policing the true reference of signs. It is these signs of law that go within and capture the subject for the institution and for law. 'The forms of action,' comments Maitland, 'are not mere rubrics or dead categories ... They are institutes of the law, they are – we say it without scruple – living things' (Maitland and Pollock, 1968, vol. 2, p.561). If the forms of action are living things, we may interpret them as living semiotically, as living within the individual who exists 'before the law', as a legal person, as someone waiting, as an upright – walking – instrument or emblem of law, a mask inhabited, a totem of personality. It is interesting to recollect in that respect that the classical sense of emblem, from the Greek *emballo*, was that of 'to throw within' and so, as regards the legal institution, its emblems are the means by which it inhabits the legal subject and dwells within the institution of personal and public life.

A semiotics of common law must thus pursue the tradition through its images, through the forms in which it works itself into the nervature of everyday life. It must account for law as a surface structure which can be evidenced in the masks of everyday life: law as repetition always and already has as its subject the mask. Law is in that sense nothing other than its image, its textuality and its rhetoric – yet as that system of fascination and conversion that institutes the human face *as* legal person or *as* a mask, that institutes life from within, law is a deep structure, a heritable discourse, a 'positive unconscious', a reservoir of symbols that take hold of the subject, a positive unconscious which is therefore legible only through its disappearance. It is because law disappears (as sign, as symbol, as trace) that it dwells within the subject. And it is only because what was without reasserts itself within, only because life represses law by repeating law, forgets law by repeating law, that law makes itself felt in the living body, in the element of everyday life, in the gravity of the normal.[1]

The Iconography of English Law

In this essay we will concentrate upon the Englishness of English law and particularly upon the images, symbols and other icons through which common law as a tradition is transmitted. In cultural and so also in semiotic terms a tradition, legal or otherwise, is not a historical discipline, nor a rational, proven or evidenced sense of the past, but much more a mythology, an unconscious reservoir of images and symbols, of fictive narratives, and oracular (or immemorial) truths. A tradition exists as a sense of familiarity, as a sign of identity, of inclusion, of 'we' as against 'them'. It is in that rhetorical sense of tradition that we will here analyse the peculiar forms, insularities and jealousies of English law. More particularly we will examine the history of the contemporary common law form, the history of its present understood as its traditionality, and seek the identity of this tradition through an analysis of its earliest texts. Our argument will revolve around a close examination of the writings of Fortescue, Coke and Davies, of the first doctrinal apologies (or defences) of English law written between the end of the fifteenth and the middle of the seventeenth centuries which reflect the symbolism and mythology of an English tradition and vernacular law in whose shadow we still live.[2]

Take as a starting point the notion propounded by one contemporary philosopher that we recognise law in much the same manner that we recognise a language even though we have no conscious grasp of its grammatical rules. The question is, what is it that we recognise, with which we are familiar or at ease? At the level of greatest generality it can be suggested that what is recognised initially – both in historical and psychological senses – is Englishness, a particular systemic context, a specific system of law tied to a unified sense of geographical and national-political identity. The uniqueness of England and the national character of the island race, the antiquity and excellence of the cultural identity underlying and expressed through the common law, is captured most vehemently and explicitly, though by no means idiosyncratically, by the early Lord Chancellor Sir John Fortescue: 'Other countries ... are not in such an happy situation, are not so well stored with inhabitants. Though there be in other parts of the world, persons of rank and distinction, men of estates and possessions, yet they are not so frequent and so near situated one to another, as in England' (Fortescue, 1470/1737, p.64). It can be suggested thus as a point of departure that we look precisely for an identity, for that which differentiates common law from other laws, the law of a nation (*ius commune*) from the law of nations (*ius gentium*). The answer is likely to be found in the language and particularly the imagery in which the common law establishes itself as a tradition, as having a separate yet identifiable history, an insular and unique sense of the past. Only once we have identified the elements of that sense of the past, of that time out of mind which is also time immemorial (classically the basic source of common law) can we endeavour to understand the nature of the English constitution or the character and colour of English law.

Time, Tradition and Source in the Antique Law

To understand the aura and imagery of the common law as a system of signs, to understand it as the sense of identity and of prejudgement with which we read the texts of that law it is necessary to approach law from a much broader definition than is currently accepted in common law jurisprudence. In virtually all its pre-classical definitions, the word law (as for example, *halacha, shari'a, Dike* or *dharma*) refers either directly or incidentally to the path, the way or the road: the comings and goings that map out our everyday lives, the 'again and again' through which a routine or a route is made across the landscape of everydayness, the chart of memory, inscribed in the heart, which circumscribes our place, and helps us find our direction, our next encampment.[3] The common law does not differ in its desire to map out both a time not yet lived and a history, to indicate at once a familiar path to the future and a conceptual lineage, to trace a genealogy and also to provide an origin and a line. In this very generic sense, the qualities of Englishness and so of an English law are well-established in the writings of its early apologists; the common law is the law of the land (*lex terrae*), a rustic law for rural types. Despite innumerable conquests, we are told by Coke and the other 'sages' of the common law, English law is sacred and stretches back to the halcyon times of King Arthur, to Cornwall, to Camelot (Coke, 1611/1777, vol. IX, p.C2a). Coke, on another occasion, also manages to refer it to Brutus, 'the first king of this land' (ibid., II b 1 a). In more generic terms it can be traced also beyond the time of memory or the imaginings of 'the best historians', to an original time and lost (temporal) place where dwell the vast hosts of the dead, the ancestors. It is from these ancestors, according to Coke, that is from the original antique and unquestionable time of the fathers of our law, that its truth derives: it is nothing other than '*testi temporum, veritatis vitae, nuncio vetustatis* – the witness of time, the life of truth, the herald of old age' (ibid., I A 4 a). The time of law is constantly specified as that of ancient custom, a time of inheritance, antiquity and establishment about which we learn through the arcane and wise books of the law, although, paradoxically, the 'reports are but comments or interpretations upon the text of the common law: which Text was never originally written, but has ever been preserved in the memory of man, though no man's memory can reach to the original thereof' (Davies, 1615, p.1b).[4] Despite the Greek, Latin and French, which even Coke recognised as elements of legal language, these books and their disparate accompanying unwritten knowledges have survived all the invasions of England and have perpetuated the ancient realm, the sceptred isle, the immemorial tongue.

It is its origin in a time outside memory, a time outside chronologies that enshrines the particular national code as an inheritance that is closer to nature and to divine law than any other existent system of laws. It is first, as we have seen, the oldest of all laws or, as Fortescue proclaims it 'nor in short, are the laws of any other kingdom in the world so venerable for their antiquity ... the laws and customs of England, are not only good, but the very best' (Fortescue, 1470/1737, pp.32–3). The law of England is thus incontestable in its truth by virtue of an antiquity that is peculiar to the discipline and external to the normal procedures of historical proof. It is an enduring law, a continuance which has a secondary implication of excellence. In Davies' strident formulation,

> this customary law is the most perfect, and most excellent, and without comparison the best ... as the law of nature, which the schoolmen call *ius commune*, and which is also *ius non scriptum*, being written only in the hearts of men, is better than all written laws ... so the customary law of England, which we do likewise call *ius commune* as coming nearest to the law of nature ... doth far excel our written laws, namely our statutes or Acts of Parliament; which is manifest in this, that when our Parliament have altered or changed any fundamentall points of the Common Lawe, those alterations have been found by experience to be so inconvenient ... as that the Common Lawe hath in effect beene restored again, in the same points, by other Actes of Parliament in succeeding ages. (1615, pp.2a–b)

It is this naturalness of a law inscribed in nature itself, in the heart, that guarantees that it will return, again and again, as the 'same' law or as the customary or unwritten law which would return as the same law were it appropriately embodied in the legal subject. This unwritten writing of a common law, the immemorial memory of a common subject, serves to validate law's unnatural nature: it returns against the written text because a written law that stays a while,[5] that remains law for long enough, becomes unwritten law – but also and already against its own practice and its own disappearing text, since the customary law is in fact not at all the customs remembered by the common people but the royal custom, a feudal law of vassalage, homage and other forms of status and service.

Texts of the First Law

As regards written law, it is for Coke and Davies an interference from
the contemporary legislature with an antique spirit and perennial
wisdom that the 'moderns' are seldom capable of understanding.
Where the legislature or written law does interfere it is more likely
than not that it will have to be corrected and absorbed again to the
true condition of the antique law, to the eternal return of the same:
'some points of ancient common law [being] altered or diverted from
his due course, yet in revolution of time, the same ... have been with
great applause for avoiding many inconveniences, restored again'
(Coke, 1611/1777, II C 3a). Lord Chief Justice Hale takes the argument even further and perhaps makes the most salient point, namely
that in the eyes of the tradition all legislation aspires to the status of
unwritten law (1975, p.4). The written law aspires, in other words, for
that acceptance of time and custom which will incorporate it into the
common law, the unwritten tradition. What written law there is in
the antique tradition can thus be suspected of having a function that
is more emblematic than administrative, a status more symbolic than
practical. Domesday Book and Magna Carta, the two most significant
symbols of written law after the Conquest, both share the peculiar
characteristic of administrative and substantive legal irrelevance
(Clanchy, 1979, Chapter 1). It is interesting that it is precisely
because they had no legal 'present' that they could so quickly come
to serve as original texts, monuments, symbols of a freedom that no
Englishman ever experienced save in the imagination of the law.

Consider then the primordial emblem of freeborn Englishness, of
ancestral honour and liberty, the *Magnae Chartae libertatum Angliae*,
the *Charta de Foresta* and particularly the Magna Carta itself, a con-
cession extracted from the crown, a royal grant primarily concerned
with the relationship between church and monarch and only incidentally with the 'amendment of the realm'. For Coke, the two charters together contain the bulk of the ancient customs, the
inheritance, the antique laws, the birthright of our land (1611/1777,
VIII L 6b). Ironically, as far as liberties are concerned and so far as
the great charters can genuinely be labelled the freedom of the community 'because they make or set us free' – *communis libertas (quia
liberos faciunt)*, or the charter of franchises – *chartre de franchises*,
Magna Carta simply extorts from the monarch the promise not to
diminish further or arbitrarily to extinguish customs and liberties
that had formerly been recognised by the crown. Thus the city of
London is guaranteed 'the old liberties and customs'; the knight's
fee will not be further raised; free men will not be forced to build
bridges to their homes nor walls around their property; merchants
were guaranteed safe passage through the kingdom.

The rights and liberties symbolically affirmed in Magna Carta are all, however, subject to the law of the earth, the realm, *lex terrae*, which is nothing other than the judgement of the king as chief justice of the kingdom (*justiciarum regni*), as maker or voice of the law. In that respect even rights as fundamental – that is to say, as ancient – as the writ of habeas corpus (who has the body?), or of the inviolability of land or of home are all provisional and defeasible. In *Darnel's Case* (1627, 3 St. Tr. 1) the writ of habeas corpus was of no use in the face of committal to prison *per speciale mandatum domini regis* (by special command of his majesty). Where the realm requires it the monarch has also always had a prerogative right of access to soil and to property, papers, diaries, even the post. Take an even more striking example, that of *The Case of the Prerogative of the King in Saltpetre* (12 Co Rep 12, 13) where the following rights and liberties of the subject are eloquently and lengthily and purposelessly rehearsed:

> the king cannot take the trees of the subject ... and he cannot take gravel ... he cannot charge the subject to make a wall around his house, or for to make a bridge to come to his house. The ministers of the king cannot undermine, weaken or impair any of my wall or foundations of any house, be they mansion houses, or out-houses or barns, stables, dove houses, mills or any other buildings ... for that my house is the subject place for my refuge, my safety and comfort of my family.

In the event, however, the crown required access to the property to extract saltpetre and no degree of antique freedom, custom or law could contradict that claim. The very title given to Magna Carta, *Charta libertatum Regni* (charter of the freedoms of the crown) indicates that these are liberties by and of the ruler, of the sovereign and not of the governed. We are left with an image of freeborn and gentle and indeed natural Englishness which is less notable for its antiquity than for its furtive insecurity: the ancient order is an order of vassalage, dominium and service, a feudal order in which every subject is a tenant of the crown and liable, when the realm so requires, to serve and to die for a soil which is not his own.[6]

Garden, Castle and Home

Who are the inhabitants of the well-mapped paths of the common law? What people is it, what subjects of law, attend upon the itinerant court? The initial answer is that in classical terms the English are a somewhat melancholic and saturnine people. They live an institutional temporality of repetition, of the immemorial coming round again, recurring eternally. The literary image of the English is of a landscape and people that do not change, that resist both revolution and any other ideas of change. If nothing happens, if nothing fundamental or 'established' can ever be altered, then a saturnine passivity in the inexorable face of the order of things is the properly melancholic image to show to the world. As Voltaire put it: if you have lost in love, if you have failed in politics and history has deserted you then nothing remains but to tend your garden. That is the Englishman's fate, but at least the law protects that secluded privacy, that walled garden, that patch of obsessively native soil so beloved of the English. We begin with the legal protection of that tellurian refuge which identifies the legal subject as a subject of common law.

The imagery is distinctive. There is first and foremost an inviolable soil:

> No man can set his foot upon my ground without my licence, but he is liable to an action, though the damage be nothing; which is proved by every declaration in trespass, where the defendent is called upon to answer for bruising the grass and even treading upon the soil. (*Entick* v. *Carrington* [1765] St. Tr. 1030, at 1066)[7]

To the inviolability of a native soil should be added the sanctity of a place, the peace, the quiet, the tranquillity of a home that is both castle, fortress and refuge, both a space of repose and of defence. The home is the safest of escapes and of refuges (*Semayne's Case* [1605] Co Rep 91a-b), so safe indeed that even after the sheriff has made a lawful entry his right to break down 'such inner doors as may happen to be shut' was still worth litigating (*Ratcliffe* v. *Burton* [1802] 27 Eng Rep 123, 126); so safe that as regards unlawful entry, Chief Justice Wilmot ventured that 'the plaintiff being a butcher, or inferior person, makes no difference in the case' (*Bruce* v. *Rawlins*, [1770] 95 Eng Rep 934).[8]

The immemorial law is an unwritten tradition, an eternally present collective legal memory, something that passes by word of mouth and it is in consequence a tacit knowledge, an attribute of honour and a criterion of manners. It corresponds to the desire of privacy, the wish of the gardening nation to turn away from the *polis*, the public realm, to avert their gaze from the political and to tend simply to their backyard, their tiny piece of national identity, their emblem and (h)earth. It is, in short, the eternal law of the land, of old England, a land peopled by the freeborn, by the gentle and honest, by justice and juries, by liberties and the continuity of custom, its speech, its books, its flowerpots. It is a countryside and the English, 'a rustic, active and generous people' (Smith, 1583/ 1906, p.61), are there bathed in the king's peace in which every

Englishman's home is his castle and in which Magna Carta secures for all time and unto heaven the innate right of the Englishman to his property and his person. The realm of privacy constitutes the political and legislative as 'other', as foreign, as something best left to those who legislate as of right and by distinction of birth.

The tacit quality of a knowledge, together with decisions that are always already made, always already there, behind the scenes, are both extremely English phenomena. It is the manners of 'good form', chivalry or a sense of fair play, that have traditionally been supposed to act as the bulwark protecting the subject of law from the tyranny of judgement. It is the aristocracy in the upper house of Parliament who have traditionally been supposed to mediate between the sovereign and the governed: 'the Lords being trusted with a judicatory power, are an excellent screen and bank between the Prince and the People, to assist each in any encroachments of the other, and by just judgements to preserve the law which ought to be the rule of all three' (Coke, 1660, A 3 b), a point to which we will return.

Time immemorial is the vanishing point of origin against which all later times of the law are to be measured. Time beyond memory is the time of foundation, the time of myth whereby history is converted into tradition and the linear temporality of historical narrative is displaced by the repetitive and symbolic time of the unconscious, an unconscious that binds our affections to very explicit and vivid images. The time of the unconscious is that other time in which the divine right of status was forged, in which the sacral quality of establishment or hierarchy was apodictically given from above, a time which we repress by repeating in habit, in instinct, in our movement through everyday life. It is to those aural and unwritten images, those oneiric or unconscious symbols of tradition as they inhabit English law, as they accompany and underpin the legal text, that we will now turn.[9]

Mystic Body and Unwritten Law

If we return to the question of the iconic unity of law as that which we recognise when we first recognise law as being our law, the image is of old England, an England that is eternal: it is our ground and our circumstance, our landscape, our nature, both mystical and thoughtless. It is at one level a purely internal history, the history of the survival of the English line, the history of the exclusion or repression of all forms of foreignness, even or especially when such foreignness is in our midst as language, as conqueror or indeed as royal family. In a secondary sense the internal character of the history of the English is a product of the fact that it is not a considered or explicit history; it is nature in the sense that it is given and indisputable: what is English, be it law or any other institution, is first and unquestionable. Its history is therefore something which can be assumed, it is internal in the sense of being inside all true English, all free English, mystical and inexplicit. In the end it is a family history, a history of a domestic constitution, a constitution that is unwritten because gentlemen do not need to put their word in writing, it is enough simply to give one's word (*Kington* v. *Preston* [1773] 99 Eng Rep 437). It is also an unwritten constitution because domestic agreements are outside the law; they are irreducible to law for the reason that law assumes that no reasonable person, no gentleman, would wish to jeopardise the harmony or honour of family agreements by taking them to court (*Balfour* v. *Balfour* [1919] 2 KB 271), just as it was until recently the case that no one could threaten a marriage by taking a husband to court for rape of his wife (*R* v. *Miller* [1954] 2 AER 529). The question remains as regards the constitution as to whose body, whose family (whose history), which line?

The authors of the ancient tradition are quite explicit, the constitution is one of 'regulated monarchy' and, as Coke also puts it, the crown is the hieroglyph of all our laws. If we turn to the icon itself, the licit representation of our nation and of our national legal system – the two are inseparable, the 'best inheritance a subject has [being] the law of the realm' (Coke, 1681, II A 2a) – it is the monarchy which paradoxically coheres both the identity of our character and the unity of the national legal system. The point is one which has been made variously in historical terms through the analysis of the *corpus mysticum* or undying royal body and its various forms of portraiture,[10] while in specific terms of the common law as it exists today, there is the exhaustive and excellent study by Tom Nairn (1988) of the quintessentially monarchical character of the historical and contemporary English constitution. What Nairn also makes abundantly clear is the dependency of the national psyche, the media, the communications industry, the entire fabric of social placement and personal differentiation upon one icon, one family, one parent, one law, one crown. If we move now to examine what it is that we belong to, what constitutes our tacit culture and our law, what it is that we know before we read any individual text, it is the monarchy that will emblematise the space of law, the deep structure, the waking and the sleeping dream. It is precisely to a monarchical culture that we belong before we read the law: it is from that culture that we make our decisions as to interpretation and state with each judgement our allegiance to a literal Englishness, to an identity that excludes all consideration of any other culture or any other way.

The elements of an unwritten constitution can be listed with relative brevity; the key to the English constitution – to how we 'stand together' (*con-statuere*) – is precisely that it is unwritten, that it is tacit and traditional: it is law as *dharma*, as way or path or road, as a manner of doing things, as good form, and not as an idea or a dialogue or even as anything to be thought about. In that sense it is pure tradition kept alive by the circulation of one symbol, one icon, one family, of what 'we are' *as represented* in the comings and goings, doings and sayings, court news and state functions of the royal family. The search for an identity could thus well begin with a statement of the obvious: the constitution as it exists today was primarily the product of the arrogation of the powers of the church to the crown in 1534. The monarch became both spiritual and secular sovereign, Leviathan twice over, the inerasible and singular image of a national legal system that had broken with Rome and with the Roman church. Law, as the frequently misread philosopher John Austin had no hesitation in specifying,[11] was best defined as being no more or less than the command of the sovereign: a command that could be positive and direct or could take the more subtle form of the adoption of existing law or tacit command as the judgements of the sovereign's judicial representatives.

As regards the spheres of adoption and tacit command we move into the realm (the *regalis*) of the unsaid or unstated of a legal system that has accumulated, discovered or 'found' law far more often than it would claim to have directly devised it. Law as tradition depends upon the notion that what is established requires no further or no rational justification; it simply belongs, it is there, part of the system of symbols that constitute a legal identity and system of law. In so far as it is surprising and could be amusing, we can borrow some statistics from Nairn (1988) to suggest the extent to which the monarchy as symbol pervades the national consciousness, and its unconscious as well. Taken from surveys in the late 1960s and 70s, we learn that 77 per cent of labour voters and 50 per cent of the unemployed would retain the monarchy (the royal family does no harm), over 50 per cent of the population indeed believed that God took a special interest in England, 'that God guides this country in times of trouble'. Finally over a third of the population had dreamt about the royal family. The statistics can be added to the other indices of a quiet but obsessive national concern with the crown, with its omnipresence in public life. The question to be posed is that of how serious that pervasive regality is in terms of the constitution of our laws.

Law, Correct Speech and the Logic of the Centre

The key to an understanding of the significance, the absolutism, of a monarchical and wholly pre-revolutionary constitution does not lie in the literal manifestations of monarchism, in its ordinariness or its triviality, but in the impossible and unspoken realm of everyday power that circulates along lines of force that emanate from the throne. Let us continue the list, but now in terms of symbols that refer the citizen, the litigant, the subject to the liturgical or inaugural space of the monarchy, of that mystic body that never dies: 'King is a name of Continuance, which will always endure as the Head and Governor of the People (as the Law presumes) as long as the People continue ... and in this Name the King never dies' (*Willion* v. *Berkley*, Plowden Reports, 3 Eliz 177a). We may go further than Justice Brown and observe that not only does the monarch as mystic body, or body politic, never die, but the political and legal attributes of that body, its mystic members, its offices and honours, statuses and creeds do not die either (Kantorowicz, 1957, pp.11–15). To adopt a classical civilian motif, *dignitas non moritur*: dignity (meaning office, honour and status) does not die, though we may certainly die for it; we may die for an office, a country, honour, a mask (Legendre, 1988, pp.33–42).

If we remain in search of the *regalis*, of the crown in public or abroad we must look to the courts. In one of its earliest guises the court was the royal court, the royal household or 'the body of persons who form the [sovereign's] suite or council' and accompany the monarch's person on its constant journey through the kingdom and other possessions (Milsom, 1981, pp.31–33). As *curia regis* (*coram rege*) it was also the first court of the common law, though the notion of the court as that which follows the crown, as a suite or continuance, provides a useful insight into both senses of court; first, as site of etiquette and decorum in the proper sense – that of ceremonies of court – and, second, as being the site of judgement or mercy, preferment or punishment. The court follows the crown, it is peripatetic as part of the royal entourage and later itinerant through delegation: the provincial courts and assizes are simply the royal court 'sitting elsewhere', the monarch's person in its capacity of body politic rather than natural being.

That the court is the royal court sitting in the absence of the monarch does not in any sense preclude the presencing of majesty. The labyrinthine structure of the Royal Courts of Justice amply indicate an architecture of place, a pageantry and regality that constitute in the most direct of senses a plastic elocution of an iconic authority: the emblematic name of the law is to be found endlessly repeated in the alternative space and the other time of the court. 'That is the great lesson of the history of ... law, that the power and authority of reason are the same thing' (Legendre, 1985, p.38).[12] In more aphoristic terms, it is through the institution of the image that the law gets under the skin. Consider the iconic order of licit representation as it is to be found in the architectural and ornamental organisation of a court, in the symbolics of its physical places, in the aura of its furniture and gargoyles, its inscriptions and devices (crests and arms), in its modes of dress and address, and finally in its terms, its moments of appearance and disappearance, of sitting and dissolution. Our concern is with that panoply of symbols that exist to create a legal place, a site or space of law, of legal annunciation[13] if that term can be so adapted from its biblical usage to indicate an announcement that is simultaneously a mode of sacral presence, the presence that has to be brought to law for it to be law. The fascination of power must always take a material form, it must be reinstituted to create a space, an architecture within which a discourse becomes solemnised, a language approaches a liturgy and the signs are all there to indicate the distances necessary to a place, that will allow the judge to speak in the mask of the Other, to speak innocently as a mouth of the law. The places are mapped according to criteria of ascension and both physically and verbally all points look up to and are directed towards the bench, upon which, after the ushers have demanded silence and respect, it is the law that sits down in the place of merely human demands (Miller, 1986). Consider too the forms of dress, the apparel of justice, always recollecting Carlyle's aphorism that 'the beginning of all wisdom is to look fixedly on Clothes' (1893, p.45). Recollect also, the order of its coming and going and the restriction upon the forms in which it can be addressed, the various metonymies as well as the sacral appellations: the court, the bench, your honour, your worship, your lordship.

What the court takes with it is the awful logic of the centre, the English tradition, the custom of the realm which is of course the custom of the crown. Consider again that English is first a language and second a law, the common law. Immediately prior to the era when Sir Edward Coke, Sir John Davies, and others were forging the records of English legal tradition and creating the secular myth of the common law, Richard Mulcaster, Henry Peacham, Thomas Wilson, Sir Thomas Elyot and others less well-remembered were nurturing English as the national and the best of all languages. English was being forged against the Latin and French of the law, although it was Latin that was most decried:

is it not a marvellous bondage, to become servants of one tongue for learning's sake, the most of our time, with loss of most time, whereas we may have the very same treasure in out own tongue, with the gain of most time? Our own bearing the joyful title of our liberty and freedom, the Latin tongue reminding us of our thraldom and bondage? I love Rome, but London better. I favour Italy, but England more, I honour the Latin but I worship the English. (Mulcaster, 1582/1970, pp.254–5)

Consider then the work of a barrister, George Puttenham, on the geography of correct linguistic usage:

> [you] shall follow generally the better brought up sort, such as the Greeks call (*charientes*) men civil and graciously behaved and bred. Our matter therefore at these days shall not follow Piers Plowman nor Gower nor Lydgate nor yet Chaucer neither shall [you] take the terms of Northern men ... nor in effect any speech beyond the river Trent, though no man can deny but that theirs is the purer English Saxon at this day, yet it is not so courtly or so current as our Southern English, no more is the far Western men's speech ... ye shall therefore take the usual speech of the court, and that of London and the shires lying about London within 40 miles, and not much above. (Puttenham, 1589, pp.120–1).

Just as the courts follow the court, English law follows the English language in respect at least of the geography of correct usage, the centrality of records and places, and the pre-eminence of manners, forms of correct behaviour and of speech as determinative of propriety (or more strongly of normality). The phonetic basis of class identity is only comprehensible to those who have lived in England: a certain tone, an accent, use of received pronunciation and standard English vocabulary are together the most powerful of indicators of class and determinative of institutional place. It is frequently the case that no more is needed than a few choice, well-spoken words; the aural signs of law are here the unwritten constitution and precede any explicit rule, or any writing, any text.[14]

Status, Honour and Spoken Law

The unwritten constitution, the English constitution, is a court-based custom, a series of conventions transmitted through an unwritten knowledge of forms and tacit rules of behaviour associated with the better classes, the better educated, the honourable and the gentle. Just as the court has its place, namely London, so the people have their places with 'every man in his room of honour according as his place requires' (Ridley, 1607/1676, p.134). The distinction of blood, of breeding, of genealogy has been as important (possibly more important) than any particular behaviour: the barrister John Legh writes in a work called *The Accedens of Armory*, one of several legal manuals of the rules and insignia of status of the period, that 'the distinction between gentle and ungentle, [is one] in which there is as much difference, as between virtue and vice' (1562, fol. ii b). It was the lawyers in the main who systematised and spelled out the system of honours, manners, proper speech and social law.[15] We can learn from them. The system of honour depicts or, better, represents the various forms of ancestral or acquired nobility, through which an unwritten but nonetheless well-marked network of power is transmitted.

As Sir John Ferne defines it, that nobility is derived as a word from the Latin *nobilitas* which in turn has a root in *nosco*, to know (1586, p.4). By extension we might argue that the system of nobility not only signifies generosity (or gentility), *viz* nobility, of blood and degree which is known by its insignia, which is represented in the 'devise' or mark or crest, but it is also a form of codification, an encoding of knowledge, a hidden language or initiate wisdom even if that wisdom is of manners and mores and little else. Through their arms the gentle, the honoured, those of social standing are known and noted. They bear their status on their breast as *symbolica heroica* (heroic symbols), as signs of dignity and of birth. What is known and noted, however, is strictly and opaquely encoded. All the treatises of armory emphasise: it is a secret science, known of God (Legh, 1562, fol. v b); it is the art 'of hieroglyphical or enigmatic symbols and signs, testifying the nobility or gentry' of the bearer (Guillim, 1610, fol. 3a); they are 'true symbols' (Fraunce, 1588, fol. H 3b), and being 'obstruse and sacred', enigmatic and holy in origin, the meanings of arms of honour are best protected by dark and foreign words (Estienne, 1643, fol. B iia). The unwritten constitution spans equally the political and legal domains. It establishes a power that is both unknown and nomadic, a moving target in that the generic secrecy of the institution means inevitably that for every success in eliciting information countless documents disappear, oral culture reasserts itself, archives sink into the flowerbeds, new laws of secrecy are passed or old laws are exorbitantly enforced. The principle involved is summarised prosaically by Nairn: 'from the 1680's to the 1980's the right of those in power to discuss nothing about the exercise of power but what suited them has been a constitutive principle of British tranquillity and decency' (1988, p.268).

The two principles of English constitutionalism, those of monarchism and secrecy, of an aura or display of power that simultaneously hides the logic of its practice, can be traced without difficulty or too great a degree of digression into the common law itself. The aura of majesty that is put in place by the architecture of the court, by the placement of the judiciary within the courtroom by the direct ennoblement of the judges, by the appropriate modes of addressing the bench, by the order of speech, by the rules of evidence, by costume, pageantry and language – all these display the making of a liturgical, legal setting. These symbols are the servants of the crown, they issue their writs by the grace of God and in defence of the faith, and in the name of the crown their space is the regal space of the law. Like the constitution, the law that they carry is unwritten: it is custom, it is tradition, it is *ius non scriptum*, unwritten reason, that can be terroristically applied as and when the judicial memory of the immemorial or of 'time out of mind' comes on the scene of the present.

The notion of time out of mind describes legal method most exactly; it is time unbound to any life or object, free of any specific temporality, a time of repetition and so a thoughtless time. It is what Legendre terms the 'delirium of the institution' which unravels itself within the discrete confines of the legal form, as a prisoner not of life but of normative governance (1976). It is in this sense that the law unfolds as a prison of the *deep structure*: a prison in the sense of a mathematic envelope, of a reality that outlasts or outlives another. The law is a prison of the deep historical structures which time treats badly. Hence time out of mind is a time of repetition but in this repetition is always and already difference, and loss: that is to say, what is repeated in the again and again of a precedent is not the same case, not the same life, not the same thought, the same rule, the same instance. The institution hallucinates standard forms of procedure and norms of usual behaviour on the strength of half-remembered arguments, through the dazed recollection of unreported cases or largely forgotten conversations:

> in those cases where judges were declaring law it was a transient, oral, informal process and only those present at the arguments could hope to achieve a wholly accurate impression of what had been decided, and then only when the judges spoke loudly enough. (Baker, 1978, vol. 2, p.159)

These were the tools of the common law, these were their memories, a *communis opinio*, a collective memory, as law. Law is a presence which implies the totality of its history, but this implication is not logical or historical; rather, it is traditional and mythic. The hallucinating mind is in strict terms a mind that wanders, that 'lucinates', that goes astray. That is the source of common law, of unwritten law, it is the meandering of the legal mind, a temporal and geographic nomadism that snakes its path across the justificatory texts, the judgements, of the year books and the law reports. Here we can understand how the text is also the unwritten structure of everyday life, a reality which time treats badly and transmits very slowly over long periods, how reason itself becomes a mask 'worn by longstanding historical and political facts, the memory of which men [have] retained over centuries,' (Braudel, 1958, p.26) how the limits 'marked by reason' have nothing reasonable about them. Herein nature, space, time, memory, reason and its images are all objects to be constructed. The perception of the past is still and always a perception, a projection and as such is essentially creative. The law as the prison of the deep structure embraces the universe of hallucinatory objects: metastable, totemic, interoceptive: the marmoreal deposits of a time out of mind, time immemorial. Yet these objects are enclosed within a life world, still bound in an elemental way to both an experiential world and a historical world: the life world takes them up into itself as 'practical structures', that is to say, as the objects of praxis. In the courts they are taken up as the burden of a legal reason always and already enchanted by the archaisms of a culture. These archaisms function as the 'handles' of a particular theory of interpretation, a particular hermeneutic, a particular rationality. The space of law is always and already carpentered; embedded systems of measurement and scales of value prompt the circular logic of repetition, mobilise an uncodified (unsupported)[16] reason that was traditionally more lyrical than rational but which now travels under the disguise of a linear and pragmatic logic of decision-making, that now travels as the lie of reason.[17]

Conclusion: *Ius Imaginarium,* the Law of Images

The protection of the sacral aura of courtroom process is one of the oldest powers known to the common law. The common law of contempt of court is indeed 'coeval with their first foundation and constitution; it is a necessary incident to every Court of Justice'. (*R v. Almer* [1975] Wilm 243, 97 Eng Rep 94) Its basis is interestingly enough forgotten, it belongs to time out of mind, it is part of the *lex terrae*, part of the very soil, the earth from which the law springs unseen and unremembered till its reinstatement as the presence of the living present. This immemorial usage has no origin, the chief justice admitting readily that 'I have examined very carefully to see if I could find out any vestiges or traces of its introduction, but can find none. It is as ancient as any other part of the common law, *there is no priority or posteriority to be discovered about it ...*' (ibid, 99–100). It is simply there, established and unchallengeable, part of precedent, part of the law even if we have no reason, no justification, no memory of why that might be – or, better, might have been – the case. The justificatory principle is classic common law logic and to return to Sir John Fortescue, this time sitting on the bench in 1458, we may cite a remarkably precise formulation: 'Sir, the law is as I say it is, and so it has been laid down ever since the law began; and we have several set forms which are held as law, and so held for good reason, though we cannot at present remember that reason' (1458, YB 36 Hen. VI 25b–26).

For amnesia to resemble reason, for anamnesis to be the proper form of legal knowledge, requires that the subject understand that what occurs in court is emblematic. To paraphrase the work of Louis Marin,

> the [law] is only truly [law], that is, [justice], in images. They are its *real presence*. A belief in the effectiveness and operativeness of these iconic signs is obligatory, or else the law is emptied of all its substance through lack of transubstantiation, and only simulacrum is left; but inversely, because its signs are the [legal] *reality*, the being and substance of the [law], this belief is necessarily demanded by the signs themselves (Marin, 1988, p.9).

The image of the court is protected in the occasion of its appearance and even more so in the public relay of that appearance through the press and other media. The law which governs 'contempt of court' is unique in that it allows summary indictment of offenders without the option of jury trial: to take some recent examples, people laughing in the courtroom; witnesses too frightened to give evidence against people they know; persons too confused to respond to judicial questions, have all been imprisoned on the spot for common law contempt of court *in praesentia*, in the presence of the court.

Two points need to be made, one spatial and one temporal. From early on in its history, the court was not geographically limited to the courtroom: it was a 'place' and it was to be protected as such, that is to say in its other offices, in its chambers, in the Inns of Court, in the chancelleries, the libraries and all the other sacred hiding places (*sacramentorum latibula*) including the royal treasure chest (*thesauria regis*) in which the records and the other writings of the law were either forged or kept. In *Thorpe* v. *Makerel*, to take a geographically extreme example, a clerk of the King's Court was urinated on in Fleet Street while on his way to Westminster, in the company of other men of the court. In the writ issued, a *venire facias*, the trespass charged was stated as having been *in presencia curiae* (1318, Selden Society vol. 74 at 79).

The point of that little history, however, is larger than is perhaps apparent: all aspects of the honour of the court and of its aura are protected: what cannot be geographically charged as contempt in the face (*imago*) or presence of the court, can be indicted as scandalising the court *in absentia*. The emblematic image, the reputation, the presence of the court and of what occurs within it is rigorously (not to say draconianly) controlled. Nothing can be published that would be, in the eyes of the court, prejudicial to any civil or criminal trial. Their vision is often surprising and it has been held, for example, to be contempt for a lawyer to show documents that had been read out in open court to an investigative journalist, even though the journalist could have obtained a transcript of the hearing (*Home Office* v. *Harman* [1982] 1 AER 532). It has been held more recently that republication of information that was already in the public domain could be a contempt of court (*Attorney General* v. *Newpaper Publishing PLC and others* [1989] *Guardian*, May 8). Further, 'any act done or writing published calculated to bring a Court or a judge of the Court into contempt or lower his authority is a contempt of court' (*R* v. *Gray*, [1900], 2 QB 36, 40). Thus any adverse criticism of any aspect of a trial, a judge, a court, or a verdict, is potentially in danger of incurring the strictures of the law. It is to be reported, in other words, according to and in its majesty; it is to be reported reverently, darkly, emblematically – for such are the characteristics of the institution. They are also embedded in its language, in its annunciation, in all its forms of appearance and disappearance, in all the icons and other totems behind which lurk the unreason of legal practice.

Notes

1. On the relation between repetition and repression, see Deleuze, 1968, especially pp.138–9 where Freud's notion of 'primary repression' is discussed in the following terms: 'one does not repeat because one represses, but one represses because one repeats'. In terms of memory one can thus argue that the primary repression establishes an unconscious that repeats so as not to remember. In Lingis' words, it constitutes 'a system that does not remember, that is, represent, its past, because it repeats it. It does not reinstate its past in the non-actuality of representation but in the actuality of its repetition' (1989, p.158).
2. There is an extensive literature on the impact of printing and so also of the vernacular, on the legal profession. The now standard work is Eisenstein, 1980. For further references and my own justification of the centrality of the sixteenth century to an understanding of the contemporary legal profession, see Goodrich, 1990, Chapter 3.
3. Specifically on *dharma*, see B. Jackson, 1978. On law as the road or way see Rose, 1988, pp.359–60. On *dike* see Benveniste, 1969, vol. 2, pp.107–110.
4. See also Sir Henry Spelman, *The Original of the Four Law Terms of the Year* (1614, pp.102–3) for further discussion of the unwritten basis of the legal text. Its inscription on the heart of man is a reference both to its divine provenance and to a curiously spurious source in the rulings of Lycurgus of Sparta against the reduction of law to writing.

5. For Peirce, the evolution of a code requires that there be a conservation and development of forms, a logic of continuity which moves language from mere marks to symbols:

    the mark is a mere accident, and as such may be erased. It will not interfere with another mark drawn in quite another way. There need be no consistency between the two but no further progress beyond this can be made, until a mark will *stay* for a little while; that is, until some beginning of a *habit* has been established by virtue of wh:ch the accident acquires some incipient staying quality, some tendency toward consistency. (Peirce, 1931–5, p.204.)

    For Peirce's influence on the legal realists, see Kevelson, 1988.
6. On *pro patria mori*, see Kantorowicz, 1965, pp.308–24, and 1957, pp.232–73. See further, the discussion in Legendre, 1988.
7. The trace itself is always and already the trace of the Other, which, even in its disappearance, its aesthetic of disappearance, is a passage to the limit, a passage across and through a boundary, and thus a movable object, a legal sign, a legal icon.
8. What better image of the difficulty of getting to know the English could one seek than that of inner doors? Each inner door is a new obstacle, a further defence, a subject of independent litigation. For a recent discussion of the concept of the home in the interesting and innovatory area of psychiatric damage cause by damage to the home, see *Attia* v. *British Gas* [1987] 3 All E.R. 455.
9. Merleau-Ponty, 1962, defines an original past as 'a past which has never been present'.
10. The best studies are not of the English monarchy but of the French, the classic study of the iconic form of royal portraiture being L. Martin, 'Le Corps Glorieux du Roi et son Portrait' in Marin, 1986. There is also his longer study (1988).
11. For discussion of such misreadings of Austin, see Moles, 1987.
12. For further discussion of this specific point, namely the inscription of law in the building, in the symbols of place, see the excellent discussion in Hersey, 1988, pp.9ff., of the etymological link between trope and trophy in architectural ornament. See also Vidler, 1987.
13. The annunciation is enunciation with a phonetically indiscernible difference. The biblical annunciation brought news of her pregnancy to Mary via the Archangel Gabriel. It was both the announcement and simultaneously presence of the Holy Spirit.
14. Interesting in this context to note that etymologically the word repetition connotes rehearsal and more distantly; re-hearing it is an auditory phenomenon before it is a matter of record. See Rose, 1984, p.102.
15. The other major works are Fraunce, 1588; Spelman, 1654; J. Logan, *Analogia Honorum*, 1677; J. Bosewell, *Workes of Armorie*, 1610. Full references can be found in Goodrich, 'Rhetoric, Grammatology and the Hidden Injuries of Law', 1989, *Economy and Society*, no. 18, p.167.

16. The term code comes from the Latin *codex* and more distantly from *caudex* meaning structure or support. The etymology is interestingly discussed in U. Eco, *Semiotics and the Philosophy of Language*, 1984, pp.164–82.
17. The lie of reason is from Nietzsche, *The Twilight of the Idols*, 1915, pp.24–5, where he argues in effect that the history of truth is the history of an error and presents the narrative of 'How the real world became a myth'. Baudrillard, 1983, translates Nietzsche's six stages of the history of an error into 'four successive stages of the image', the last of which is that the image 'bears no relation to any reality what-soever, it is its own pure simulacrum'. While this translation provides a semiotically interesting variant of Nietzsche's theme it misunder-stands Nietzsche's principal conclusion, namely that with the sup-pression of the real world the world of appearance is also abolished. Only theatre and mask, truth as fiction and fiction as truth remain.

References and Further Reading

Works preceded by an asterisk are those most likely to act as suitable introductory readings on semiotics and semiotics of law. The *International Journal for the Semiotics of Law* appears three times a year and is now in its fourth volume. It promises to cover most areas of the discipline and is open to different perspectives although contribu-tions have so far been predominantly from structuralist and analytical orientations. The annual proceedings of the Roundtable on Semiotics and Law are published from the Centre for Semiotic Research in Law, Government and Economy, Pennsylvania State University, Reading, PA, and are edited by Professor Roberta Kevelson (1988–90). Of more general interest is the journal *Semiotica* which often carries work on law. In terms of general philosophical introductions to a supplemen-tary jurisprudence of signs a major source of inspiration is Nietzsche (1910) *The Genealogy of Morals*, Edinburgh: Foulis.

Baker, J.H. (ed.) (1978) *The Reports of John Spelman* (London: Selden Society).
*Baudrillard, J. (1983) *Simulations* (New York: Semiotexte).
Benveniste, E. (1969) *Le Vocabulaire des Institutions Indo-Européenes* (Paris: Editions de Minuit).
*Blonsky, M. (ed.) (1985) *On Signs* (Oxford: Basil Blackwell).
Braudel, F. (1958) *On History* (London: Fontana).
Carlyle, Thomas (1893) *Sartor Resartus* (London: Murray).
Carty, A. (1989) 'Of Crabs and Constitutions', *International Journal for the Semiotics of Law*, no. 5, p.215.
Carty, A. (ed.) (1990), *Post-modern Law* (Edinburgh: Edinburgh University Press).
*Carzo, D. and Jackson, B. (eds) (1985) *Semiotics, Law and Social Science* (Rome: Gangemi and Liverpool Law Review).

Clanchy, M.T. (1979) *From Memory to Written Record* (London: Arnold).

Coke, Sir Edward (1610) *A Book of Entries* (London: Streeter).

Coke, Sir Edward (1611/1777 edn) *The Reports* (London: J. Rivington).

Coke, Sir Edward (1660) *Political Catechism* (London: Field).

Coke, Sir Edward (1681 edn) *The Second Part of the Institutes of the Laws of England* (London: Rawlins).

Davies, Sir John (1615) *Le Primer Report des Cases & Matters en Ley Resolves & Adjudges in les Courts del Roy en Ireland* (Dublin: J. Franckton).

Deeley, J. (1982) *Introducing Semiotic* (Bloomington: Indiana University Press).

*Deeley, J. *et al.* (1986) *Frontiers in Semiotics* (Bloomington: Indiana University Press).

Deleuze, G. (1968) *Difference et Repetition* (Paris: PUF).

Douzinas, C., McVeigh, S. and Warrington, R. (1991) *Postmodern Jurisprudence* (London: Routledge).

Eco, U. (1984) *Semiotics and the Philosophy of Language* (London: Macmillan).

Eisenstein, E. (1980) *The Printing Press as an Agent of Change* (Cambridge: Cambridge University Press).

Estienne, H. (1643) *The Art of Making Devises* (London: Holden).

Ferne, Sir John (1586) *The Blazon of Gentrie* (London: Winder).

Fortescue, Sir John (1470/1737 edn) *De Laudibus Legum Angliae* (London: Gosling).

Fraunce, A. (1588) *Insignium Armorum, Emblematum, Hieroglyphicum et Symbolorum* (London: Orvinus).

*Goodrich, P. (1987) 'Review', *Modern Law Review*, no. 50, p.117.

*Goodrich, P. (1990) *Languages of Law: From Logics of Memory to Nomadic Masks* (London: Weidenfeld & Nicolson).

Goodrich, P. (1990) 'We Orators', 53 *Modern Law Review*, p.408.

Guillim, J. (1610) *A Display of Heraldry* (London: Rycroft).

Hachamovitch, Y. (1990) 'From the Tooth to the Triangle: A Semiotics of Moveable Bodies', in Kevelson (ed.), (1990) pp.93–113.

Hale, Sir Matthew (1975 edn) *The History of the Common Law of England* (Chicago: Chicago University Press).

Hersey, G. (1988) *The Lost Meaning of Classical Architecture* (Cambridge, Mass: MIT).

Jackson, B. (1978) 'From Dharma to Law', *American Journal of Comparative Law*, vol. 45, p.163.

Jackson, B. (1985) *Semiotics and Legal Theory* (London: Routledge).

Kantorowicz, E. (1957) *The King's Two Bodies* (Princeton: Princeton University Press).

Kantorowicz, E. (1965) *Selected Studies* (New York: Augustin).

Kevelson, R. (1988) *Law as a System of Signs* (New York: Plenum).

*Kevelson, R. (ed.) (1988-90) *Law and Semiotics*, 3 vols. (New York: Plenum).

Legendre, P. (1976) *Jouir de Pouvoir* (Paris: Editions de Minuit).

Legendre, P. (1985) *L'Inestimable Object de la Transmission* (Paris: Fayard).

Legendre, P. (1988) *Le Désir Politique de Dieu* (Paris: Fayard).

Legh, G. (1562) *The Accedens of Armory* (London: Totil).

Lingis, A. (1989) *Deathbound Subjectivity* (Bloomington: Indiana University Press).

Maitland and Pollock (1968) *History of English Law* (Cambridge: Cambridge University Press).

Marin, L. (1986) *La Parole Mangée* (Paris: Klinckseick).

*Marin, L. (1988) *Portrait of the King* (London: Macmillan).

Merleau-Ponty, M. (1962) *Phenomenology of Perception* (London: Routledge & Kegan Paul).

Miller, J.A. (1986) 'Jeremy Bentham's Panoptic Device', October 3.

Milsom, S.F. (1981) *Historical Foundations of the Common Law* (London: Butterworth).

Moles, R. (1987) *Definition and Rule in Legal Theory* (Oxford: Basil Blackwell).

Mulcaster, R. (1582/1970) *The First Part of the Elementary* (London: Menston).

Murphy, T. (1991) 'The Oldest Social Science? The Epistemic Properties of the Common Law Tradition' (forthcoming), *Modern Law Review*.

*Nairn, T. (1988) *The Enchanted Glass* (London: Radius).

Nietzsche, F. (1915) *The Twilight of the Idols* (Edinburgh: Foulis).

*Pierce, C. (1931–5) *Collected Papers* (Cambridge, Mass: Harvard University Press).

Puttenham, G. (1589) *The Arte of English Poesie* (London: Field).

Ridley, T. (1607/1676 edn) *A View of the Civille and Ecclesiasticall Law* (Oxford: H. Hall).

Rose, G. (1984) *Dialectic of Nihilism* (Oxford: Basil Blackwell).

Rose, G. (1988) 'Architecture to Philosophy – The Postmodern Complicity', *Theory, Culture, Society*, no. 5, p.357.

Smith, Sir Thomas (1583/1906 edn) *De Republica Anglorum* (Cambridge: Cambridge University Press).

Spelman, H. (1654) *Aspilogia* (London: Martin & Allestry).

Vidler, A. (1987) *The Writing of the Walls* (Princeton: Princeton University Press).

English Constitutional Law from a Postmodernist Perspective

Anthony Carty

The Idea of the English Legal Order

This chapter will explore some historical roots of the idea of an English legal system. It will examine the implications of a very simple hypothesis, that the English legal system is an expression of a national *Volksgeist* which was given shape by the Elizabethan theologian Richard Hooker and the great theorist of the English Civil War, Thomas Hobbes. They developed a theory of law and the state which has remained essentially the same up until the present analytical school of law. Their central thesis is that the very idea of law, of its sovereignty, must mean that all sectors of society abandon their autonomy of legal interpretation (that is, of the extent of their obligations) in favour of a single national interpretative authority. In other words there is not so much a coercive monopoly of legal meaning as an inevitability of legal unity seen as central to the very idea of legal order.

The chapter will demonstrate in the first instance that the unity of the legal order rests upon an Anglican idea of the polity, that the entire English people consists of a single presence in the crown in parliament, itself the Christian Commonwealth seen in its political aspect. The notion of 'presence' is elusive and a large part of the chapter will attempt to elaborate it. It is fundamentally a theological idea. In its religious aspect, the English people are a single, complete, church, in the sense that the 'presence' of God/Christ guarantees the essential unity and harmony of the people. There is no likelihood of a principle of internal contradiction or anything which might disturb this harmony. Its law is an expression of its identity, not something imposed from outside and in no sense a critical principle. So there is no need for a separation of legal powers within its 'body' nor does it make any sense to speak of an external critical legal principle. That would be merely a reintroduction of the notion of a universal church, the very idea of which Anglicanism was founded to deny.

The essay will go on to consider the attempts of Blackstone and later Burke to rewrite the Anglican polity in terms first of customary/

established/common law. The formal characteristics of the Anglican legal polity are retained, the idea of the sovereign unity of the law, its homogeneity and, above all, the law as an expression of a presence, now no longer explicitly an Anglican Christian Commonwealth, but more an 'establishment' in the 'present' of a continuing identity, the English people. Rationality in law is openly resisted in the sense that there is now a much more familiar resistance to the idea of a charter of the rights of man, a rejection of the idea of the separation of powers and the continued refusal to look upon law as an independent standard of criticism of society. It remains the principal form through which the English people express their identity.

Finally the chapter will consider the attempts of Dicey and more briefly, the analytical school of law, to 'modernise' the idea of an English legal order. It is to be separated from history and tradition and given a formal character independent of politics and morality. The principle of the sovereignty of parliament does not open up the threat of tyrannical power. It is simply seen to be the logical foundation for the unity of the legal order. The absence of limits upon the legal duty to obey the law equally expresses merely the effortless homogeneity of the legal order. The very idea of law, within this system of thought, can still not conceive of the necessity for such foreign, rationalist ideas as the separation of powers and independent standards of human rights. As a modernist concept of law it depends, above all, upon the notion of the autonomy of law as an independent discipline or phenomenon in reality which can only be properly understood and appreciated as existing in and for itself: law for law's sake, as art for art's sake. It is the predominant view that theoretical study of the English legal order has, at present, achieved this goal.

The presentation of this chapter will have a rudimentary postmodernist pretention. It will have the very deliberate and simple objective to demonstrate that the modernist attempt to transform the English legal tradition into an analytical legal structure based upon the sovereignty of parliament is, in a sense which evidently cannot be expressed succinctly or abstractly, absurd and meaningless. It is hoped to demonstrate this thesis through a deconstruction of familiar texts. This brings me to a closer or more extensive account of how I understand postmodernism in this context. There is a very consistent argument to postmodernity which stands or falls as a readily verifiable historical proposition. Modernity purported to secularise thought, to render it independent of a religious or metaphysical ground of being, to liberate it from the 'darkness' of history, tradition and authority. Its model of law is above all perfectly clear. It is, at least, what society at present actually accepts as law. As such it is self-justifying, if indeed one can even pose the question whether justification is needed. Society recognises or constitutes a system of institutions, procedures and so on, which provide a structure in which to place and understand individual rights and claims. About this there is no mystery. There is no need to reach out to ultimate foundations. A perfect clarity illuminates society's understanding of itself in its world.

Such a modernist project can be understood most clearly through a comparison with what it purported to replace. This chapter considers a postmodern perspective on how modernity appears to have failed in its own terms, precisely in that it incorporates fundamentally religious/metaphysical assumptions into its own categories of thought. As a leading French exponent of postmodern thought, Derrida, puts it, metaphysics are a white mythology (1986, p.213). This is even explicit, in my view, in England in the writings of Hobbes who assigns all semiotic significance or meaning to the state. The deconstruction of secular rationalism is a central feature of postmodernism. Derrida suggests how far the imagination – or, if one prefers, the intellect – is as much spellbound as subject to the white mythology which it thought it had exorcised. The implications for modernist law are never far away. In other words postmodernism marks the reintroduction of ontology into law, not as a solution to the question of the foundation of law, but as a firm assertion that law has no foundation. Put concretely, in the context of the present chapter, basic or central English legal forms are adrift, no longer embedded in a definite cultural identity. Thus the supposed strength of modernity, its quest for autonomy and distinctiveness, becomes a mark of aimlessness and directionlessness.

Nihilism, as it presents itself at the end of this chapter, is therefore not simply, or even at all, a morally destructive perspective. Rather it is a reassertion of the ontological question, 'why anything at all?', a searching out, with a stylistic mixture of rhetoric and parody, of how this question is suppressed and excluded. Although this chapter is a cultural history of the specifically English understanding of constitutional law, it is not making a contribution to an analytical understanding of law as an order or system by, for instance, finding alternative structures hidden at a deeper level within already elucidated structures. In different ways the English analytical school of law consists of structuralists making explicit how 'naturalist' or 'prelegal' notions of subjectivity are enmeshed (and none the worse for it) in structures of meaning which are, nonetheless, juridical. The particular form of poststructuralism upon which I am engaged is simply to show, as a matter of historical fact, that the soul has gone out of a culture, that what we are studying are fossils, ghosts, dead memories.

Constitutional Theory and Political Theology in the Sixteenth and Seventeenth Centuries

My presentation of Hobbes's classic *Leviathan* as an exercise in political theology follows very closely the work of Carl Schmitt, in part his *Political Theology*, but more particularly his own study of Hobbes (1938). Schmitt is a well-known proponent of the thesis that political ideas are, as a matter of history, secularised theology. So the state was accorded omnipotence in the making of laws and was considered to be the final arbiter of any dispute, where, *ex hypothesi*, there was no agreement as to how a supposed norm was to apply. It creates law out of chaos. Thus, outside the state there is no law. At the same time the state is not itself law, but precedes it and is not dependent upon it (ibid., pp.50–3, 69, 74). That is to say, the state absorbs into itself all rationality and legality. Outside it there is only a state of nature. The state has its order within itself, and depends for nothing outside itself (ibid., p.75). Hobbes is anxious to absorb the traditional medieval right of resistance to the state into the state itself so that it is simply nonsensical to speak of a right of resistance on the same level of legality as the state itself (ibid., p.71).

Schmitt uses the expression *rechtlich widersinnig* (juridically senseless) to describe the idea of a legal right to resistance, for he is concerned with the notion of the state as a symbol. Either the state makes all subjective and objective law itself, or it simply does not exist; it is not present (*vorhanden*) (ibid., p.72). The right of resistance means simply the right of civil war, of state destruction. Hobbes did not propose to hand over the insecure individual to a terrifying state, but to end feudal, estate and church rights to resistance, by setting against them an unambiguous effective system of legality (ibid., p.113).

A decisive aspect of the absorption of all symbols of legality into the state is to unify the religious and the political. In other words *Leviathan* follows an Anglican view of church and state which adheres very closely to the theory of the state outlined by Hooker in volume VIII *Of the Laws of Ecclesiastical Policy* (1981). Why Hobbes felt compelled towards this course he makes plain when he says in Part III of *Leviathan* (*Of A Christian Commonwealth*) that the reason for the right of the sovereign to appoint pastors is that the right of judging what doctrines are fit for peace and to be taught to subjects must rest in the sovereign civil power, whether it be one man or an assembly of men. The reason is obvious: 'that mens actions are derived from the opinions they have of the Good, or Evil' (Hobbes, 1968, Chapter 42, p.567). Where pastors do not receive their authority from the civil state they 'sliely slip off the Collar of their Civill Subjection, contrary to the unity and defence of the

Commonwealth' (ibid., p.570). What follows is in the spirit of Hooker. The sovereign has supreme power in all causes Ecclesiastical as civil,

> as far as concerneth actions and words ... and these rights are incident to all Sovereigns, whether Monarchs or Assemblies: for they that are the Representatives of a Christian People, are Representants of the Church: for a Church, and a Commonwealth of Christian People, are the same thing. (ibid., p.576)

Concerning who may make what laws for the affairs of the church, Hooker argues that all free and independent societies must be seen as indivisible unities. It is for the whole and not any part of the polity to make laws, and the first thing that laws must consider is the service of God:

> When we speake of the right which naturally belongeth to a Commonwealth we speake of that which needes must belong to the Church of God. For if the Commonwealth be Christian, if the people which are of it doe publicly embrace the true religion, this very thing doth make it the Church. (1981, vol. 8, Chapter 6.4–6.6, pp.390–1)

Hobbes ties his view of the unity of church and state to his treatment of the absolute duty of the individual to obey the law in Chapter 18, in Part II, *Of The Commonwealth*. When he begins his extensive controversy with the Roman Catholic, Bellarmine, he declares: 'I have already sufficiently proved that all Governments which men are bound to obey, are Simple, and Absolute'. Of course it does not matter if the form is democratic, aristocratic or monarchic. 'And of the three sorts, which is the best, is not to be disputed, where any of them is already established'. The essential point is that the power it has be 'an Absolute Sovereignty' (Hobbes, 1968, pp.576–7). In Chapter 18 he rejects a form of covenanting Presbyterianism in a few words of Anglican political theology:

> And whereas some men have pretended for their disobedience to their Sovereign, a new Covenant, made, not with men, but with God; this also is unjust: for there is no Covenant with God, but by mediation of some body that representeth Gods Person; which none doth but Gods Lieutenant, who hath the Sovereignty under God. (ibid., p.230)

Considering almost at once the question whether a sovereign can be said to have covenanted himself with his subjects, Hobbes makes clear his objection to any type of covenanting tradition. If anyone pretends a breach of any covenant by the sovereign and the latter disagrees, 'there is in this case, no Judge to decide the controversie: it returns therefore to the Sword again' (ibid., pp.230–1). Hobbes may be taken to be making a purely logical, analytical point. In Chapter 17, the first in *Of The Commonwealth*, he simply states that a commonwealth must mean the reduction of a plurality of wills to one will. This text however appears to me to equate polity repeatedly with unity, and, of course, quite explicitly with one God. So the question is how to erect a 'Common Power', to confer all power upon one man or one assembly to reduce all wills to one will, to appoint one man or one assembly of men. Clearly Hobbes is not thinking of a single personal sovereign. The notion of unity is the essential feature of the oneness which he so constantly repeats. 'This is more than Consent, or Concord; it is a reall Unitie of them all, in one and the same Person.' What concerns him is not what this one will do, but that all individual people have precluded themselves from independent action. This Mortal God is a sovereign power precisely in the sense that 'he is enabled to forme the wills of them all' (ibid., pp.227–8).

I would like to stress the sense in which Hobbes identifies sovereignty with unity in the second, the civil, and not simply the third, the *Christian Commonwealth* part of the *Leviathan*, and to suggest, through further comparison with Hooker, how far he is giving a particular definition of sovereignty, understood in the sense of a focal point absorbing all the symbols of public action into one unity. I will not go so far as to say that Hobbes upholds the doctrine of parliamentary sovereignty as such. However, in my view he explains exactly what such a doctrine means if one makes an equation between the crown in parliament and the commonwealth as he understands the term. The equation of the terms is clearer in the writings of Hooker.

So Hobbes explains why the commonwealth cannot be subject to the civil law (that is to say, what the commonwealth has already commanded). To my mind the religious tone of the following expression is clear, remembering that Hobbes has already equated the political and religious commonwealths. This can be seen in the reference to binding and loosening, an analogy with the scriptural authority for ecclesiastical authority and papal infallibility:

> The Sovereign of a Common-wealth, be it an Assembly, or one Man, is not subject to the Civill Lawes. For having power to make and repeal lawes, he may when he pleaseth, free himself from that subjection, by repealing those Lawes that trouble him ...: Nor is it possible for any person to be bound to himself; because he that can bind, can release. (ibid., Chapter 26, p.313).

Here we have the doctrine that parliament cannot bind its successors, built into the very idea of law in the English tradition.

Again in the *Civile Commonwealth* Hobbes comes to grips with a crucial question in religious controversy: who has the authority to interpret laws. Hobbes represents the view that 'All Laws, written and unwritten, have need of Interpretation' (ibid., Chapter 26, p.322). He makes clear that the idea of the law as such must be absolutely subordinated to the question of who interprets it. The law is binding because it is, even if by some steps removed, 'the Sovereigns sentence' (that is the Judges take all of their authority from the Sovereign) (ibid., p.323). Hobbes is repeating his thesis that law must, and can only, constitute a unity as a single expression of the will of a single commonwealth. So when he comes to consider whether any effective appeal can be made to divine law, Hobbes comes down firmly on the side of Anglican political theology. It may be noted that he has already said that the 'Law of Nature' as such 'is become of all Laws the most obscure' and most in need of sovereign interpretation (ibid., pp.322–3). He goes on to say:

> for if men were at liberty, to take for Gods Commandments, their own dreams, and fancies, or the dreams and fancies of private men; scarce two men would agree upon what is Gods Commandment; and yet in respect of them, every man would despise the Commandments of the Commonwealth. I conclude therefore, that in all things not contrary to the Morall Law (that is to say, to the Law of Nature,) all Subjects are bound to obey that for divine Law, which is declared to be so, by the Laws of the Commonwealth. (ibid., p.333)

In my view we have here the roots of the denial that any alleged doctrine of natural or divine law can negate the legal quality as such of English law, thereby furnishing the cultural barrier to the development of doctrines of fundamental law or natural rights such as might provide the framework for a written constitution. In no sense does Hobbes deny that such values exist. Rather, they are already incorporated into the unitary spirit of English law.

So Hobbes never denies that individuals can rebel against a law or against an interpretation of the law, but if they do so individually it is merely a private affair. If they do so in significant numbers the commonwealth as such simply ceases to exist. As a manmade construction it is just no longer there. To repeat a point which I have already noted him as making:

> If any one, or more of them, pretend a breach of the Covenant ... there is in this case no Judge to decide the controversie: it returns

to the Sword again; and every man recovereth the right of protecting himselfe by his own strength, contrary to the designe they had in the Institution. (ibid., Chapter 18, p.231)

In other words people who devise constitutions in which there is some limit on sovereign power are simply going round in circles, chasing their tails. There is no real alarm or menace in what Hobbes is proposing. This is because underlying his conception of the sovereign is his view that the polity is in itself a natural unity, a point which I will try to trace to Hooker. So Hobbes continues this part of his argument in a virtually bantering tone:

It is therefore in vain to grant Sovereignty by way of precedent Covenant ... But when an Assembly of men is made Sovereign; then no man imagineth any such Covenant to have past in the Institution; for no man is so dull as to say, for example, the People of Rome, made a Covenant with the Romans, to hold the Sovereignty on such or such conditions; which not performed, the Romans might lawfully depose the Roman People. (ibid., p.231)

The notion of the unity of the polity is in Hobbes's hands an aversion to any form of intellectual activity which might have an independent character. He anticipates a human rights tradition, as well as any attempt to judge the polity in a comparative perspective, as simply so many ways of weakening the polity. To contemplate that the sovereign power might be divided is to divide the power of the commonwealth, for powers divided mutually destroy each other. What Hobbes has in mind is very specific, an independent learned class. He continues: 'And for these doctrines, men are chiefly beholding to some of those, that making profession of the Lawes, endeavour to make them depend upon their own learning, and not upon the legislative Power.' (ibid., p.368). This is a matter of the reading of books, imagining the exploits of the Greeks and Romans in overthrowing tyrants. Here men find words such as regicide, tyrannicide, subjects enjoying liberty and slaves under coercion, and imagine they can rebel lawfully if they use the right words (ibid., p.369). He goes on immediately to deplore the Doctors who say that there be three soules in a man; so there be also they that think there may be more than one soul in a Commonwealth. They set up a Ghostly authority against a Civill 'working on mens minds, with words and distinctions, that of themselves signifie nothing, but bewray (by their obscurity) that there walketh (as some think invisibly) another Kingdome, as it were a Kingdome of Fayries, in the dark.' (ibid., p.370). For Hobbes any such animated discussion about legitimacy can only be unsettling. He questions whether such books should be allowed to circulate. The reason is simple. In his discussion of the supposed distinction between temporal and spiritual he sees only anarchy. 'For seeing the Ghostly Power challengeth the Right to declare what is Sinne it challengeth by consequence to declare what is Law, (Sinne being nothing but the transgression of the Law;)' (ibid., p.371).

Commonwealth is also a central word in Hooker's vocabulary. It is the focal point of his sense of the unity of the English polity.

> So albeit properties and actions of one kinde doe cause the name of a Commonwealth, qualities and functions of another sort the name of a Church to be given unto a multitude, yet one and the self same multitude may in such sort be both and is so with us, that no person appertayning to the one can be denied to be also of the other. (Hooker, 1981, p.319)

Hooker calls church and commonwealth properties and actions of one subject (ibid., p.325). The Bishop of Rome divides the body of the Commonwealth into two diverse bodies, but within the Realme of England one societie is both the Church and the Commonwealth.

> In a word our estate is according to the patterne of Godes own ancient elect people, which people was not parte of them the Commonwealth and part of them the Church of God, but the self same people whole and entier, were both under one cheif Governour, on whose supreme authoritie they did depend. (ibid., p.330)

Reading Hooker as a forerunner of doctrines of institutional sovereignty is not straightforward. I am trying to tease out his contribution to the 'essence' of the unity of the polity. So he denies that kings might exercise supreme authority against the ancient laws of nations (ibid., pp.347-8). He firmly distinguishes Christ's headship from that of kings. It is the former whose power is absolute. Kings are restrained in the manner just mentioned (ibid., pp.361-2). However, the crucial step is taken, in my view, where Hooker discusses the relationship between Christ and the visible church. Christ, while 'touching visible and corporeal presence', is as removed from the visible church as heaven is distant from earth. Yet visible government is necessary for the church and how is it possible without 'sundrie visible governours whose power being the greatest in that kind so farr as it reacheth ... Heads indued with supreme power extending a certaine compasse are for the exercise of visible regiment not unnecessarie' (ibid., pp.370-1). A fundamental difficulty for Anglicans was to explain how Christ could, as one person, have numerous heads of separate churches. Hooker responded to this crisis by saying that there can be many churches, 'every of them a body perfect by itself', with two heads and the magistrates, the particular heads. The latter do not have to be some one person. There is no difficulty that 'in Popular States a multitude should to it self be both body and Head' (ibid., p.373).

The equation of church and civil society has an entirely egalitarian aim. Hooker wishes to deny any special authority of a clerical class (which might later as an intellectual class have independent pretentions to authority) over the rest of society. As the natural subject of power to make civil laws is the commonwealth, 'so we affirm that in like congruitie the true original subject of power also to make church lawes is the whole intire body of that church for which they are made. Equalles cannot impose lawes and statutes upon their equalles' (ibid., p.386). To make laws is the mark of any free independent society. This includes laws for the service of God, which is the first thing the law should care to provide. It is at this point in his argument, where supreme law-making is attached to the fact of political independence, that Hooker takes the vital step which, in my opinion, explains the virtually mystical doctrine of unity which underlies his understanding of the polity:

> When we speak of the right which naturally belongeth to a Commonwealth we speak of that which needes must belong to the Church of God. For if the Commonwealth be Christian, if the people which are of it doe publiquely embrace the true religion, this very thing doth make it the Church, as hath been shown. (ibid., p.391)

There follows a complete statement of the supremacy of Parliament as that within which the entire Realme of England is present, both civil and spiritual. The king is very much under and a part of this Realme, not separate from it. There can be no question of disobedience or rebellion, not simply because all of this is instituted by God, as indeed is the church, but because everyone present can already be taken to have consented. Equally, in the interpretation of law there can be no disunity, because all conflicts eventually return to the commonwealth which itself has power to make law. Finally to subject the king as the representative of the commonwealth to judgement is simply to defeat, by contradiction, the sense that he is the supreme authority.

Taking up the theme whether a civil authority can legislate on ecclesiastical matters Hooker says this:

> The Parliament of England together with the Convocation annexed thereunto is that whereupon the very essence of all

government within this kingdome doth depend. it is even the
bodie of the whole Realme, it consisteth of the King and of all that
within the Land are subject unto him for they all are there present
either in person, or by such as they voluntarily have derived their
very personall right unto. (ibid., p.401)

The authority to legislate for the ecclesiastical sphere is in fact the
means whereby all become bound by laws made and why there
cannot normally be a right of resistance. After noting how
Parliament is made for more than such supposedly temporall
matters as meddling with leather and wooll (ibid., p.402), Hooker
says that however much wisdom there may be amoung pastors and
bishops, it is the general consent of all that give their counsel the
form of laws. They would otherwise remain as no more than the
counsels of physicians to the sick, 'but laws could they never be
without consent of the whole Church ... which is the only thing
that bindeth each member of the Church to be guided by them'
(ibid., p.403).

The religious sense of presence could not be plainer in the following passage which shows how little the divine right of kings had
root in Hooker's political theology. The essential feature of Christ's
Church is that it is everywhere in the Realme of England; it is that
Realme present in its Parliament. The laws do not take their force
from power which the Prince communicates to Parliament or to any
other Court under him,

> but from power which the whole body of this Realme being natu-
> rally possessed with hath by free and deliberate assent derived
> unto him that ruleth over them so farr forth as hath been
> declared. So that our lawes made concerning religion do take origi-
> nallie their essence from the power of the whole Realme and
> Church of England then which nothing can be more consonant
> unto the lawes of nature and the will of our Lord Jesus Christ.
> (ibid., p.405)

The whole problematic of constitutionality is quite simply subsumed under the ultimate power of the commonwealth to interpret
all law. There is no need for an absolute distinction between giving
and interpreting laws. 'All decisions of things doubtfull and correc-
tions of things amisse are proceeded in by order of law ... It is
neither permitted unto Prelates nor Prince to judg or determine at
their discretion, but law hath prescribed what both shall doe ... the
entire communitie giveth generall order by law how all things pub-
liquely are to be done'. The king merely assists in the framing and
execution of the law (ibid., pp.434–5). The question whether the

king can be subject to judgement is treated in the context of excom-
munication. He rejects the idea that the ecclesiastical authorities
should attempt to stand over him. Within their own dominions the
kings can have no peers. How could any coercive power be exercised
when such a power would make that person so far forth his superior's superior ruler and judge? (ibid., p.445).

In any case, at a more general level, the question of a need to
reject, in any radical sense, an existing constituted authority is difficult to pose in Hooker's scheme of the polity as unity. It is not
simply that all powers are of God, that power is of divine institution, whether directly from God or from men by light of nature.
Rather the question is how can conflict arise if the power is of all
sorts of superiours made by consent of commonwealths (ibid.,
p.398)? 'For if that be accounted our deed which others doe whom
we have appointed to be our agents how should God but approve
those deeds even as his own' (ibid., p.399).

The 'Everywhereness' of Parliament and the Unity of Law with Itself: the Christian Commonwealth Becomes 'Established'

Sovereignty is more unitary than unconditional. Supremacy is totality. Everywhereness is togetherness. In his classic statement, given
in the year 1765, Blackstone shows us how the sense of supremacy is
one of completeness. There can be no one outside it to judge it, and
all who are within comprehend it. Dicey's well-known quotation of
Blackstone vibrates with the emotion of the oracle. He himself
begins by quoting Coke. The power and jurisdiction of Parliament is
'so transcendant and absolute, that it cannot be confined either for
causes or persons, within any bounds' (Blackstone, 1979, p.156). The
language of final religious authority runs through the whole para-
graph. Parliament has 'uncontrollable authority concerning matters
of all possible denominations, ecclesiastical or temporal' (ibid.). This
is the place of 'that absolute despotic power which must in all governments reside somewhere'. All mischiefs which transcend the ordinary course of the laws are within the reach of this extraordinary
tribunal. It can alter the succession of the crown, established religion
and the duration of parliament. Blackstone continues: 'It can, in
short, do everything that is not naturally impossible; and therefore
some have not scrupled to call its power, by a figure rather too bold,
the omnipotence of Parliament. True it is, that what the Parliament
doth, no authority on earth can undo' (ibid.).

Blackstone says that government should be lodged in those
persons who possess those qualities 'which are amoung the attributes of him who is emphatically stiled the supreme being', wisdom,

goodness and power (ibid., p.48). There must be in every government:

> a supreme, irresistible, absolute, uncontrolled authority, in which the *jura summi imperii* or the rights of sovereignty, reside. And this authority is placed in those hands, wherein the qualities requisite for supremacy, wisdom, goodness and power, are the most likely to be found. (ibid., p.49)

In the case of the British constitution they are lodged in the crown in parliament which possesses the three divine qualities. The King represents power, the Lords, wisdom, and the Commons, virtue (ibid., p.51).

Nothing could be more remote from Blackstone's mind than a doctrine of the separation of powers, Montesquieu-style. Sovereignty is togetherness. 'For a state is a collective body, intending to act together as one man' (ibid., p.52). He elaborates on the theme in his chapter on the royal prerogative. The law attributes to the king a great and transcendant nature by which the people are led to consider him in the light of a superior being, to pay him awful respect (ibid., p.234). Blackstone refers in particular to the statutes of Henry VIII which declare the king to be the supreme head of the realm in matters both civil and ecclesiastical and as a consequence inferior to no man upon earth. He means specifically that if any foreign jurisdiction claimed power, as was formerly claimed by the pope, the independence of the kingdom would be no more (ibid., p.235). It is clear that Blackstone is here speaking of the king as the crown in parliament because he concludes by saying that if a domestic tribunal had power to try him this would destroy the free agency of one of the constituent elements of the sovereign legislature.

So it is the unity and completeness of parliamentary sovereignty which renders any outside critical power, of which judicial review is just one imaginable, quite superfluous. Thus Blackstone tells us that law as such is incapable of distrusting those whom it has invested with any part of the supreme power, since such distrust would render the exercise of such power precarious. Oppression may occur, but law as such cannot by its nature remedy this. This is inevitable given the element of completeness in Blackstone's understanding of supremacy. 'For, wherever the law expresses its distrust of abuse of power, it always vests a superior coercive power in some other hand to correct it; the very notion of which destroys the idea of sovereignty' (ibid., p.237). The supposition of law is that neither the king nor either house of parliament is capable of doing wrong, since in such a case the law feels itself incapable of furnishing any adequate remedy. For this reason all oppressions which may happen to spring from any branch of the sovereign power must necessarily be out of the reach of any stated rule or express legal provision (ibid., pp.237–8).

Edmund Burke is another expounder of Englishness who writes shortly after Blackstone, equally stressing the 'established' character of the Anglican polity. It will be seen later how Dicey quotes him as an authority on the representative character of the House of Commons. Inspired by an ascendant principle of unity, Burke tells us how the elected representative is taken up into the governing circles of the land. The popular representative is taken into a government already complete in all its ordinary functions. The representative separate from the other parts 'can have no existence' (Burke, 1960, pp.183–4). In other words parliament is always there. Its 'beingthereness', an essential part of its 'everywhereness', precedes all elections. So:

> With us the representative, separated from the other parts, can have no action and no existence. The government is the point of reference of the several members and districts of our representation. This is the centre of our unity. This government of reference is a trustee for the whole and not for the parts. So is the other branch of our public council, I mean the House of Lords. With us the King and the Lords are several and joint securities for the equality of each district, each province, each city. (ibid., p.184)

– as far away as Scotland and Cornwall. In Burke's mind 'they' are the new French Assembly where an elective body is the sole sovereign, of which all the elected members are integral parts.

What could be more natural than that such a parliament should be able to change the rules for election of its representative part? It clearly precedes the electoral process. As a being with a trinity of divine qualities, parliament goes well beyond any mere contemporary events. It is an eternal concept of representation which imbues the British constitution:

> We have consecrated the state ... It is a partnership between those who are living and those who are to be born ... a clause in the great primaeval contract of eternal society ... He willed therefore the state – He willed its connection with the source and original archetype of all perfection. (ibid., pp.93, 95)

Nothing should be less surprising than that such a state can do no wrong. Burke tells us that the courts will not review the king's conduct any more than that of the Lords or Commons 'who in their several public capacities can never be called to account for their conduct' (ibid., p.27).

The Presence of Establishment as the Absence of Popular Sovereignty, or the Petulance of the Spirit of Criticism

For Blackstone the prospect of modernity or even Enlightenment does present itself, but it is deftly handled. When he has finished his classic statement on parliamentary sovereignty, Blackstone remarks that it should be owned how Locke believes there must be inherent in the people a supreme power to remove a legislature which has betrayed the trust of those who set it up. Now such a devolution of power to the people means an annihilation of all sovereign power, a desperate situation in which all legal dispositions are ineffectual (Blackstone, 1979, p.157).

Blackstone recognises that it is inconceivable that conflicts should not arise between society at large and the magistrates delegated by society. Locke is definitely correct in his theoretical statement of the position. The question is how to explain the resolution of these conflicts after the event, so to speak. Thus, for instance, to provide principles of justice to explain the events of 1688 is much less wise than to treat the matter as established. The formulations of zealous republicans such as Locke risk the dissolution of all society and with it all distinctions of honour and property, inevitably involved in it being left to the people to erect a new system of state and polity. Hence the 1688 'incident' is best left as an abdication which produced a vacancy. Establishment is a matter of letting sleeping dogs lie. The great merit of Blackstone is that one can understand what he is talking about. To look for reasons for a political event:

> might imply a right of dissenting or revolting from it, in case we should think it unjust, oppressive or inexpedient. Whereas our ancestors having most indisputably a competent jurisdiction to decide this great and important question and having in fact decided it, it is now become our duty, at this distance of time to acquiesce in their determination; being born under that establishment which was built upon this foundation, and obliged by every tie, religious as well as civil, to maintain it. (ibid., p.205)

Blackstone is drawing upon the all-embracing concept of supremacy in the sense that he is excluding any possibility of an independent standard of criticism. It is the very unity of law, the very 'everywhereness' of sovereignty which makes it impossible to stand so outside of it as to imagine what it would be like to begin afresh from some such starting point as Locke's state of nature. Given that sovereignty is indivisible, it is not surprising that Blackstone should say that no practical system of laws can set out beforehand those eccentrical remedies which emergency may justify. Locke's republicanism contradicts Blackstone's holistic concept of society, because it purports to give to every individual the right of determining this expediency. So the notion of popular sovereignty is seen as individualist. It is a doctrine productive of anarchy and in consequence equally fatal to civil liberty, a tyranny itself.

> For civil liberty rightly understood, consists in protecting the rights of individuals by the united force of society; society cannot be maintained, and of course can exert no protection without obedience to some sovereign power: and obedience is an empty name, if every individual has a right to decide how far he himself shall obey. (ibid., p.244)

As a footnote it might be worth mentioning that Burke follows Blackstone's interpretation of the events of 1688 and the use of the word establishment, although at a rather polemical level. However, in one respect he is more suggestive than Blackstone, and that is in his characterisation of intellectual criticism of the English polity. With 1688 in the background he identifies the notion of a contract between monarch and people, an elective monarchy, as reminiscent of an 'archpontiff of the rights of man, with all the plenitude of the papal deposing power [who] proclaims usurpers by circles of longitude and latitude (Burke, 1960, p.12). He is conscious of precedents of the impudent French revolutionary intellectuals. Following Blackstone, he insists that the events of 1688 do not allow one to turn a state of necessity into a rule of law (ibid., p.15). The enemy is the critical intellectual, the cabal calling itself philosophical (ibid., p.86), an atheistical gang with a bigotry of their own, who have learned to talk against monks with the spirit of the monk (ibid., p.108). In England writers were and are wholly unconnected individuals (ibid., p.86):

> instead of quarrelling with establishments as some do, who have made a philosophy and a religion of their hostility to such institutions, we cleave closely to them. We are resolved to keep an established church, an established monarchy, an established aristocracy and an established democracy, each in the degree it exists, and in no greater. (ibid., p.88)

English Legal Positivism as Failed Modernity: a Postmodern Deconstruction of Diceyan Parliamentary Sovereignty

The postmodernist approach to law presented here is deconstructionist in the perfectly clear sense that it uncovers the metaphysical and religious ghosts hidden in an apparently modernist attempt to construct an autonomous constitutional order resting upon the independent 'will' of a purely secular power. In fact close analysis of supposedly logically coherent analytical structures reveals innumerable contradictions. The object of this chapter, however, is not to pursue a cult of the incomprehensible or the simply absurd. It is to demonstrate an entirely historical argument that far from heralding Enlightenment or Emancipation, such as in terms of a liberal polity, legal positivism merely marks the partial disintegration of the comprehensive Anglican polity marked out by Hobbes and Hooker. It had already become dogmatic and even deliberately 'senseless' with Blackstone and Burke. With Dicey it is visibly crumbling. The task of the postmodernist critic is the easy one of tracing the pre-modern ghosts in cracked skeletons of modernity.

Parliamentary sovereignty is the recognised pillar of British constitutional law. Its authoritative modern exponent is the Victorian Oxford Law Professor, Dicey, whose treatment of the subject in his *Introduction to the Study of the Law of the Constitution* (first published in 1885), is still regarded as definitive. At the time he swept away all opposition. In the light of what has been said already it should become clear that Dicey's work is an exercise in partial amnesia. It is full of quotations whose historical inevitability is obvious but whose full meaning appears to escape him. A particularly distinctive feature of Dicey's work is the insertion into his text of page-long quotations, without any accompanying analytical comment. Thus there are the two pages from Blackstone on parliamentary sovereignty which is supposed by Dicey to be 'a classical passage' (Dicey, 1957, pp.41–2; Blackstone, 1979, p.156), and a full page from Burke, coming at the end of a discussion on representation and the House of Commons, (Dicey, 1957, pp.84–5; Burke, 1960, pp.183–4). One might suppose that at the very least Dicey agrees with what he quotes Blackstone and Burke as having said. Yet this does not allow one to suppose that Dicey either has or wants to have a sense of historical continuity. On the contrary he supposes that his legal discipline has an entirely autonomous task. It is supposed to be simply to identify the whereabouts of a sovereign power in the state. As Dicey puts it, that is how the term constitutional law appears to be used in England. We look for the rules which identify the members of the sovereign power (Dicey, 1957, p.23). It does not matter whether the argument as to parliamentary sovereignty has any logical, philosophical or other foundation. Nor does it matter whether this type of constitutional framework does in fact exist in any other country. It has its ground in no theory, conscious act or comparison, but in an even duller and more obtuse version of Establishment than Blackstone's. 'In England we are accustomed to the existence of a supreme legislative body, i.e. a body which can make or unmake every law; and which cannot therefore be bound by any law' (ibid., p.72).

However, a possible hermeneutical approach to Dicey's whole project might mean understanding that a distinctive feature of modernity is the attempt to break with what is seen as the dead weight of tradition. This Dicey sees as central to his positivist enterprise. His wish to define clearly the nature and scope of constitutional law means for him the need to make a distinction between law and history. It makes him hostile to history for its own sake. He is aware of the tendency or practice of regarding the longevity of English institutions with awe and undertakes a modernist rejection of this. The first essential feature of the modernist approach is the rejection of the past in favour of the present. Law as a validating force is not an accumulating memory but an actually present and, as will be seen shortly, self-creating force:

> antiquarianism is not law and the function of the trained lawyer is not to know what the law was yesterday, still less what it was centuries ago, or what it ought to be tomorrow, but to know and to be able to state what are the principles of law which actually and at the present day exist in England. (ibid., p.14)

Thus modernity in law is above all law as completely present. The supreme sovereign power is a body which can make and unmake every law now. Nothing from the past can weigh it down. Dicey has only a withering disdain for the common law of the famous ancient and feudal constitution of England. As for its arch-priest the early seventeenth-century Chief Justice, Sir Edward Coke, no one could have been more unhistorical, artificial or pedantic in his reasoning (ibid., p.18). Indeed to consult our uncultured Anglo-Saxon ancestors about our 'modern constitutional freedom' makes as much sense as asking what a Cherokee Indian would have thought of the claim of George III to separate taxation from representation. Dicey does not mention a law of progress, but it seems implied in his disdain for the concept of time implicit in tradition. A knowledge of the turmoil of the seventeenth century:

> guards us from the illusion, that modern constitutional freedom has been established by an astounding method of retrogressive progress; that every step towards progress has been a step backwards towards the simple wisdom of our uncultured ancestors. Our respectable Saxon ancestors were respectable barbarians. (ibid., pp.17–18)

Part of the great memory of the common law is the doctrine of precedent. The idea of retrogressive progress is merely one form of the appeal to precedent. Precedent is merely fictional, confusing students of constitutional law as to whether judges are legislating. Antiquarianism is permissible only if it joins forces with formalism (ibid., p.19). For Dicey the constitution has to be a positive creation. It must exist in the present.

So Dicey is trying to mark a transition from the pre-modern to the modern in the notion of an English legal system and constitution. He is concerned about the modernist revolutions in France and the United States. 'Can it be that a dark saying of Tocqueville "the English constitution has no real existence" contains the whole truth of the matter?' Dicey is clearly concerned that the constitutional question should not only belong to historians and specialists in political ethics (ibid., p.22). Indeed at the very beginning of his work he states quite honestly his envy of his American 'rivals'. He is worried that English constitutional law appears to have no foundation point, no starting point; clearly no small matter for someone who despises historical tradition. In the United States matters are quite different. The historian may go back as far as he pleases, to colonial times, even to England itself. However, the American constitutional lawyer, such as Story or Kent, need not go beyond 1779 (ibid., p.15). The lawyers may begin with the constitution of the Founding Fathers.

Postmodernist deconstructive analysis helps to give a critical perspective on Dicey's task quite simply by undertaking a detailed textual study of the contradictions in his arguments. These are to be traced to the partial historical amnesia which his work represents. Dicey wishes to be modern. So he defines his professional task in terms of contemporary comparisons. What ought the constitutional lawyer to do? 'He ought to expound the unwritten or partly unwritten constitution of England in the same manner in which Story and Kent have expounded the written law of the American constitution' (ibid., p.32).

Well, how is this to be done? We have already had Dicey tell us that in England we are accustomed to a supreme legislative body, a body which can make and unmake every law (ibid., p.72). Another way that he puts the same idea is to say that the doctrine of parliamentary sovereignty is fully recognised by the law of England (ibid., p.41). Yet how can this be possible? He also explains that the lawyer 'may search the statute book from beginning to end, but he will find no enactment which purports to contain the articles of the constitution; he will not possess any test by which to discriminate laws which are constitutional or fundamental from ordinary enactments' (ibid., p.6).

We must look to history for the foundation of parliamentary sovereignty. 'This supreme legislative authority of Parliament is shown historically in a large number of instances' (ibid., p.43). It might appear that Dicey is committing what the modernists call a category mistake. This is rather more sophisticated than simply noting that Dicey has already told us that law is one thing and history another. It is a matter of understanding the object of the great modernist enterprise in law. It has to be remembered that for the artificial and pedantic ancestor-worshipping Coke the law goes back well beyond our respectable Saxon barbarians. Since it has no beginning it needs no foundation. Not so with Dicey. Modernity is something which starts. This is the essential meaning of the notions of foundation and of 'basic'. Clearly it must start at some point in time. Yet once it has started, it keeps going by its own momentum. There is no need to return to the point when it began. What is even more important is that there should be no need to ask how history brought about the English constitution. Otherwise the positivist modernist enterprise will have failed and people will not have constructed an autonomous system of law.

Dicey is going to rely on an historical event, and this is contradictory if it is all he does. Yet he does more. He considers one particular historical event as transformatory. Dicey decides that there is no single statute which is more significant, either as to the theory or to the practical working of the constitution, than the Septennial Act (ibid., p.44). The king and the ministry (at the beginning of the Hanoverian succession) were convinced, 'with reason', that an appeal to the electorate (many of whom were Jacobites) might be perilous not only to the ministry but also to the tranquillity of the state. So (ibid., p.45) the parliament then sitting was induced to pass the Septennial Act, a statute 'justified by considerations of statesmanship and expediency', which prolonged the life of parliaments (starting with the one that passed the Act) from three to seven years. Not surprisingly this measure gave rise to some controversy. Dicey, as a true modernist, prefers clarity of thought and categorical assertion to woolly and spurious reliance upon fictitious tradition (ibid., p.46). There should be no pretence but that this was an unprecedented act. Those who objected that the House of Commons must be chosen by the electorate, that it had been chosen to sit for three years only, made an essential point, in Dicey's view. To go beyond three years was to exceed their function as delegates. What was startling, Dicey notes well, 'was that an existing Parliament of its own authority prolonged its own existence' (ibid., pp.46–7). What fascinates Dicey is that parliament appears to be creating itself. It is an autonomous being. His conclusion is:

Parliament made a legal though unprecedented use of its powers ... That Act [the Septennial] proves to demonstration that in a legal point of view Parliament is neither the agent of the electors nor in any sense a trustee for its constituents. It is legally the sovereign legislative power in the state, and the Septennial Act is at once the result and the standing proof of such Parliamentary sovereignty. (ibid., pp.47–8)

The linear time of tradition has been broken by the circle of autonomy. The Act is both a result and a proof of the argument. Dicey is engaged not in a traditionalist search for depth in the past, but in a modernist assertion of a fundamental starting point. This particular seduction of parliament by 'the Ministry' marks the English equivalent of the American Declaration of Independence and of the French Revolution. This is why he treats a particular incident at one point in time as both the result of and the standing proof of a legal principle. He does remark, *en passant*, that 'there are countries, and notably the United States, where an Act like the Septennial Act would be held legally invalid' (ibid., p.47).

Thus we have an apparently anti-modern denial of the principles of popular sovereignty and democracy which is put together in a thoroughly modern way. While the principle of constitutional validity has its origin in a particular historical moment, it is its own independent justification and foundation. Yet it refers to absolutely no legal principle or political idea except an unexplored English notion of parliament. The bridging point chosen is Dicey's assumption that what the judiciary would determine is conclusive of every issue. The latter know nothing of the sovereignty of the people as a legal doctrine, so that is an end of the matter. Criticism of Dicey's style has to be a central part of postmodernist deconstruction. He becomes more dogmatic and even petulant as the historical amnesia progresses. He declares bombastically against Austin: 'Nothing is more certain than that no English judge ever conceded or under the present constitution, can concede that Parliament is in any legal sense a "trustee" for the electors' (ibid., p.75). What needs to be 'worried' is the notion that it is the judiciary which should be so emphatic that they are not needed. The essential trace which remains lodged in Dicey's mind is that somehow the apparently unlimited sovereignty of parliament is really no cause for concern. Parliament is supreme in that it is everywhere. There cannot be judicial review because the judiciary cannot stand outside the realm of England which is parliament. As Sir Thomas Smith has already said: 'For everie Englishman is entended to bee there present' (ibid., p.79). We must seek after the wonderful 'everywhereness' of the English parliament. This means looking to Dicey's footnotes, and especially to Blackstone on the doctrine of parliamentary sovereignty.

The supreme legislative body is not accountable to the electorate, and, yet, somehow that is not a matter of concern. So to the argument that members of the House of Commons are merely trustees for the electorate, that they are delegates, Dicey responds fiercely, as we have just seen with Austin: 'Nothing is more certain than that no English judge ever conceded, or under the present constitution, can concede, that Parliament is in any legal sense a trustee for the electors. Of such a feigned "trust" the courts know nothing' (ibid., p.75). Nonetheless Dicey feels no concern that parliament could be tyrannical. He concludes his chapter on parliamentary omnipotence with very reassuring words. The external limit on any sovereign power is disobedience of the bulk of the subjects (ibid., 76–7). An internal limit rests in the social sense of the sovereign power, its actual historical character. Representative government diminishes the divergence between the external and internal limits of sovereign power. The 1688 Revolution ensured that the rulers were induced to make their wishes accord with the will of the nation (ibid., pp.82, 83). Thus:

> the essential property of representative government is to produce co-incidence between the wishes of the sovereign and the wishes of the subjects; to make, in short, the two limitations on the exercise of sovereignty absolutely coincident. (ibid., p.84)

This must surely be something of an anti-climax to a very elaborate 80-plus pages of text designed to show that English constitutional law is based upon the absolute sovereignty of parliament. What on earth is the point of this exercise? It seems that there is some abtracted entity, parliament, which is in no way a trustee of the English people, which can do exactly as it pleases in law, in the most absolute legal terms possible, and yet which is, by virtue of the principle of representation, bound to be coincident with the wishes of the subjects. If there is to be a coincidence of the wishes of sovereign and subjects, why are they not simply one and the same?

Law as 'Dead' Tradition and Parliamentary Sovereignty as an Absent 'Everywhereness'

As Dicey puts it, in England we are accustomed to the existence of a supreme legislative body. If all of us object to this order, it disappears. If only some of us do, it remains unaffected. At present the great debate among theorists of the English legal order is as to whether we submit to this order out of habit or some form of intention. A radical view is that those who actively operate the system do so intentionally. Within this debate the argument never goes beyond asking to what extent officials and 'subjects' habitually obey or consciously recognise what they are doing. The question is how can popular submission and obedience as such constitute a sovereign? The answer is determined by the agenda set by Blackstone and Burke, popularised by Dicey. The nineteenth century Austinian view that sovereignty is constituted merely by habitual obedience is now regarded as too primitive. So the most popular legal philosopher since the 1960s and 70s, Hart, favours the view that 'the solution' is no longer to regard the attitude of the 'subjects' as one of simple obedience but to replace this with a supposed practice of legal officials who accept constitutional rules (see the chapter by Fitzpatrick in this volume).

Thus it might be said that now 'progressive' research shows how it is realised, for instance by the great liberal reformer of the nineteenth century, Jeremy Bentham (see Postema, 1986, pp.235–7, 242), that 'subjects' obey the laws of the sovereign and for that reason can be said to respond intentionally towards one another in their submission. That is, it is now 'realised' by progressive research that intentionality is interactive and therefore social. The legal order can only be undermined if there is a virtually total withdrawal of adhesion. Even then its disappearance is merely registered as a fact. The English are then no longer accustomed to the existence of a supreme legislative body. This evidences a consensus that the English constitutional order does not have any notion of limit or critique built into it. This is the vital 'everywhereness' of its being. So the absence of any common signal marking the juncture for general resistance is what makes English sovereign authority indefinite. Whether such a signal exists is a purely contingent/conventional (why not also historical?) fact (ibid., p.244). Yet it is such a fact that becomes forgotten in the transition from Blackstone, through Bentham, to Dicey. Bentham is repeating Blackstone's criticism of Locke when he says that the individual obligation to obey the law (ibid., pp.248–9) is a matter of individual utility not yielding a public standard affecting the status of the law. The latter can only be a matter of the social facts of coordinated recognition. Thus there is no conceivable way to introduce an independent critical element into the legal order, as a legal element. Law's 'everywhereness' guarantees its unity.

Yet another essential feature of this legal order is its 'alreadythereness'. What counts is not what is decided but what has already been decided. It is past common consent which binds and because it is past and not present. This one can trace in Dicey's circular argument that English law recognises the sovereignty of parliament. It is much clearer in Blackstone's acceptance of what has been established, since the divine analogy is much clearer in the eighteenth century.

In one major study of the influence of sixteenth and seventeenth century Anglican political theology on the English legal order, Little stresses the circuitous character of the English legal tradition, in particular tracing the influence of Hooker's Anglican political theology on the developing seventeenth century constitutional order. Where the word 'realm' is understood as 'structured' in the modern sense, it can be said that, in Little's paraphrase of Hooker's thought:

> the law is determined by the realm, and the realm was determined by the law ... The way in which the realm is [has been] structured is the way in which the realm ought to be structured ... The very formation of the realm becomes the 'right' prescription for its formation; circularly, however the realm set itself up, it ought to have set itself up ... Just as what ought to be for succeeding generations emerges from what already is, so what ought to have been for the 'ancient realm' proceeded from the actual manner of its constitution. One is reminded here of Hooker's statement, 'All things that are, are good' ... It is noticeable, however, that the act of deciding, of electing in itself – as the primary and continuing basis for true order – receives no attention from Hooker. What is central is what has been decided, and what is therefore given ... Hooker rejects elections as the basis of political order. Social status and function are ascribed, the patterns of social life predetermined. (Little, 1969, p.165)

So for the dominant English tradition in analytical legal theory the concept of custom, or customary acceptance, will not mean a reference to a living or vivid historical tradition, but merely a repetition of the notion of establishment as a circular process. In this respect it pays lip service to modernity in its very shallow understanding of its own past. The 'alreadythereness' of the 'everywhereness' of the legal order is a flight into amnesia. With Blackstone and Burke the exclusion of a critical dimension is intentional and even intelligible. With Dicey and his successors it is simply a fetish. It is as ghosts that we reflect on what we accept, without realising that in our mirrors we are only reflecting ourselves as dead. Typical of this fetishising of legal thought is the major recent offering of Postema's. It concerns his so-called interactional (not individual, but social) model of customary regulation:

> This custom generates the 'constitutional' rules which define the powers of the sovereign (as well as potentially limit those powers). In turn this practice itself can be shaped by the exercise of the sovereign legislative power it confers, and so can be seen as, in part issuing from the sovereign, though ultimately it rests on the practice of the people. (Postema, 1986, p.237)

Conclusion

I have outlined a simple substantive argument: that the doctrine of parliamentary sovereignty and the companion doctrine of the duty to obey the law without any legal limits are rooted, in England, in certain historical traditions which are perfectly clear in pre-Dicey classics such as Hooker, Hobbes, Blackstone and Burke. It is a historical fact that the English combined spiritual and temporal authority in their parliament which they saw, in any case, as a complete expression of their national identity. It is also a fact that a nominalist tradition of political philosophy favoured a view which put an absolute primacy on the location of the final interpreter of the law. The content of the law was all penumbra of doubt resolved by authoritative interpretation. These two facts merged well together with the unity of the English people in their parliament.

The question I have posed is what on earth does Dicey do with this tradition? Abroad, political modernity as represented, for instance, in the US, meant a modern constitutionalism, with a consciously agreed starting point with the Founding Fathers. Dicey takes the form of modernity without the content. He cuts English constitutional theory off from the history which gave it a sense. He rejects the organic notion of authority implicit in the common law which at least purported to rely upon the historical experience of the people. In its place there is a spurious basic norm of parliamentary sovereignty rooted in the arbitrary, explicitly anti-democratic Septennial Act. He follows with an insistence that this fact of sovereignty will not be questioned by the judiciary, simply because this idea is 'unthinkable'. So modernity turns an intelligible history into a blind acceptance of 'facticity'. Why? What is the point?

References

Blackstone, W. (1979) *Commentaries on the Laws of England*, Vol. 1 (facsimile of 1st edn of 1765), introduction S.N. Katz (Chicago University Press).

Burke, E. (1960) *Reflections on the Revolution in France*, introduction by A.J. Grieve (London: Everyman).

Derrida, J. (1986) *Margins of Philosophy* (Brighton: Harvester).

Dicey, A.V. (1957) *Introduction to the Law of the Constitution*, 7th edn, ed. E.S. Wade (London: Sweet & Maxwell).

Hobbes, T. (1968) *Leviathan*, ed. C.B. McPherson (London: Penguin).

Hooker, R. (1981) *Of the Laws of Ecclesiastical Polity*, Book VIII, ed. P.G. Stanwood, The Folger Library Edition of the Works of Richard Hooker (Cambridge, Mass: Harvard University Press).

Little, D. (1969) *Religion, Order and Law, A Study in Pre-Revolutionary England* (New York: Harper & Row).

Postema, G.J. (1986) *Bentham and the Common Law Tradition* (Oxford: Oxford University Press).

Schmitt, C. (1938) *Der Leviathan in der Staatslehre des Thomas Hobbes. Sinn und Fehlsclag eines Politischen Symbols* (Hamburg: Steinbeck).

Index

207

Truth, 145, 146, 179
  see also legal truth

Unconscious and law: see law
Unity, 187
  church and state, of: see church
    state, of: see state
Universal reason: see Marxism and
Universalisability: see Kant, test of
Universalism: see contractual rela-
    tions, of; jurisprudence and;
    reason, of
Universalism in jurisprudence: see
    jurisprudence
Universality of law: see law
Universities, 38, 40, 61
  reform of, 53
  role of, 38
  see also education, legal
Unwritten law: see law, unwritten
Unwanted pregnancy: see pregnancy,
    unwanted
Use value, 117
Utilitarianism, 45, 46, 47, 57
  see also Bentham, J.; Mill, J.S.
Utopianism: see feminism and

Voltaire, F., 166

Weber, M., 68, 82, 92
Welfare state, 72
  criticism of, 72, 74

West, R., 152–3, 154
Western culture, crisis in, 74
Willion v Berkley, 170
Winch, P., 9, 17, 26, 30, 62
Wishik, H., 143–4, 151–2, 155
Wittgenstein, L., 3, 4, 5, 9, 10, 15–16,
    23, 30, 31
  notion of family resemblances,
    15–16
  see also rules and games
Wollstonecraft, M., 134, 135
Women:
  exchange of, as basis of culture, 139
  experience of, 142, 145–7, 148,
    153, 154–5
  epistemology and, 142–9
  jurisprudence and, 95
  legal profession, entry of, into: see
    legal profession
  legal subject, as, 108
  law and, 95
  oppression of and law: see
    oppression
  private property, as: see private
    property
  social construction of, 146
  subordination of, 126
    Marxism and, 126
  see also objectification of; sexuality,
    women's
Women's Law, Institute of: see
    Institute of Women's Law